D1338103

SECULAR BEATS SPIRITUAL

Secular Beats Spiritual

*The Westernization of the
Easternization of the West*

STEVE BRUCE

OXFORD
UNIVERSITY PRESS

OXFORD
UNIVERSITY PRESS

Great Clarendon Street, Oxford, OX2 6DP,
United Kingdom

Oxford University Press is a department of the University of Oxford.
It furthers the University's objective of excellence in research, scholarship,
and education by publishing worldwide. Oxford is a registered trade mark of
Oxford University Press in the UK and in certain other countries

First Edition published in 2017

Impression: 1

Published in the United States of America by Oxford University Press
198 Madison Avenue, New York, NY 10016, United States of America

British Library Cataloguing in Publication Data

Data available

Library of Congress Control Number: 2017943302

ISBN 978-0-19-880568-7

Printed and bound by
CPI Group (UK) Ltd, Croydon, CR0 4YY

Preface

It may help the reader to say a few things about the general perspective of this book and a convenient way of describing its ethos is to reply to the criticisms of the sociological profession made in the back-cover summary of an excellent study of yoga in the USA. In puffing the book's virtues, the blurb says:

> [The author] departs from conventional approaches by undermining essentialist definitions of yoga as well as assumptions that yoga underwent a linear trajectory of increasing popularization. While some studies trivialize popularized yoga systems by reducing them to the mere commodification or corruption of what is presented as an otherwise fixed authentic system, Jain suggests that this dichotomy oversimplifies the history of yoga as well as its meaning for contemporary practitioners.

Like a stern glance from my mother, those two sentences convey a list of reproaches to which, on behalf of all purveyors of 'conventional approaches', I will reply.

We can certainly agree that supposing that any widely held and enduring belief system has a single and unchanging essence is usually a mistake. Grand contrasts—yoga in India in the eighteenth century is one thing; yoga in London in the twenty-first century is something else—tend to the essentialist but such simplification is entirely reasonable if the point we wish to make would stand even if we spent more time describing the variations to be found in either time and place. Dogs differ enormously in size and temperament, but the hotelier's 'No dogs allowed' reasonably treats them as if they were all the same for the purpose of admission. Essentialism is a problem only when, and to the extent that, it misleads.

The same pre-emptive response can be offered to the criticism of presenting some change as 'linear'. For many explanatory purposes, it does not matter whether a trend of increasing popularity followed a straight line or went round the houses twice. What usually matters are the prevailing direction of change and its endpoint. As the subtitle of this book makes clear, one of my concerns is to show that (insofar as they have become popular in the West) eastern spiritual beliefs and practices have fundamentally changed to become more secular. This does not require that the religion in question was entirely without secular elements in its original environment. It does not preclude the possibility that some innovation was pre-emptively secularized 'in the East' in anticipation of problems in selling it in the West. Nor does it rule out the interesting possibility that 'the West' in such a proposition includes those class fractions in eastern countries that have adopted certain western values.

Trivializing is an interesting intellectual crime. I confess to a certain irreverence. I feel no need to treat religious beliefs with any more solemnity than I would political ideologies or secular cultural trends. That someone presents an absurdity as a path to spiritual growth should not prevent us pointing out that it is an absurdity. The promoters of the idea that the enlightened can live without food or water or that water containing homeopathic dilutions (that is, plain water) can cure AIDs are dangerous charlatans and should be treated as such. Nor should vices go unremarked because their promoters present them as ways to enlightenment. We would be failing in our responsibility to describe accurately if we hid the fact that many of the male spiritual leaders discussed here were sexually predatory exploiters of their followers. And we would similarly be failing in our scholarly responsibilities if we did not at least note that many of the alternative therapies discussed in this book contradict well-established principles of anatomy and, when they have been subjected to rigorous testing, have failed miserably.

I do not, however, judge the supernatural core of the religious and spiritual beliefs discussed here, nor do I judge between them. Which of Zen Buddhism or Scientology is correct is unknown to anyone this side of the grave, and there is nothing in the training of social scientists that gives us any greater insight into the existence of God or Gods than is possessed by anyone else. We practise methodological agnosticism. We report the religious beliefs of those we study: we do not evaluate them.

Finally we come to 'oversimplifying'. This is not a failing to be corrected: it is a necessity of writing. Jain's study of one small slice of one particular formerly eastern religious practice took 230 pages and that despite making almost no mention of anything outside the USA. My book covers many more beliefs and practices and includes a sociological explanation of the ways in which they have changed in the West. I would remind every reader who finds that what are for them important details have been omitted that to give to every topic and theme the treatment they might wish for their interest would have rendered this book too long to be published. Compression and elision are necessary. Those who wish to know more about any of the topics discussed here will find detailed sources listed in the notes.

Something should be said about the book's concentration on Britain for illustrative material. Many of the religious innovations I discuss were invented in the USA, and, because of their relative size, most of the specific movement organizations had far more adherents in the USA than in Britain. I focus on Britain for two reasons. First, it is one of the most secular societies in the world and thus offers a prime site for testing theories about the contemporary fate of religion. Second, it is small enough to calculate degrees of penetration with some accuracy. This is important, because the proliferation of new expressions of religious and spiritual interest is, of itself, a mark neither of popularity nor of social importance. For reasons explained in the text, the decline of the size and social power of the Christian churches makes innovation easy. Hence we would expect seculariza-tion to be accompanied by an *increase* in the range of religious and spiritual products on offer in Britain but a *decrease* in the overall take-up of religious and spiritual practices. To establish that we need to be able to estimate the proportion of the population that is engaged in such innovations. A small country, with an effective national census to give accurate population baselines, is ideally suited to such estimation.

Acknowledgements

As always, there are obligations to be acknowledged. I owe an inestimable debt to David Voas of University College, London. In a profession that is notoriously chippy, it is worth recording that I have never heard a bad word about David, who is unfailingly polite and helpful. Although we have never worked together on original research, we have co-authored many essays and journal articles and the experience (for me at least) has always been both educational and enjoyable.

I am also greatly indebted to my former colleague Tony Glendinning. Having originally trained as a mathematician, he is a first-rate social statistician, and his contribution to both the design and the analysis of the religion module in the 2001 Scottish Social Attitudes survey and to the analysis of other large-scale datasets was a major help in my work.

My third inspiration is Paul Heelas, formerly of the University of Lancaster and now resident in Stockholm. For many years I broke my journeys from the north-east of Scotland to places in England to stay with him and we enjoyed very many long evenings of argument. Our disagreements about the significance of what he calls holistic spirituality are discussed in Chapter 6, but without him I would never have become interested in the topic.

Four sources of funding have made the research that informs this book possible. Between 2007 and 2009 I was allowed to research full-time by a Leverhulme Senior Research Fellowship and since then I have used only Unilever soap products (shares in which fund the Leverhulme Trust). I would like to thank Lord Lever (1851–1925), the Trustees, and the Director Prof. Gordon Marshall (whom I first met when he beat me in the Scottish Daily Express Schools Debating Championship in 1970). I am also beholden to the Economic and Social Research Council for the grant that allowed Glendinning and me to mount a module of religion and spirituality questions in the 2001 Scottish Social Attitudes survey. The legacy of another wealthy man—the Carnegie Trust for the Universities of Scotland—has funded my research travel on a number of occasions. Finally, I should thank the University of Aberdeen (and behind it the Scottish

Funding Council) for allowing me to research and lecture on aspects of what follows.

On a number of occasions I have visited the Findhorn Foundation, the Samye Ling Tibetan Buddhist monastery, the Throssel Hole Zen Buddhist Priory, the Manjushri Centre in Cumbria, and London's annual Festival of Mind, Body, Spirit. I have also taken part in a very large number of the activities described here and have often been the subject of various forms of spiritual healing. I owe an enormous debt to the very many organizers and other participants at such events and to the individual practitioners who have taken the trouble to talk to me.

However, as always, my greatest debt is owed to the late Roy Wallis. Wallis taught me at the University of Stirling and in 1978 gave me my first job at the Queen's University of Belfast. His *Elementary Forms of the New Religious Life* was immensely influential, as were our many arguments. Had he not been drawn into university management and then died young, he would surely now be one of the most significant sociologists of religion in the anglophone world. Insofar as this book has any merit, I would like to dedicate that to his memory. In the memorable metaphor of Isaac Newton, Wallis is the giant on whose shoulders I have stood.

Contents

Contents

List of Figures and Tables

FIGURES

TABLES

1

The Secularization of the Wes

Holwick is a cluster of houses on a single-track road on th
of the river in Teesdale.[1] An Ordnance Survey map fror
shows a chapel to the south of the road, at the end of the
opposite the old school, but I could not see it. There wa
orderly pile of stones in the next field, and I wondered if
remains. And then I noticed that a garage next to the road
blue metal doors, had a lintel visible between the two do
the doorway below it had been filled in. And above the
doors there were traces of high windows, now filled in. M
chapel had become a double garage.

It is interesting to rank redundant churches and chapel
how much their current use would offend the original bu
could hardly object to private homes. Housing cars rather
seems a little impious, but the lead miners and farmer
the Holwick chapel would approve of modern engines.
Victorian chapelgoers would have denounced (and, if they
afforded it, renounced) rich living means they would prol
their Bethels and Zions becoming restaurants. The Cleckh
dence Congregational chapel was described by Nikolaus
the Yorkshire volume of his *Buildings of England* series as
pompous for a religious building. More like a town hall than
It was turned into the Aakash curry house by a local busine
left the organ and balcony in place and painted an ornate
ceiling.[3] More objectionable would be the frequent convers
and bars. Not all Victorian Christians were paid-up teet
almost all churchgoers would have been mindful of Pr
'Wine is a mocker, strong drink is raging: and whosoever

thereby is not wise.' Indeed. Most Christians would also have been suspicious of people who were overly concerned with their appearance and hence would hardly have approved of the fate of the Primitive Methodist chapel in Barnard Castle. It was demolished, and the site is now occupied by a fetching sandstone block of flats with a shop on the corner at street level. In 2010 the premises were occupied by a tanning and beauty salon.

But the prize for the most offensive use of a former house of worship must surely go to the former Congregational Chapel at Lane End, near High Wycombe. It is a beautiful neat flintstone building that sits low to the ground, as though praying, with just a tiny bit of ostentation in the pointed decorative stone work on the corners and the roof apex. In 2010 it was a photography studio. But not any photography studio. It was FYEO, which a little investigation reveals to stand for 'For Your Eyes Only'. This is boudoir photography. Women who want to give their lovers a souvenir can book a make-up session and have themselves photographed—by women photographers to maintain the proprieties—in little or no lingerie. The original occupants would have given their loved ones a grim-faced head-and-shoulders portrait and a suitable Bible text. The current owners produce tasteful erotica.

Some churches and chapels became redundant because the people they served moved. Rural English churches stand empty because the many ploughmen whom Thomas Gray could have watched plod their weary way home when he was composing his 'Elegy in a Country Churchyard' in 1750 moved to towns and cities as they were replaced by one man on a large tractor. The Holwick chapel, built in 1843 for the grand sum of £34, fell into disuse because the Teesdale lead mines closed. At its most popular it had some twelve members, attendances of around twenty-five souls, and an average Sunday School of fifteen. By 1935 it had eight members, but attendances were now hardly larger. Services became irregular during the war, and it formally closed in 1945.

Some rationalization of plant was necessary because of mergers. When the three strands of Scottish Presbyterianism reunited, many towns and villages were left with two spare churches. The same was true with the 1932 merger of the various Methodist bodies. And even when the churches and chapels were popular, they were too many of them, and many were too big. Victorian confidence often led to such over-provision that many towns and villages had twice as much seats

in churches as there were people to sit on them, even if every adult attended at the same time.[4]

But the primary cause of redundancy has been a seismic shift in cultural preferences.[5] The Christian churches have declined at a rate that a sympathizer has called a 'nose dive'.[6] In 1851 the government conducted its one and only census of religious worship. The administrative structure responsible for the normal population census was tasked with the additional work of identifying every outlet for religious worship and distributing a questionnaire that asked for details of the history of the building, its seating capacity, and attendances at all the services on 30 March. We cannot be sure of exactly how many people went to church that day, because the census forms recorded attendances rather than attenders, and many people attended more than once. But we can readily see both ends of the possible range. If anyone who attended any service attended only one, then the number of attenders is the total of attendances at all services. If everybody attended twice then—because not even the keenest Christian could attend the same service twice—the total is simply the number who were at the most popular service. Roughly speaking, the minima is 40 per cent and the maxima is 60 per cent, so for ease of comparison we can say that in 1851 half the population attended church.[7]

The government never repeated that experiment, but in recent decades Peter Brierley and the various organizations for which he worked conducted similar censuses by asking every known worship outlet to count and report numbers attending on a particular Sunday. Some did not respond, and Brierley had to fill the gaps with some judicious guessing, but we have two reasons to be confident in his results. First, the non-responders were usually small, and so their absence from the record will have little affected the overall results. Second, Brierley has always projected five and ten years from his censuses, and when they have subsequently been repeated, the actual results have turned out to be very close to his projections. Brierley showed a church attendance rate in England of 12 per cent in 1979, 10 per cent in 1989, and 6 per cent in 2005.[8]

Brierley's census results are more reliable than data based on what people tell surveys about their church attendance.[9] People exaggerate, in part because they present an idealized version of themselves (and thus report what they 'normally' would have done rather than what they actually did) and in part because they feel some slight pressure to give the right answer.[10] An important source of information that avoids such compliance effects is the Time Use Diary survey. The UK 2001 study recruited respondents who agreed to note on a printed sheet what they were doing every ten minutes and to tick boxes to show whether that activity was at home or outside the home and whether it was something done alone or in the company of others. It showed that, in a typical week, only 8.3 per cent of people engaged in any religious activity lasting more than ten minutes. And almost all that activity lasted more than fifty minutes, was done in the company of others, outside the home, on a Sunday morning.[11] Which looks like church-going. Because it becomes important later, we should note that there was very little evidence of the 'alone and at home' religious activity that might indicate meditation, Buddhist chanting, or private prayer.

All of which is a long way to the conclusion that between 1851 and 2001 churchgoing changed from something that most people did to being an interest of only a very small minority of the population.

Those who wish to deny that religion has declined in popularity may assert that churchgoing is a poor measure of religious interest. It is often said, usually by non-churchgoers, that you do not have to go to church to be a Christian. Actually you do. Every Christian organ-ization, large and small, either requires or strongly encourages its members to gather regularly to encourage each other and to learn what their faith requires but most importantly to worship God. The Catholic Church makes failure to take Mass on Sunday without good reason a sin, and the small evangelical Protestant sects will expel members who fail to attend regularly. That what the churches demand is reflected in the behaviour of their supporters can be demonstrated from surveys that ask the same people if they identify with any par-ticular religion, if they regularly attend church, and if they hold certain religious beliefs. The three types of responses do not map on to each other perfectly, but, when graphed for a very large number of people over a long period, the three lines move in tandem.[12]

In sum, there is no evidence (and wishful thinking is not evidence) that there are many people who take seriously Christian beliefs but do not attend church.

Not all committed believers are secularization deniers. Some, such as Brierley, are realists who suppose that decline is best combatted with accurate information. Some conservatives actually revel in the evidence of decay since their church abandoned the Latin Mass, the Book of Common Prayer, the King James translation of the Bible, or whatever it is they hold to be the best expression of God's will. Some observers have sought comfort in blunting the implications of decline by reinterpretation. For example, Grace Davie subtitled a book 'Believing without belonging' and argued that what had declined was not interest in religion as such but only interest in public association.[13] This was made plausible by its coincidence with a popular argument made by the American sociologist Robert Putnam in his celebrated *Bowling Alone*.[14] In the 1950s people went ten-pin bowling in teams that competed in local leagues; bowling was a social activity that brought together local communities. Bowling is now as popular as it was then, but most bowlers are individuals or couples, so the activity no longer forms part of the wider social fabric. Putnam uses this example to illustrate his general case that Americans are losing their taste for public association. Davie takes up the theme and shows that cinema-going, trade-union membership, and football spectatorship have all declined since the end of the Second World War. So too has churchgoing; not because people have lost faith in Christianity but because they have lost interest in the social organizations that represent that faith.

There is a good case to be made that, however well Putnam's analysis fits the USA, it does not work well for the UK and that much of its apparent plausibility stems from a failure to notice new forms of association that have replaced the old.[15] But there is no need to argue about what is after all an analogy when we can examine directly what really interests us. It is certainly true that when, for any particular time and place, we compare a measure of religious activity (such as churchgoing) and a measure of belief (such as agreeing that one believes in God), we find that belief is always more popular than any activity predicated on such beliefs. But what was missing from Davie's assertion was any consideration of how those two measures were changing over time. When we graph religious identification, religious activity, and religious belief over time, we find that all three declined in largely similar trajectories over the twentieth century.[16]

EXPLAINING THE DECLINE

The decline of religion, common across the developed world and now evident even in the USA, is not an accident and nor is it the work of committed atheists. It is an unintended consequence of a series of

subtle social changes. Modernization changes the status and nature of
religion in ways that weaken it and make it difficult to pass successfully from generation to generation.[17]

Religion's Shrinking Range

With industrialization, affluent societies have become more internally
complex: areas of life have become more clearly distinct spheres, each
with its own values, and developed specialized institutions to perform
particular social functions. In the Middle Ages the Christian Church
provided much of the state's public administration, education, relief
for the poor, and social control. It controlled elements of economic
behaviour (by, for example, setting 'just prices' for commodities) and
it shaped politics. The churches now have little influence on the
polity, less on the economy, and their education and welfare work is
dwarfed by that of the secular state, from which it is now little distinguished. They have no social control functions. If the Church of
Scotland now tried to punish a member for the marvellously named
sin of haughmagandy (in the demotic: 'putting it about'), the member
could simply leave.

As the churches lost functions, they lost social prestige, and,
literally as well as metaphorically, they lost touch with the people.
In the Middle Ages, everyone had frequent contact with the churches
and the clergy. Now those of us who are not Christians can pass our
entire lives without ever entering a church or meeting a cleric. Even
the great rites of passage need no longer bring people into contact
with religion: baptism is no longer normal, weddings are more often
secular than religious, and even death can be managed without the
benefit of clergy.[18] At the last two cremations I attended, the depart-
ure of the coffin to the ovens behind the curtain was accompanied by
Frank Sinatra singing 'I did it my way' and the more thought-
provoking choice of Ken Dodd singing 'Happiness. Happiness. The
greatest gift thing that I possess'.

The Decline of Community

Another major change is the decline in the traditional community.
When people worked where they lived, shared similar lives, and
frequently interacted over a very wide range of concerns, it was

possible for a single church to be an effective centre of life—providing a religious gloss to the seasons and to the stages of lives lived in common. Modernization undermined the community by increasing the range of life situations so that people objectively had less in common with each other in this life and were thus less likely to share a common vision of this life or the next. Mutual bonds between neighbours that endured over generations were replaced by the much narrower ties of contract. Where one worked and where one lived often became separated. Movement became easier and hence more common. As a consequence of the change that Ferdinand Toennies described as community being replaced by voluntary association, people lost the ability to monitor and censor each other in support of a shared community culture.

In Protestant societies, such social fragmentation was often accompanied by the division of the once-dominant single national church into a series of competing fragments. Later immigration added further diversity. Before the eighteenth century, most European states responded to diversity in much the same way as Islamic terrorists now do in the Middle East: expel, murder, or forcibly convert the heretics. But modernization in the West included an element—the growing recognition that all people were in some foundational sense the same—that made enforcing conformity ever more difficult to justify, especially when coercion failed to discourage dissent and when states came to realize that a shared religion was not essential for national stability. Change was slow. Britain did not allow Catholics the vote until 1829, and it was only in the 1870s that Oxford and Cambridge admitted students who were not members of the Church of England. But across the West modernization has meant religious freedom, and, as religion has become a matter of choice, so the state has had to give up sponsoring one particular faith. This can produce some accidental drollery. An American President, elected by appealing to right-wing religious conservatives who on religious grounds wish to ban the teaching of evolution, homosexuality, and abortion, refrains from sending Christmas cards. Instead he spends mid-December signing cards that wish the recipient 'Happy Holidays'. One area that very clearly shows the gradual shift to religious neutrality is education. Most schools in the West no longer teach that Christianity is the one true faith. Instead they teach *about* a variety of religions as though they were all equally true. Which is the same as teaching that they are all equally false.

In addition to the social structural consequence of making the public space increasingly neutral, religious diversity (and that includes an increasing number of people who choose to have no religion) has an important effect on the social psychology of the way we can hold our beliefs. Put simply, it is very hard now to be convincingly dogmatic. Even committed believers know they are a minority, and, unless they insulate themselves in an artificially created and sustained sub-society bubble, they will interact positively with people who do not share their religious beliefs and they will discover by personal experience that such people do not have horns and they may even marry them. This in turn brings the issue of how children should be raised and, even if a mixed-religion couple agree to raise the children in one faith, those children cannot have the certainty of their ancestors, because their personal experience will undermine any suggestion that a particular religion has a monopoly of the virtues. Which explains one well-founded observation about the family transmission of the faith. For the second half of the twentieth century, the success rate of single-religion couples was 50 per cent: if they had two children, one would continue in the faith and one would not. For mixed-religion marriages (even when the mix was as little as Church of England and Methodist), the transmission rate is halved. For one child to grow up religious, the couple would need to have four children.[19]

To summarize, because modern societies no longer have shared religions, supported by the state and by influential social institutions such as education and the mass media, into which all people are indoctrinated, and which are reinforced by repeated everyday inter-action, religion has become a matter of individual preference. If you wish, you can have one, but you do not have to have one, and anyway you will decide what it will be and how far you will commit to it. For many of us religion has become like any other consumer product.

Science and Technology

Where does science feature in this story? It is often thought that science has undermined religion by showing that many traditional Christian beliefs are false: the earth is not flat; heaven is not just above our heads nor is hell just below our feet; the earth moves round the sun and not vice versa; the earth and human life are vastly older than the biblical accounts suggest; and almost all scientists agree that an evolutionary model along the lines of Charles Darwin's theory of evolution by natural selection offers a far better explanation of the origins of species than does the divine creation account given at the start of the Bible. Though such arguments fascinated literate Victorians, I doubt that science as a body of discoveries is that important. After all, when many westerners can believe that the moon landings were faked and that the US government blew up the Twin Towers, it is difficult to suppose that one body of ideas displaces another simply because it is better supported by the evidence. That is, being true and being plausible are not the same thing.[20]

What has been much more important than science as ideas is science as the basis for technology. Technically efficient machinery and procedures have two important consequences. They reduce our need for the supernatural and they change our sense of self-importance and self-worth. People used to sprinkle holy water on their sheep. There is simply no need to turn to God for help with ringworm when you can buy a drench that has proved over and over to be an excellent cure for the condition, even in sheep owned by atheists. When people had no way of preventing plague, turning to God, with weeks of fasting and special prayers, was a popular response. Now that we know a great deal about diseases and can manage and even eradicate them, a whole series of occasions for the expression of religious interest has been lost.

The decline of resort to religious solutions in everyday life is obvious. The second change is more subtle. As we have become more effective in controlling our environments and engineering change, we have become less likely to think of ourselves as the victims of fate or the subjects of an all-powerful and erratic divinity. Disasters, natural and social, still befall us, but we are nothing like as helpless as the medieval peasant and we do not feel it. With pretty good reason, we suppose that we can solve problems. The culture of the West is now pragmatic. A good example is the control of Ebola in Guinea and neighbouring countries in 2014–15. Ebola is a virulent and deadly disease that was first identified in 1976. Between then and 2013, twenty-four outbreaks, involving fewer than 2,000 people, were recorded by the World Health Organization. But in 2013 an epidemic broke out in West Africa that, as of writing, has killed over 11,000 people. Although the virus is contagious and deadly, it does not survive long away from a host body, and it is easily killed—by heating, for example. The initial reaction to the current epidemic was something close to panic, but the intervention of western agencies effectively ended it. Quarantine arrangements were imposed, and efficient and safe method of disposing of bodies was arranged, and good nursing and hygiene even allowed many sufferers to survive, which in turn increases the chances of vaccines being developed. The epidemic subsided and with it the panic.

That technology and efficient social organization have given us much greater control over life than was enjoyed by the medieval peasant does not prevent us believing in God, but it does change how we see ourselves in relation to some deity or divinity. We can still be religious, but the attitude of prostration assumed in the idea of 'worship' is now alien.[21] A few of us have self-esteem problems, but our culture generally thinks pretty well of itself, as is inadvertently indicated in that term 'self-esteem'. We might consult God. We might even periodically seek his approval. But a people that esteems itself does not easily worship.

The above is an extremely abbreviated version of the argument that in a wide variety of subtle ways modernization changes the social environment to create a society where religion is a matter of individual choice, where the rich diversity of religious cultures makes it hard to believe that one's faith is uniquely right, where social institutions do not indoctrinate citizens in a single faith, and where everyday interactions do not reinforce a shared faith. This erodes the intergenerational transmission of faith and creates both religious indifference and the new sort of believer we will meet in the following pages: selective, assertive, and autonomous.

The Supply-Side Alternative

There is an elaborate alternative to the secularization thesis.[22] In the 1830s Alexis de Toqueville, a minor French nobleman, toured America and made a series of penetrating comparisons of the old world of Europe and the new world of the United States. He was particularly struck by the irony that in France, where there was just one church, many people ignored or hated it. In America, where there were many competing denominations and sects, most people were committed adherents.[23] De Toqueville's observations have been taken up enthusiastically by American sociologists, who have combined them with the principles of free market economics (what is now called 'neoliberalism') into a general theory about the operations of religious markets. For them religious activity in Europe has declined, not because religious ideas have become less plausible, but because defects in the structure of the religious market mean supply has failed to meet or stimulate inherent demand. Where religion is voluntary and there is a lot of choice, it will remain popular; where there is one dominant church (especially if it is state supported and publicly funded) and thus little or no competition, religion will decline. The supply-side argument is complex, but the following will give some flavour of it.

First, there is a link between politics and religious disaffection. In Revolutionary France, where the Catholic Church was firmly on the side of the old social order, those social classes that wanted to challenge that order became disillusioned, not just with the Church, but with religion itself. As there was no state church in America promoting the interests of the ruling class, those people who wanted to express social and political dissent could do so without also abandoning religion. If they did not like one church, they could join another or found a new sect.

Second, there is a question of clergy motivation. The state church system contains little incentive for the clergy to recruit a congregation. The Church of England vicar derived his living from the rental value of lands given to the church centuries earlier by monarchs and pious lords. There was no direct material reason for such a clergyman to increase his congregation or to make himself more popular. For personal reward and advancement, it was much more important that he curried favour with social superiors who controlled church appointments. Operating in a voluntary religious market, the clergy of the American churches only ate if they recruited a congregation to feed them. If they wanted to become rich and famous, they had to do it, not by sucking up to the elites, but by appealing to potential congregants.

A free market also allows new entrants, while a state church either prevents competition or imposes artificial costs on it. The proliferation of alternatives is beneficial because, the more competing religions there are, the more chance there is that people will find something that meets their needs. With religion as with car manufacture: a competitive free market leads to more consumption.

It is not hard to find local examples of the value of competition. In 1858 the Shetland Methodist Ministers Quarterly Meeting minutes noted:

the value of the [Methodist] mission must be estimated—not by numerical results alone—but also by the indirect benefit which has resulted to the common cause of Christianity. The mission . . . has quickened the Church of Scotland into some additional effort. The mission has also given impulse to effort on the parts of the Free Church, Congregationalists and others.[24]

It is also easy to find examples of state religion producing slothful and indolent clergy. The novels of Jane Austin and Anthony Trollope are replete with accurately drawn examples of clergy who took the stipends attached to their posts and performed their jobs minimally or not at all while paying a curate a fraction of their income to do the work for them.

But there are also obvious problems with the supply-side alternative to secularization. If it works at all, the idea that a state church alienates people from religion if they become alienated from the old social order works only for Catholicism. Because Catholicism argues that the Vatican has a monopoly of religious truth, it encourages a forced choice. You either buy what the Church says or you abandon religion. Hence one has the pattern in twentieth-century Spain, Italy, Portugal, and France of society dividing into two big competing blocks: the Catholic Church on the one side and, on the other side, the secularism of communist and socialist parties. But in Protestant countries, even those that had a state church, there was always the possibility of breaking away. If you believe that all people can equally well discern the will of God and that there is no need for bishops and priests, then you can form your own religious organization. And many British people did just that. If they did not like the close ties between squire and vicar, they became Methodists, and if they felt that their Methodist chapel had become lifeless and formalistic, they could form a Primitive Methodist chapel. In the late eighteenth and nineteenth centuries, the state Church of Scotland had competition from the Relief Presbytery, four brands of Seceder Presbyterian, and the Free Church, and still most English dissenting movements found a foothold. The contrast between established religion and voluntary religion does not work well for Britain, where it was quite possible for those people who were alienated from the state churches by their political associations to set up their own dissenting sects and denominations.

The point about the incentives to clergy to build congregations is a good one, but again it fails to explain the differences between Britain and America. Although the clergy of the state churches had no financial incentive to be popular because they were paid from what was in effect a land tax, there were plenty of ministers in the dissenting denominations who had every good reason to work hard to become and remain popular. By the 1850s half of Britain's clergy were outside the state churches.

But the biggest problem with the supply-side alternative to the secularization thesis is that it does not fit the big picture. While there are short-term and local benefits from competition, over any long period of time, a society with a single religion to which everyone belongs (and which is supported by the government and other vital social institutions such as the schools) has proved more resistant to secularization than has a competitive religious environment. In Europe, the Catholic monopolies of Poland and the Irish Republic remained religious longer than the fragmented religious economies of England or Holland. Narrower comparisons reinforce this conclusion. The three Baltic states of Lithuania, Latvia, and Estonia are similar in their political histories and their economies, but they differ in their religious make-up, and, of the three, the homogenous Catholic Lithuania remained more religious than the religiously divided Latvia and Estonia.[25] We see the same picture when we compare three Scottish islands: Orkney, Shetland, and the Outer Hebrides. They were part of the same state, subject to the same laws, and had very similar economies: a mix of subsistence farming and fishing.[26] In 1900 they were similarly religious. By the 1970s they were very different. Orkney and Shetland had gradually secularized in much the same way as the rest of Scotland, while Lewis in the Outer Hebrides had so patently remained churchgoing and Sunday observant that it was used to signify being irritatingly pious. If Scots comedians wanted to poke fun at religion, they put on a Lewis accent. And the key difference was diversity. Orkney and Shetland, like lowland Scotland, had a number of competing denominations. In Lewis almost everyone belonged to the evangelical Free Church, and its popularity allowed its values to become deeply entrenched in everyday life, to be monitored by close community supervision, and to be reinforced by everyday interaction.

Not Decline Just Change

It is possible to accept all the explanatory elements of the secularization thesis but reject the conclusion that the consequence of modernization is secularity. One could suppose that a completely voluntaristic religious culture, in which most people have no faith and the remainder construct their own idiosyncratic packages, offers a stable environment for religion. It has not declined (despite the obviously growing number of people who say they are not religious); it has just changed.[27] We now have a clear choice. The 'not-decline-just-change' school thinks consumerist religion will endure as well as the old authoritarian community religion. The secularizationists think that consumerism is one of the causes of secularization.

Consumerist religion suffers two obvious problems. The first is that the solidarity and collective action that would give it weight beyond the sum of its parts is impossible. A highly sympathetic anthropologist has referred to the New Agers of Glastonbury as a 'tribe' but, as we will see in Chapter 2, her own account shows them unable to create and sustain social institutions. To the extent that each person insists on the right to decide what to believe, social action is difficult. This is particularly the case with intergenerational transmission. As we will see in Chapter 6, New Agers are less successful at passing on their interests to their children than are conventional Christians. And that is no surprise. A faith based on the proposition 'Only believe what seems true to you' will not be inherited or reinforced by frequent interaction with like-minded people. It will need to be invented by every individual spiritual seeker and it will die with that seeker.

There is also a question of commitment. It is a sad fact that, left to our own devices, we are unlikely to commit or sacrifice much. It is no accident that the successful models for overcoming addictions are those such as Weightwatchers and Alcoholics Anonymous, where the group both controls its members via fear of embarrassment and supports them. If we are the sole arbiters of what is required, we will find ways of persuading ourselves that what we want to do is what should be done. The biography of one of the founders of the Findhorn Foundation (of which more in the next chapter) shows someone persuading himself that the sexual affairs in which he repeatedly indulged were exactly what was required for his spiritual development and, by the way, were also good for his abandoned partners and the Foundation.[28] We need social pressure to counter our natural tendency to sloth, self-deceit, and self-indulgence. Without others to chivvy, nudge, and nag us, we will do what we want to do, and for any religious or spiritual beliefs that means that, instead of some religious innovation changing us, we will tend to pick the bits that fit most comfortably with our current preferences. I do not mean to suggest that people never change or that serious commitment to an idiosyncratic and self-selected package of new spiritual expressions is impossible. I mean only that the average levels of commitment in shared communal religion will be higher than those prevalent in religious cultures where people claim the authority to determine their own levels of involvement.[29]

In summary, the 'not-decline-just-change' view seems a little like wishful thinking. Aside from the overlooked matter of the rapidly growing numbers of the avowedly religiously indifferent, many of whom are quite happy to declare that they are neither religious nor spiritual, to the sociologist, the 'just change' religion has some obvious weaknesses.

DEFINITIONS

In social science, as in natural science, precision is important, but the social changes being described and explained in this book are so large and clear that the accuracy of either description or explanation is unlikely to depend much on any particular use of terms. Hence those who just want the big picture can probably skip this section with little loss.

We can begin with some rather loose definitions and then refine these later if further precision becomes useful. Given that the rest of the book contains very many illustrations of what is here defined, some loose formulations are sufficient to start with.

This book treats the religious and the secular as comprehensive and complementary alternatives—like smoking and not smoking—rather than as mirror images. By religion I mean beliefs and actions predicated on the existence of some supernatural being (or, to encompass karma, some impersonal agency) with the power of moral judgement. To placate the divinity and to increase the odds on a good life now and a better life in the next world, we must do some things and not do others. Spirituality is more difficult to define. Especially for older people, spirituality may be just the personal component of being religious; spiritual being the equivalent of pious. For those who consciously choose spiritual rather than religious as a self-description, spirituality involves beliefs and actions predicated on the existence of some supernatural power that is no longer external to us but is already inherent in all of us, if only we knew it.[30]

By secular I mean simply the absence of the religious and spiritual. Obviously people can be more or less religious or spiritual, but there is a point of being less of either that deserves to be labelled secular and is actually so labelled by the formerly religious or spiritual when they talk about having lost their faith. Secularization is the process of becoming more secular and secularity is the state of being secular. A secularist is someone who approves of and promotes the expansion of the secular sphere at the expense of the religious sphere.

For completeness, I should clarify one frequent source of misunderstanding. As should have been clear from the above, the historical process of secularization owes almost nothing to avowed secularists. Their role is usually confined to coming along after some change has occurred and giving it their approval.[31] Most of the crucial elements in the proposition that modernization undermines religion are unintended consequences. For example, when various waves of dissenters broke away from the national churches, they intended to weaken (so they could replace) only the national church and not religion as such. But the long-term effect of each sect wishing to protect itself from other churches and sects was to force the state to become religiously neutral, to turn religious education in schools from the promotion of a particular religion to teaching about all religions, and to create an environment in which religion changed from a community-enforced expectation to a matter of free choice.

I have just defined religion in terms of what I (and, more importantly, most people) take to be its substantive characteristics. Some sociologists define it in terms of its social functions—for example, religion is that thing which unites a body of people—and this finds echoes in the popular business of asserting that this or that is 'the new religion'.[32] This unhelpfully muddies the waters. It may be that this or that secular social institution or activity performs functions that were once the province of religion: following a football club or dancing at drug-fuelled all-night raves may provide the fan or raver with some of the sensations or social benefits that were enjoyed by the pious Christian in the nineteenth century.[33] But to *define* following football as a religion is to achieve by fiat what needs to be established by empirical comparison. And when we make that detailed comparison we can immediately see many ways, substance apart, in which religion and football differ. Few football fans martyr themselves for their club; few will marry only supporters of the same club; few believe their clubs to embody comprehensive explanations of life or guides to achieving salvation, or even ethical systems; and few fans regard other clubs as the embodiment of evil. It seems obvious that, when some fans say 'football is my religion', they mean only that they take football unusually seriously.[34]

The terms church, sect, denomination, and cult will be used a number of times in ways that make their meaning fairly clear; they are defined fully in Chapter 7. Because they are more immediately significant, I will introduce the contrast pair of world-affirming and world-rejecting religion.

Roy Wallis presented a wide-ranging overview of the new religious movements (NRMs) of the 1960s and 1970s in which he divided them into two based on their orientation to the world. Some, such as the Unification Church (aka Moonies), were world rejecting.[35] They saw the human self as essentially bad and becoming good only under external discipline. They promoted asceticism, encouraged adherents to withdraw from conventional social roles to work full time for the movement, and concentrated on the next life. Others, such as est and Scientology, were world affirming. They saw the self as essentially good and improvable by its own efforts. They aimed to improve people's experience of this life in one of three related ways. They promised to help people become more successful: a weekend of est or Insight training would help you win that promotion. They promised to help you fill the emotional vacuum left by too-vigorous striving for material success. A participant in an Actualizations training seminar said:

All my life, I've been an achiever. I've always won all of the 'Best of Everything' awards. I've been rising fast in the corporation I work for, looking forward—somewhat uneasily—to the day when they make me president of the company. It's a goal I have absolutely no doubt that I'll achieve. There's just one drawback. I feel the closer I get, the less human I am. It's robbing me of my humanity.[36]

Third, to the extent that circumstances could not be altered, they helped you to accept your life as it is: to feel that things were just as they should be and hence you should not feel frustrated and embittered by your situation. And many world-affirming movements promised to do all three.

There are good reasons for regarding world-affirming NRMs as being more susceptible to secularization than their world-rejecting counterparts.[37] Because they assume that humankind is essentially good and can be improved by its own devices, the drift to purely secular psychotherapies is a short one. One needs only to drop the idea that the self is perfected by connection with the cosmic consciousness and replace claims that are patently supernaturalist or bordering on the supernatural with entirely secular views. So the 'power within' that Findhorn talks of becomes simply our own innate human potential. And we go back from Carl Jung and Bhagwan Shree Rajneesh's spiritualized psychotherapy to Sigmund Freud's secular original. In saying this, it is important to distinguish causal claims from tautologies. I am not *defining* world-rejecting and world-affirming movements as respectively 'really religious' and 'really secular'. World-affirming religions can be thoroughly religious; Scientology is an example. In practice, and as we will see, world-affirming religions do often attenuate religious characteristics and for that reason they can be way stations on the road from the religious to the secular.

One final element of theoretical introduction will be useful. The subtitle of this book—the westernization of the easternization of the West—is a slightly tongue-in-cheek reference to Colin Campbell's *The Easternization of the West*.[38] In this seminal work, Campbell argues that the culture of western societies has changed, not just because eastern religions have become more popular, but also because, at a much deeper level, 'essential primary assumptions concerning reality and truth, time and history, the cosmos, and the nature of humankind' in the West have become more like those prevalent in the East.[39] I largely sympathize with this argument. As will become clear, I disagree only in that I think Campbell gives too much weight to two embodiments of that process: new religious movements and New Age spirituality. And, though he often acknowledges it, I do not think he gives enough weight to the way in which our cultural borrowings have been 'westernized' in the process of being borrowed.

CONCLUSION

All the above is background to the argument that will be advanced in this book. My primary concern is to demonstrate that the 'not-decline-just-change' rebuttal of the secularization thesis is just another unconvincing attempt to deny what to those who have no interest in asserting the continued social importance of religion seems obvious.[40] In what follows I will seek to demonstrate that the NRMs of the late 1960s never recruited anything like the number of people needed to sustain the 'just change' view; that those that did best were the least religious; that world-affirming movements (which by and large are most secular) did better than world-rejecting ones; that most of those that survived more than a decade did so by becoming more, not less, secular; that attempts to measure serious interest in spirituality have failed to find any evidence that it is in any conventional sense of the word 'popular'; and that, while it is the case that eastern religious themes have proved attractive to some in the West, they have been changed in ways that look like capitulation to the secular culture of the West. That is, rather than providing evidence against the secularization thesis, the fate of key innovations actually demonstrates the power of the secular.

NOTES

1. Traditionally the Tees divided County Durham from the North Riding of Yorkshire, but in 1974 Holwick and Lunedale were transferred to Durham.
2. N. Pevsner, *Buildings of England: West Riding of Yorkshire* (London: Penguin, 1967), 163–4. The pungent remark is actually made about Cleckheaton's Central Methodist chapel. The Providence entry that follows immediately after says: 'The same applies here.'
3. C. Hirst, 'A Converted Chapel in Yorkshire is Just the Right Setting for Aakash, a New Curry House Offering Heavenly Flavours', *Independent*, 25 August 2001. Unfortunately the owner of the Aakash over-reached and went bust.
4. R. Gill, *The Empty Church Revisited* (Aldershot: Ashgate, 2003).
5. Identifiers with non-Christian religions, mostly immigrants since the 1960s and their descendants, comprise around 6% of the population and so do not much affect the overall levels of personal religious adherence.
6. P. Brierley, *Pulling out of the Nosedive* (London: Christian Research, 2006).
7. For a detailed account of the 1851 Census, see E. Higgs, The Religious Worship Census of 1851, Online Historical Population Reports <http://www.histpop.org/ohpr/servlet/View?path=Browse/Essays%20(by%20kind)/General&active=yes&mno=2062> (accessed November 2016).

8. Brierley, *Nosedive*, 12.
9. It might be supposed by the sceptical that the clergy exaggerate their attendances, but, in thirty years of collecting church attendance and membership data generated in a variety of ways from a wide variety of organizations, I have seen no evidence that this is the case.
10. An attempt to test the reliability of survey data by comparing the evidence of clergy reports with what a representative sample of residents of Ashtabula County, Ohio, said in response to a telephone survey showed claimed attendance 83% higher than actual attendance. See C. K. Hadaway, P. L. Marler, and M. Chaves, 'What the Polls Don't Show: A Closer Look at US Church Attendance', *American Sociological Review*, 58 (1993), 741–52.
11. S. Bruce and A. Glendinning, 'The Extent of Religious Activity in England', *Future First*, 29 October 2013, pp. 1, 4.
12. D. Voas and A. D. Crockett, 'Religion in Britain: Neither Believing nor Belonging', *Sociology*, 39 (2005), 11–28.
13. G. Davie, *Religion in Britain since 1945: Believing without Belonging* (Oxford: Blackwell, 1994).
14. R. Putnam, *Bowling Alone: The Collapse and Revival of American Community* (New York: Simon and Schuster, 2000).
15. P. A. Hall, 'Social Capital in Britain', *British Journal of Political Studies*, 29 (1999), 417–62.
16. I am indebted here to the pioneering work of Alasdair Crockett and David Voas.
17. For a book-length elaboration of the secularization thesis, see S. Bruce, *Secularization* (Oxford: Oxford University Press, 2012).
18. Data on all these measures are presented in S. Bruce, 'Appendix Two: Fifty Years On', in B. R. Wilson, *Religion in Secular Society Fifty Years On* (Oxford: Oxford University Press, 2016).
19. Voas and Crockett, 'Religion in Britain'.
20. This distinction, as much else in my work, is owed to P. L. Berger and T. Luckmann, *The Social Construction of Reality* (London: Penguin, 1973).
21. I am indebted to David Voas for drawing my attention to this.
22. For examples of the supply-side school of thought, see L. Young, *Rational Choice Theory and Religion: Summary and Assessment* (New York: Routledge, 1997).
23. A. de Toqueville, *Democracy in America* (Chicago: University of Chicago Press, 2000).
24. Shetland Methodist Church, *Records of Ministers Quarterly Meeting*, 20 May 1858. Shetland Archive CH11/79/1/8.
25. S. Bruce, 'The Supply-Side Model of Religion: The Nordic and Baltic States', *Journal for the Scientific Study of Religion*, 39 (2000), 32–46.

26. Details of the comparison of the three islands can be found in S. Bruce, *Scottish Gods* (Edinburgh: Edinburgh University Press, 2014), ch. 2.

27. Arts and Humanities Research Council, 'British Religion Has Changed Dramatically and the Implications for Policy and Practice Are Far Reaching', 10 May 2012 <http://www.ahrc.ac.uk/newsevents/news/britishreligionpolicyandpractice> (accessed May 2017). See also L. Woodhead, 'Mind, Body and Spirit: It's the De-Reformation of Religion; Church Attendance May Be Declining, But Real Individual Religion has Undergone a Huge Revival in The Past 30 Years', theguardian.com, Monday, 7 May 2012. It is worth noting that in 1966 Bryan Wilson, widely regarded as the progenitor of the modern secularization approach, gave an effective rebuttal of the 'just-change' view in *Religion in Secular Society* (London: C. A. Watts, 1966), pp. xiv–xvii.

28. P. Caddy, *In Perfect Timing: Memoirs of a Man for the New Millennium* (Forres: Findhorn Press, 1995). Peter had an affair with a young Swedish student to whom he gave an inordinate amount of influence over the community before he departed for the USA, leaving Eileen and the young woman to sort out the obvious conflict of authority. In his new life as 'planetary ambassador' he managed to add two marriages to his previous three.

29. This point is developed by Rosabeth Kanter into an explanation of why some intentional communities last longer than others. See R. Kanter, *Commitment and Community: Communes and Utopias in Sociological Perspective* (Cambridge, MA: Harvard University Press, 1972).

30. For a more detailed depiction, see P. Heelas and L. Woodhead, *The Spiritual Revolution* (Oxford: Blackwell, 2005), 24–30. On the difference between religion and spirituality, see B. J. Zinnbauer, K. J. Pargament, B. Cole, M. S. Rye, E. M. Butter, T. G. Belavich, K. M. Hipp, A. B. Scott, and J. L. Kadar, 'Religion and Spirituality: Unfuzzing the fuzzy', *Journal for the Scientific Study of Religion*, 36 (1997), 549–64.

31. Even where secular ideologues do seem to be influential, it is usually because circumstances have created the conditions they sought to promote. For example, the position of religious tolerance enshrined in the US Constitution owed far more to the fact of the early colonies having a number of competing churches and sects than to the work of theorists such as Thomas Paine.

32. It is worth noting that those sociologists who are often described as advancing a functional definition of religion seem on close examination to be doing no such thing. Robert Bellah, in *Tokugawa Religion* (Glencoe, IL: Free Press, 1957), 6, says: 'It is one of the social functions of religion to provide a meaningful set of ultimate values on which the morality of a society can be based.' If religion is not just the functions it serves, then it must be identifiable separately from those functions. As

has often been noticed, functionalists often fall back on conventional substantive definitions. Jack Goody says of Talcott Parsons and Bellah 'it is perhaps significant that in their pragmatic treatment of religious phenomena the above authors adhere much more closely to the "traditional" sphere of discourse' (J. Goody, 'Religion and Ritual: The Definitional Problem', *British Journal of Sociology*, 12 (1961), 154).

33. On fandom, see J. O. Bickerdike, *The Secular Religion of Fandom* (London: Sage, 2015). On ravers, see G. Lynch and E. Badger, 'The Mainstream Post-Rave Club Scene as a Secondary Institution: A British Perspective', *Culture and Religion*, 7 (2004), 27–40.

34. Equally unhelpful is the habit of discovering religion by giving religious names to secular attitudes. One detailed study of young people's religious beliefs that showed very clearly that most did not have any called what did interest them 'immanent faith', though its primary components were almost entirely secular: fondness for family and friends and an interest in developing an authentic 'self'. Not being religious but occasionally worrying about things becomes 'bedroom spirituality'. See S. Collins-Mayo, B. Mayo, S. Nach, and C. Cocksworth, *The Faith of Generation Y* (London: Church House Publishing, 2010).

35. R. Wallis, *The Rebirth of the Gods? Reflections on the New Religions in the West* (Belfast: Queen's University of Belfast, 1978). When this inaugural lecture was expanded as *The Elementary Forms of the New Religious Life* (London: Routledge and Kegan Paul, 1984), Wallis added an intermediate 'world-accommodating' position. As that refinement is not particularly relevant to my argument, I have stuck with the initial dichotomy. Carrette and King have an alternative based on eight reactions to, or preconditions for, being exploited by neo-liberal capitalism. As well as being more detailed, this typology, they claim, solves the problem of resting on an intersubjective agreement of the nature of the world that people are either affirming or rejecting. I do not believe that they have solved a perennial problem of social scientific explanation or that the eightfold distinction sufficiently adds to the analysis to justify the additional clunkiness. See J. Carrette and R. King, *Selling Spirituality: The Silent Takeover of Religion* (London: Routledge, 2005), 20.

36. J. M. Martin, *Actualizations: Beyond est* (San Francisco: San Francisco Book Co., 1977), 55.

37. Note that this discussion is confined to religion in the formerly Christian West. That the former hegemonic religion was, in theory at least, world-rejecting has created general cultural expectations of what religion is like.

38. C. Campbell, *The Easternization of the West: A Thematic Account of Cultural Change in the Modern Era* (Boulder, CO: Paradigm, 2007).

39. Campbell, *Easternization*, 363.

40. Normally I would not try to explain the errors of colleagues by their material interests. After all, the private reasons for advancing one theory rather than another are irrelevant to its evaluation. For that, what matter are the internal consistency of argument and the fit with the evidence. However, I cannot resist pointing out that in the UK the 'not-decline-just-change' position is far more popular with theologians and scholars in Religious Studies departments (that is, people whose work assumes the continued importance of religion) than with social scientists, who can be indifferent to the fate of religion.

2

Contemporary Spirituality

INTRODUCTION

Edward Cayce was an American mystic responsible among other things for popularizing notions about the supposed lost ancient and magnificent city of Atlantis. It is thus appropriate that it was a speaker from the Edward Cayce Foundation who in 1980 was very nearly killed by a 2-pound crystal while talking at the Findhorn Foundation's Universal Hall. The whole notion of crystals as a source of power was controversial. The Foundation had been joined by a group who believed that certain crystals could channel energy from Atlantis. When the Universal Hall was being built, they lobbied for the inclusion of their occult designs:

> A specially cut quartz crystal, about the size of a grapefruit, was prepared and suspended on gold wires in the centre of the Hall. The gold wires led to the supporting pillars, from which silver wires led down into the foundations. In the basement, a smaller crystal was embedded in the floor and a small piece of meteoric iron sat above it. A third crystal was fixed to a light in the centre of the ceiling. . . . a special service of invocation was held to inaugurate the energy transfer.

Two years later the wires snapped and dropped the sharp-edged heavy ball of glass onto the middle of the floor. Perhaps warned by his psychic powers, the speaker was standing off to one side and was hit only by some fragments. Eileen Caddy, one of Findhorn's founders and an opponent of occult practices, had the bits gathered up, and, following her intuited guidance, they were buried.[1]

FINDHORN

Now one of Europe's oldest New Age[2] centres, the Findhorn Foundation on the Moray coast in Scotland had its inauspicious origins in the sacking of three English people from their jobs running the Cluny Hotel in Forres. Peter and Eileen Caddy and their friend Dorothy Maclean moved into the cheapest accommodation they could find: a shabby caravan on a shabby holiday caravan park.[3]

To highlight the miraculous nature of Findhorn's creation, histories tend to tell the story as though it had no background, but the Caddys and Maclean had long been involved in the fringe milieu of esoteric knowledge. Peter Caddy had been in the Rosicrucian Order Crotona Fellowship—a group barely larger than its name that studied esoteric subjects from lectures, plays, and correspondence material prepared by their inspired master George Sullivan. Peter also attended meetings at the Pimlico flat of Sheena Govan, whom he married in 1948. Govan had a caravan in Glastonbury, and her followers were familiar with the various groups that saw it as a place of particular spiritual power.[4] Caddy's RAF career allowed him to visit India and Tibet, where he found themes for his own personal bricolage. It also led him to meet Eileen, who became his second wife. Maclean was also part of the Govan circle. It was Govan's decision to move to a tiny isolated cottage in Glenfinnan that brought the three to Scotland, and, after a few years of unemployed poverty, all three found work running a large hotel in Forres. By their account they turned a white elephant into a profitable concern, but their employers—perhaps disturbed by the sensationalist coverage of Sheena Govan's circle in a number of popular Scottish papers in 1957—moved them to the Trossachs Hotel for a season and then fired them. That led to the three spending what they assumed would be a temporary sojourn on the Findhorn caravan park. Desperately poor, they began to grow their own vegetables.

> Dorothy meanwhile had had messages come through to her in meditation, to feel into the nature forces such as the wind, and then the higher nature spirits of clouds or vegetables. She had discovered to her surprise that her entry into that realm was welcomed by those spirits. At Peter's request that she ask for help with the growing of the vegetables, she found she was able to attune to the essence of the garden pea.[5]

Initially the least assertive of the trio, Eileen had a power that Peter
lacked: having first heard an 'inner voice' in a church in Glastonbury,
she became a channel for regular messages of spiritual guidance.

> As soon as my pen touched the paper it was like switching on an electric
> current. The words flowed. I was told: 'I work through each of you in
> different ways. You know when you need guidance from Me, you can
> receive it instantaneously. Like a flashing of lightening it is there. You
> can find the answer immediately; therefore you hold great responsibil-
> ities in your hands.'[6]

She initially regarded her revelations as coming from God traditionally conceived. Later she came to an internalist view: 'There is no
separation between ourselves and God, there is only "I am". I am the
guidance. It took me so many years to realize this.'[7]

The Caddys first attracted attention for their spirit-assisted gardening: 'stories of plants performing incredible feats of growth and endurance: 40-pound cabbages, 8-foot delphiniums, and roses blooming in
the snow'.[8] As an aside it is worth noting that the miracle vegetable
stories were the work of people who knew nothing of Findhorn's
environment (which in the 1930s was described by tourism promoters,
with only a little wishful thinking, as the Moray 'Riviera') and assumed
that anything 'up north' must be snow covered. It very rarely snows on
the Moray Coast, and, without any assistance at all from Maclean's
devas, the neighbouring town of Forres has repeatedly won the Scotland
in Bloom title.

Gradually the caravan park attracted like-minded people. Initially
they were elderly long-term habitués of the English cultic milieu, but
the trickle turned into something of a rush in the late 1960s, when the
hippie counter-culture produced a surge of interest in communal
living.[9] It is hard in retrospect to imagine this, but for a short period
it seemed to many that individualistic capitalism was about to be
replaced by communal socialism; that 'revolution in the air' was not
just the title of a flimsy Thunderclap Newman pop hit. In 1969 the
caravan park had about 600 visitors and in 1970 the group grew from
17 to 42 adults and 9 children. In the spring of 1973, the BBC ran a
prime-time documentary about the growing community. The 1975
publication of an entirely flattering portrait brought the group to the
attention of an international audience.[10]

The modern community owes much to two changes that show the
shift from world-rejecting to world-affirming religion: the Caddys'

conversion to optimism and input from an American couple. The Caddys originally saw themselves as a saved remnant in a largely bad world from which they would be rescued by Venusian spacemen. On Whitsun 1966

> a group of about sixteen carefully selected people (plus a few gatecrashers) gathered with us at Findhorn. We had been told to expect an attempted landing by our space brothers, so we all assembled on the beach at the landing site we had prepared and built up in our meditations over the years. Those with inner sight actually described a spaceship as it came in and hovered overhead; I saw nothing, of course, but when Roc was told to stand in the centre, where a beam of light would be focused on him to 'raise his vibrations', even *I* saw him disappear briefly! It gave me quite a shock. Yet while nothing else seemed to happen afterwards—according to the sensitives, the spacecraft flew off again—all of us there were filled with a tremendous feeling of upliftment, as if something very profound had changed and things would never be the same again.[11]

Eileen's inner voice announced:

> Let none of you have any feeling of disappointment regarding last night.... All was in preparation for something far, far greater than any of you have ever contemplated. Raise your thinking and you will raise your living to an entirely new level. Do it this instant, going your various ways, knowing that this is actually happening to you. Rise together.[12]

Just as many Christian sects that mistakenly predicted the end of the world explained their apparent failure by claiming that their good work had bought the human race extra time, so Eileen's guidance went on to say that sufficient Light had been anchored on the planet (presumably by the work of the Caddys and like-minded souls) that destruction was now no longer inevitable: 'the spacecraft that had come, as we thought, to arrange . . . evacuation had in fact "popped in" to tell us that everything was all right'. Clearly there might be a lot of retrospective rewriting in this account produced thirty years after the event, but Peter Caddy saw the Whitsun 1966 spacecraft visit as 'a turning point in human history'.[13]

The second significant change was the arrival of David Spangler, a young American who has a reasonable claim to have been one of the devisers of the concept of the 'New Age'. Active in psychic circles in California since 1965, Spangler first visited in 1970 and then moved permanently to Findhorn in 1973. He and his wife, Myrtle Glines, put the educational work of the community on a firm footing and encouraged the expansion that in 1975 saw the purchase of the Forres hotel from which the Caddys had been sacked. In 1983 the community's base was secured when it bought the caravan park. It was also gifted the tiny tidal island of Erraid off Mull and a house on Iona, both of which were run as outposts of the Foundation.

Histories of the Foundation often describe it as miraculously self-generating: proof that 'manifestation'—present your needs to the spirit world and they will be met—worked. A more rational reading is possible. Peter Caddy did not wait for the spirit world to deliver. He assiduously cultivated key figures in the esoteric milieu. Robert Ogilvie Crombie (the 'Roc' in the Venusian story) and Sir George Trevelyan of the Wrekin Trust were friends. He acquired the mailing list of well-known psychic Liebe Pugh and used it to sell Eileen's spiritual guidance and to solicit donations. Essentially Caddy garnered publicity by exaggerating Findhorn's size and achievements, committed to building projects the community could not afford, and hoped that enough people or donations would be attracted to make real the exaggerated claims.

With his marriage to Eileen in trouble, Peter began to spend more time advertising the community abroad, and he left it finally in 1979. Eileen also retreated from active involvement in day-to-day running of what was now a considerable bureaucratic operation.

Since 1979 the Foundation has had to be restructured a number of times as ambitious plans for growth brought debt problems, and its reluctance to adopt a strong management structure caused repeated difficulties in determining its purpose, limiting its membership, and protecting its resources. But it has survived by clearly separating its strands and by making its purpose more mundane but sustainable. As the revolution for which it was to be the catalyst never occurred, it settled for being a base for the spiritual education for a transient population. A core of about 150 staff services a regular programme of instruction for visitors: about 5,000 a year in the 1990s; perhaps 2,000 a year in the 2010s. Visitors spend a week in group meditations and instruction classes. They also do much of their own housekeeping and work with the staff in such domestic tasks as gardening and food preparation. For many, Experience Week is enough; they go home and add what they have learnt to their other spiritual practices. A few come back for further and longer periods and a handful who are acceptable to the core staff are invited to become resident members. By creating a controlled route into membership, the Foundation resolved the swamping problem of the early days when there were no formal mechanisms for rejecting people who wanted to join.

In addition to the staff core, there are perhaps 400–500 sympathizers and ex-staff who live in their own properties in Findhorn village and the surrounding area and who provide some services to the Foundation and support its activities. The Phoenix is a large organic and wholefood store and bookshop (which stocks an eclectic range of spiritual and religious books, DVDs, and CDs). The Apothecary supplies homoeopathic and herbal medicines. The Universal Hall provides a large modern auditorium for music and dance events. One strand of work that has proved particularly attractive to the wider world is ecologically sensitive development. To the original interest in organic horticulture, later generations have added sustainable forms of electricity generation, waste-water purification, and environmentally sensitive forms of building.

As an aside, and because numbers become important in Chapter 6, it is worth noting that the Findhorn Foundation recruited almost no Scots. Its founders were English and Canadian. Key later figures were American, Australian, and English. The vast majority of people attending Experience Week are continental Europeans: Scandinavians form a large bloc. Although large numbers of people have benefited from the Findhorn experience, they represent a trivial fraction of the total population from which they are drawn—which is pretty well the entire Anglophone world and Europe, minus Scotland.

Exactly what Findhorn teaches has varied with the interests of the residents and of the wider New Age community. The second generation, exemplified by David Spangler, brought a political and social critique of capitalist society.[14] Under the leadership of Craig Gibsone (1989–93) the 'holiotropic Breathwork' style of psychotherapy popular at the Esalen Institute in California was promoted. This involves beliefs about the importance of birth experiences for later psychological development and uses hyperventilation to help the psyche cure itself. It was suspended after complaints about health implications led to a critical report from academics.[15] The dispute over Atlantean power-generating crystals has already been mentioned. Insofar as there has been a common core, it is a combination of environmentalism, personal growth psychology, and the power of intuition.[16] A variety of rituals (using, for example, dance, guided meditation, and music) offer participants ways of transcending their personal problems and becoming happier more effective people. Although some activities borrow from paganism (especially Wicca), there is a clear break with traditional religion—which Eileen clearly expressed in her changed views of the source of her inspired writing— in the sense that rituals are thought to help people discover the power they *already* possess rather than give them access to external power. A favourite Findhorn phrase is 'coming into your own power'. This emphasis on personal growth (rather than on social revolution) has allowed a rapprochement with capitalism.

Since its inception, the Foundation's more outré beliefs have been dropped. Residents no longer expect to be lifted out of this life by space ships. Communitarianism has been ditched: the houses on the caravan park site are privately owned and visitors are confined to the programmes for which they have paid (and physically kept separate on the hotel site). It no longer publically describes itself as a 'centre of Light'.[17] The hippies who saw Findhorn as an alternative to 'the Man' have been replaced by professionals who boast of selling their services as consultants in conflict resolution to BP, GlaxoSmithKline, Price-Waterhouse Cooper, Standard Life, Shell, and the Royal Bank of Scotland.[18] In a gesture of mainstream assimilation, Eileen Caddy was awarded an MBE for services to 'spiritual enquiry'.[19]

THE HEALER'S TALE

By her own account 'a very ordinary woman',[20] Dorothy Lewis trained as a teacher after her marriage broke down and she was left with four children to raise. Originally from Hull, she was persuaded after a winter holiday in Yorkshire's Wensleydale and Swaledale that she belonged closer to nature. Her move is told as a series of con-firming coincidences: the external world regularly reassured her by unexpectedly meeting her needs.[21] She found a house in Reeth that would cost £12,000; she managed to sell her Hull bungalow for exactly £12,000. She needed somewhere to live while the Reeth house was renovated; friends lent her their holiday home. 'I can't believe it was all just "luck". I *needed* to trust an intuitive move. I needed to uncover so much of myself that had been lying hidden for nearly fifty years.'[22] Failing to find a teaching job, she decided to operate a bed-and-breakfast house. Adverts in a Quaker magazine brought Quaker customers.

> Many others had no apparent religious belief, but found something up on the moors that to them was 'other' and renewing. I respected this as a spiritual link—different but no less of worth than that of those who needed a formal pattern for their spirituality.[23]

If discovering the power of intuition was her first spiritual experience, her second was an episode of dissociation.

> I awoke one morning to find that the fells suddenly looked like cardboard theatre props. My head and reason told me quite clearly that if I walked up there, the ground would be as usual, and I would walk over into the next valley. But my eyes told me they were not 'real'. They could almost be lifted up and put away. I didn't understand this and found it very scary. What was happening? I think now that I was actually moving into a different stage of awareness. What I was seeing, or being shown, was a first glimpse of the difference between inner reality and outer unreality.[24]

Note the agency in that last sentence. Something or someone was showing her.

A son sent her a book on dowsing and ley lines. The phrase 'ley line' was coined in 1921 by amateur archaeologist Alfred Watkins, who believed he could identify ancient trackways in the British landscape. Watkins later developed the idea that these alignments were created for ease of overland trekking by line-of-sight navigation during Neolithic times, and had persisted in the landscape over millennia.[25] Watkins was an intensely rational man who thought he was engaged in secular archaeology. The spiritual dimension was added in the late 1960s, when ley lines were assimilated to Chinese feng shui—the idea being that they were significant channels of the earth's spiritual energy.[26] Hence meditating in a place (such as Glastonbury) where major ley lines converge or cross is more spiritually powerful than meditating at Junction 10 of the M25 London orbital road. Lewis was interested enough to find a local dowser and to discover that she had the power to dowse water. She felt this had something do with healing.

The next step on her journey involved meeting a woman who was training to be a Transpersonal Psychology Counsellor in London. Lewis was interested in something that involved study 'not only of the conscious and the unconscious but also [of] the *super*conscious, or transpersonal, or "other"'.[27] The first weekend involved exploring the self through fantasies. Lewis had a fantasy that involved a newborn tan-and-white calf. On her first walk in Swaledale after the weekend course, she came across a cow giving birth to a tan-and-white calf. 'This was synchronicity, a reality I experienced time and time again, as did my clients, when inner and outer lives merged. Often it was a signal for new creativity.'[28]

The next stage in Lewis's journey is unusual (or perhaps her being so forthright is unusual). She decided the bed-and-breakfast business was not paying well enough and looked for a way to monetize her newfound interests: 'I started looking for the next outer move, delving into a thick paperback that listed all sorts of New Age occupations—alternative medicine, healing, readings, communities, activities. I was looking for any form of healing that included dowsing and colour.'[29] She became interested in Radionics. Radionics practitioners believe that healthy and unhealthy people can be distinguished by the 'frequencies' of energy in their body. Fancy devices that look like early radios can diagnose such frequencies (in the sense of the Chinese Qi rather than the electronics sense) and heal by applying the appropriate curing frequency. Radionics originated in the early 1900s with Albert Abrams, who became a millionaire by leasing out Radionic machines to practitioners.[30] The use of these varied, but most users claimed to be able to identify disease by connecting a hair or a blood sample of a patient to the dial-covered box. *Scientific American* was sure the boxes were useless, and even the users lack a convincing theory of how they work, especially when they are not provided with any power supply.[31]

Lewis describes her contact with a nearby Radionics healer:

> I was told that as soon as possible she would do a full analysis of my energy systems, write to report on this, and then treat me for a month, all for the initial fee. I should note that the analysis was not the same as a doctor's diagnosis, as it related to the energy systems so to speak 'behind' the physical presentation.[32]

I quote that sentence because two features—the 'so to speak' and the quotation marks around 'behind'—suggest a lack of certainty about causal mechanisms common to many alternative therapies. The healer told her to lay off beef and tomatoes, which apparently cleared up a previously intractable gut problem. Lewis decided to undertake Radionics training: two years by correspondence course. Interestingly, she was not taken with the fancy machines but instead decided that her intuition was sufficient to diagnose energy imbalances and that she could convey healing by thinking of, and mentally conveying, an appropriate colour. She next met and learnt from a healer who had her own system of 'mental colour healing', and again Lewis adapted what she had learnt: 'Over the next two years she taught me a system which I loved, and still use, though in a personally modified way.'[33]

By now she was dowsing, using Radionics and colour healing, and still periodically attending a Transpersonal Psychology counsellor. Unsure as to whether she should pursue a career as a healer, she was advised to consult an astrologer, who encouraged her. She also took up meditating and studying the works of Alice Bailey, a former Theosophist who between 1919 and 1949 published many works of arcane wisdom, most of which were apparently 'dictated' to her by one of Theosophy's 'hidden Masters'.[34]

Finally she began to take paid clients and heal them. But this was not the end of her journey of spiritual discovery. She saw an angel: 'Huge and magnificent, he filled the skyline on my right, wings outspread, light all around. It was awesome.'[35] She also took up visualization: a method of guiding people through spiritually enlightening thoughts by asking questions and suggesting images:

> Anything can happen on these journeys. Some people have highly coloured fantasy experiences, meeting angels and other beings, landing on mountain tops and vividly extending their perceptions of their own strengths or potential. Others chug along in very ordinary ways, but the information that comes through from the unconscious is nevertheless exactly what they need.[36]

From this point on Lewis made a living offering one-to-one healing and running groups. At one stage she recorded and mailed out cassette tapes of healing visualizations, and those turned into the basis for publications.

THE SEEKER'S TALE

Isabel Losada was a single-parent out-of-work actress living in London whose *The Battersea Park Road to Enlightenment* is a useful catalogue of the many forms of New Age enlightenment on offer in any major city.[37] It is clear that her spiritual seeking was conducted with at least half an eye to publication and a good part of the other one looking for a man. Hence her rate of experimentation is unusually high and her attention often seems to wander, but her account is still valuable as an introduction to the New Age milieu.

Her initial entry came with an acquaintance inviting her to an Insight Seminar. Insight is one of the oldest human potential movements operating in the UK. In 1979, Bernard Levin, an elderly journalist renowned for his prickly personality, and his young lover Arianna Stasinoupolou, an ambitious recent Cambridge graduate, promoted weekends of self-realization and spiritual growth.[38] As in Findhorn's philosophy, the theory is that each of us has within us a 'centre' that already knows everything we need to know. What we need to do is get

> free of the melodrama which goes on in our heads most of the time; the fear, anxiety, guilt and recrimination; the burden of the past which dominates our present responses and produces exaggerated or inappropriate reactions; free from crippling images and beliefs, which make us feel we are not terribly worthwhile, which sabotage us at crucial points, which make us feel we simply *can't do it*—but also the contrast with that, the images of ourselves as perfect, leading to self-judgement, guilt and a burden of blame; free from the sense of oneself as victim, as the passive recipient of life's circumstances. Thus the training purveys the view that we are 'totally responsible for our lives'.[39]

Next Losada tried T'ai Chi while on holiday in France, and at the time it seemed to offer prospects of personal insight and control, but it proved too demanding when she returned to London and work, and she dropped it. Then she signed up for a weekend retreat with Christian nuns. She had been an evangelical Christian for a couple of years but had decided she did not share the beliefs, could not accept the conservative morals, and, most importantly, was not willing to surrender her right to decide what, if anything, she would believe. A two-day silent guided retreat might be acceptable. At the Anglican Community of St Mary the Virgin she listened to the nuns sing hymns, ate her meals in silence, and practised guided meditations. She took a long walk and listened to bird song. Though she found the weekend profoundly moving, 'the problem is that despite dancing joyfully at Insight, walking down cul-de-sacs with sage-like Frenchmen and a heavenly weekend at a convent, in-between times I go on being as grumpy as ever'.[40]

Next she had a consultation with a professional astrologer who told her a great deal about her personality on the basis of the alignment of the planets at the time and place of her birth. Then she signed up for a 'Goddess weekend', which promised 'a unique experience of yourself as a woman and your feminine power'.[41] This took the form of the small number of attenders talking a lot about their personal problems. 'The morning went well with some great exercises. The usual: listening skills, expressing anger, nothing I hadn't done before. I was much more comfortable.'[42] She was less so with one woman who felt the room was full of 'negative energy' and tried to cleanse it by burning sage. Or with an exercise that involved dancing in mirror image with other participants and then taking all her clothes off to learn that all body shapes are beautiful. The next day all participants turned up in flowing dresses and danced to music they had brought.

> Then a third got up and I saw pain dance. Can you imagine seeing pain? She cried out in pure grief and with the despair of all women. I'm not sure what century we were in at this stage nor who I was in the room with. . . . then joy stood up. Dancing to the old pop tune 'My Sweet Lord'. She danced naked before her Lord and I thought of my statue exercise. Here was a woman giving thanks to her God in her dance— thanks for her breasts, for her body, for being alive. We all smiled for her. We beamed at her. She radiated her joy into us, expressing complete freedom and self-love. . . . Finally it was my turn. I felt as if I had not been born. One of the women had offered me a simple white dress and it seemed very appropriate. I was a girl among these women, forgetting that I was older than many of them. Bach sounded and I began to cry. I looked around the circle. Faces of wise women who knew who they were. My job was to let the girl come out and dance.[43]

Next Losada tried a weekend of Tantric sex, which proved a disaster because the man she fell for was already attached. Then she attended a series of meetings in a Twelve Step programme for people who were 'co-dependent' rather than alcoholic. Five sessions persuaded her that, whatever problems she had, she was not co-dependent. So she tried colonic irrigation and three weeks of crank food under the instruction of a spiritual nutritionist: 'Very warm, motherly and quite sophisticated with an intelligent version of the New Age smile. She had the long flowing hair and long flowing skirts one would expect from a wise Mother-Earth-type but she also had a professionalism that was re-assuring.'[44]

If one supposes we are essentially good and are made bad only by experiences that can be stripped of their negative effects by talking about them to a trained counsellor, and if one believes in reincarnation, it follows that one will have to work through the problems accumulated in past lives and that is exactly the premise of Past Life Regression, which Losada tried next.

Then she got Rolfed. Ida Rolf (1896–1979) was an American biochemist who became convinced that bodily posture not only was important for physical well-being but also affected spiritual well-being. Her Structural Integration therapy teaches that 'a body which becomes more structurally upright, provides greater emotional, psychological and spiritual uprightness'.[45] Losada tried a self-explanatory Anger Release Day. She also tried Neurolinguistic Programming (NLP). This is an approach to communication, personal development, and psychotherapy developed by two Californians in the 1970s. Richard Bandler and John Grinder claimed that neurological processes, language, and learned behaviour patterns are related in a way that allows them to be changed to achieve specific goals in life.[46] Practitioners also claim that serious problems such as psychosomatic illnesses, allergies, and learning disorders can be cured in just one or two treatment sessions.

Finally, Losada's exhausting programme ended with a course called 'Working with Angels, Fairies, Muses and Nature Spirits'. Here she was taught about her energy field, and how to open her heart chakra.

> I stared at the sea and the sea stared back. It made nice wave noises to me. I thought of my energy and imagined it expanding to embrace the horizon. I visualised energy coming from out of my crown, looping around and coming back to me through my feet. Then I reversed the loop. I opened my soul in every way I knew how to receive the power and gentleness of the tide.[47]

By her own admission, Losada's extensive experience dabbling in alternative therapies and revelations did not make her very much more 'spiritual'. In the end she resolved to be a better person and to live more in the moment: two conclusions to which she could probably have come with a great deal less effort. Nonetheless her account is useful in showing the range of spiritual activity anyone in a major city can enjoy in little over a year.[48]

GLASTONBURY: FROM ENGLISH HIPPIES TO BEYONCÉ

The small Somerset town of Glastonbury has featured a number of times in the history of English mysticism. One recurring legend has Joseph of Arimathea (or in some versions his son Josephus) bringing the Holy Grail—a cup containing some of Christ's blood—to Glastonbury. A variant has Christ himself as a young man visiting the Somerset Levels—a myth popularized by the William Blake lyrics that are now sung as *Jerusalem*:

> And did those feet in ancient times
> Walk upon England's mountains green
> And was the Holy Lamb of God
> On England's pleasant pastures seen?[49]

In 1191, monks at the abbey claimed to have found the graves of the mythical King Arthur and his wife Guinevere to the south of the Lady Chapel of the Abbey Church, which was visited by a number of contemporary historians including Giraldus Cambrensis. The remains were supposedly later moved and then lost during the Reformation.[50] As the Wikipedia entry neatly puts it: 'Many scholars suspect that this discovery was a pious forgery to substantiate the antiquity of Glastonbury's foundation, and increase its renown.'[51]

As if Christ, the Holy Grail, and King Arthur were not attraction enough, in 1934 artist Katherine Maltwood claimed that the landscape around Glastonbury Tor formed an enormous and ancient zodiac.[52] Her claims were thoroughly debunked by serious historians in the 1970s, but this did not prevent them attracting young hippies such as Paul Weston to the Glastonbury music festival:

> I'd also heard of an alleged vast terrestrial zodiac, lying hidden in the landscape there, marked out by roads, and rivers, hills and fields. The festival, on the surface, was another great opportunity for me to continue my teenage pattern of seeing bands live and taking drugs. That was never my main reason to go there. My real focus was the mystery of the mystical capital of Britain.[53]

After two small trial events, 1971 saw the first proper Glastonbury festival.[54] Headliner David Bowie was a commercially successful pop musician, but hippie bands filled the schedules, and the music came from a stage built as a one-tenth replica of the Great Pyramid of Giza

on a spiritually auspicious site chosen by dowsing.[55] For the seriously
drug-addled Paul Weston, the climax of the performances was a
synthesizer and light show that accompanied the words:

> Pyramids and Stonehenge are ley lines to this place,
> City of Revelation, that governs inner space.
> So now, tune in your auras, let solstice music sound
> and build New Age vibrations and feed them into the ground.
> For here, inside these valleys, that are so full of energy,
> we'll build a New Jerusalem, with love, from you to me.[56]

At one point dancers in front of the stage sang the Hare Krishna
mantra and then parted to allow pass a slow-moving car containing
the 13-year-old Perfect Master Guru Mahari Ji. The Guru addressed
the audience from the pyramid stage: 'Every materialistic thing is
perishable. You should know such a thing as the un-perishable, the
Holy Knowledge of God and that is within you.'[57]

Though I must confess to once owning it all, the music of Soft
Machine, Mighty Baby, Gong, Steve Hillage, and the like never
became more than a footnote to popular music, and, as the festival
became more and more popular, its headline acts become more
mainstream, with Oasis (2004) and Beyoncé (2012) attracting protests from the old hardcore base. With attendances growing from the
original few thousand to over 100,000, organization had to become
more professional and bureaucratic. Originally the festival was free; in
2015, it cost £220 a ticket.

The town of Glastonbury itself continued to be a magnet for people
seeking or offering a wide range of New Age ideas and therapies.[58]
The New Age in Glastonbury estimates that in 1990 some 700 or so
people in a town population of 7,500 were 'alternative'.[59] Many
attempt to make a living as astrologers, healers, artists, jewellers, or
as instructors in meditation and yoga and T'ai Chi. Regular events
such as Goddess festivals are held in the town's Assembly Rooms.
There are shops selling New Age books, crystals, healing herbs, and
astrological instruments. And the activities of the town's alternative
residents are coordinated by *The Oracle*, a free occasional magazine
that advertises them and the many one-to-one services that can be
purchased.

A detailed ethnographic study of Glastonbury New Agers claimed
that they 'sustain a mode of social organization and a body of beliefs
and ideas whose features in many crucial respects display striking

similarities with the social and cultural forms of "original human society"—that is to say, human society in its evolutionary basic form'.[60] Hardly. New Agers may see themselves as having much in common with a romanticized vision of the primitive tribe but it is not obvious why we should accept their self-understanding for our analytical purposes. The Glastonbury New Agers talk a good critique of the dehumanizing nature of modern work, the unsustainability of western high maintenance lifestyles, and the virtues of self-sufficiency in a subsistence economy but many are parasitic on the capitalist economy they affect to despise. Far from being the peasants *de nos jours*, many are what used to be called 'remittance men': recipients either of inherited wealth or of state welfare payments. Others live by providing luxurious fripperies: candles, incense, soaps, magazines, and massages. Whatever else this may be, it is not an alternative to capitalism.

Despite the communitarian rhetoric, the Glastonbury New Agers found communal activity difficult. A group of friends talked of forming a spiritual community 'that would meet on a regular basis, so that, in a stable environment, they might share their spiritual experiences'. The idea was discussed for several months before the first meeting, when 'it quickly became clear that those involved had very different expectations'. They disagreed over whether the group should be open or closed and whether it should involve children. The following week the group was smaller: the two couples with children had dropped out. The third week the conversation turned to the fact that 'nearly all the people there had been involved either in a new religious movement, or a more traditional one, or had closely followed the teachings of one particular teacher'. What they had in common was the experience of feeling 'too confined ... their individuality had been threatened'. The group continued to meet for several weeks, getting smaller all the time, until it petered out.[61] The one attempt to create an alternative school was hardly more successful. The parents fell out with the original trustees and with each other, and the school closed after a year.[62]

KEY CONCEPTS

The more specifically Hindu- and Buddhist-influenced strands of religious and spiritual innovation are discussed at length in later chapters. Here I will try to summarize the key ideas in the spiritual seeking I have described thus far.[63]

The Enduring Self

A crucial New Age theme is a preference for the heart over the mind. Too much rational thought inhibits us.[64] We need to have faith in our inner selves, which is the place where we find our energy, which is also the world's energy. As Dorothy Lewis shows, we should trust to our intuition and to synchronicity. If we can just attune (in the Findhorn phrase) to reality and manifest our needs, we will find peace and success. In recognizing that, we also recognize that we are solely responsible for our lives.

Contemporary spirituality represents a 'subjective turn' in two senses. First, the divine power is no longer out there, but within us all, if only we knew it. Second, each of us is the final arbiter of truth. Sir George Trevelyan, one of the doyens of the British New Age, concluded a talk by saying: 'This is what things look like to me. If it doesn't seem like that to you, you don't have to accept what I say. Only accept what rings true to your own Inner Self.'[65]

The New Age is individualistic in *epistemology*—that is, in the theory of knowledge or in how we distinguish the truth from falsity. The crucial test is whether it works for us. We are used to individualism in the *behaviour* sense: I do not like country music, but I accept that others have a right to sing maudlin ballads with titles such as 'Little Sister, throw your red shoes away'. We are used to individualism in *political choice*: we accept that everyone has a right to express a preference in choosing the government. But conventionally we have supposed that there is an objective reality and that truth is a matter of expertise, not preference. As someone once said: 'You are entitled to your own opinions. You are not entitled to your own sets of facts.' The individualism of the New Age goes much further than individualism in behaviour in that it replaces an objective notion of truth with endless subjectivism. The individual consumer is not only the final arbiter of what he or she likes but is also the final arbiter of truth and falsity. In that sense, tolerance taken into the world of epistemology produces complete relativism. There is no longer a single truth. There is your truth and there is my truth.

We should note that, contra critics of contemporary spirituality, it does not automatically follow that epistemological individualism produces selfishness. It is quite possible for a solipsistic person to be generous. What does follow, however, is that such generosity will be on the individual's terms. However, at least in its more popular forms, New Age individualism does tend to the self-regarding. The stories flagged on the front page of one edition of *Spirit and Destiny* (the only UK holistic spirituality publication to make it into the top 400 magazines according to the Audit Bureau of Circulation) are as follows:

- The magic of mirrors: transform your self-esteem with your reflection.
- Grab back some me-time: how to put yourself first.
- 'Spirit medics help me heal the sick.'
- Sleep cures for perfect summer slumber.
- Do the dead send gifts to the living?
- Native Spirit oracle.
- Best holidays for health.
- Energy cleanse your home.
- Easy ways to eat fibre.[66]

Of those nine items, at least five are primarily concerned with the individual reader's problems and only one is patently concerned with those of other people. The Buddhist notion of 'self-compassion' is supposed to be a precursor to compassion for others, but when it is reduced to 'aim to discover what you want to do, not what you think you should do', it does seem the 'others' are going to have to wait a while.[67]

Degrees of involvement are also determined by the individual. One possible reason why New Agers are comfortable paying for enlightenment is that the commercial transaction allows them to retain guilt-free control of their commitment. Like the wandering Ms Losada and the eclectic Dorothy Lewis, one might try a very wide range of therapies and revelations. Almost all such will charge fees and, precisely because of that, one can leave without feeling guilty. This is important. One theme that repeatedly recurs in accounts of the New Age is rejection of external authority. The Brethren do not charge but they expect the interested to experience their faith in the manner prescribed by the Brethren. Jill Purce charges for her week-long course in the techniques and spiritual benefits of Tibetan Overtone Chanting and, if you lose interest on Wednesday, you can walk away.

The Effective Self and Intuition

The self not only persists but is immensely powerful. James Arthur Ray, whose ineptly managed 'sweat-lodge' ritual resulted in the death of three participants in 2009, said: 'We can all determine our own fate. Energy we receive from the universe is the same as we put in . . . You were born into greatness and you have been conditioned into mediocrity. Go out and create the universe you desire.'[68] The spiritual techniques of manifestation (show the universe what you need) and visualization (imagine what you want) offer the same message. If you just want something in the right way, you will get it. The potency of self is inflated to a point that defies the normal rules of causation. A graduate of est training working in telephone sales told Stephen Tipton: 'Here I sat, dialling the phone, hour after hour—nobody home. Finally I realized that it was me who wasn't "home".'[69] In essence there is no economy, polity, or society and, if you are unemployed or unable to afford decent housing, it is your own fault for not manifesting and visualizing in the right way. The enlightened or trained or awakened self can create its own reality.

In this sort of thinking, the 'self' is not the rational mind but our intuition: the heart rather than the head. As we saw with Dorothy Lewis, decisions are often made not by rational evaluation but by feeling (sometimes supported by channelled message). If one is, in the Findhorn Foundation phrase, properly 'attuned' to the earth and the cosmos, then one will just know what is the right decision. So Hope Tod, a Somerset healer and channeller, *felt* that the old farmhouse she fancied was intended for her, and her 'Group' of spirit guides and companions confirmed her intuition. The plan appeared to go pear-shaped when it was sold at auction for more than she could afford. But the sale fell through and the owner was happy to accept her original offer. 'So the Old House *had* been waiting for us all the time, just as the Group's message had promised.'[70]

References to Christian ideas have become less common with the decline of the churches, but it is still common to hear New Agers quote Jesus as saying 'the kingdom of God is within you'. Actually that King James version translation of Luke 17: 21 has generally been superseded by 'the kingdom of God is among you' or 'in the midst of you', but 'within you' perfectly captures the importance of intuition in contemporary spirituality.

Reincarnation and Cultural Inversion

Most core New Agers believe in reincarnation. They believe they have lived previous lives and will enjoy lives after this one. The underlying logic of New Age notions of reincarnation is importantly different from that which underpinned it in its original Asian contexts. There the goal of enlightenment was to be released from the necessity of being reborn (and the suffering that accompanied it). The aspiration was to be absorbed into the cosmic consciousness, and choosing to come back when one had reached a sufficient level of enlightenment to obtain release was the mark of the saint. The original reincarnation idea rested on the belief (which well fitted the reality of life for most people in the Indian subcontinent) that we were insignificant—less than the smallest speck of dust on a mirror. In the New Age view of reincarnation, the self is preserved because we are far too important just to vanish.

This is clear in the nature and status of claimed previous lives. I have yet to come across anyone whose previous life matches the norm for the period in question: that is, insignificant. Apparently, no hewers of wood and drawers of water get reborn. For example, one spiritual seeker who sought the advice of a channeller about his growing affection for another man was told that he and his potential lover had met in three previous lives. In one they had been monks, in another 'Celt warriors in Scotland', and in a third 'young artists in Florence'. They were not just any residents of medieval Florence: 'Always you were great painters, musicians, writers and poets. Your creativity has always brought you into your full lovingness.'[71]

As an aside we can note that New Age use of reincarnation is often inadvertently racist in the way its pillages the cultures of disadvantaged but exotic minorities. An American Indian woman neatly punctured the pretensions of many white middle-class women when she entitled a critique of New Age use of Indian ceremonies: 'For all those of you who were Indian in a former life.'[72]

Lack of Divide between Living and Dead

Spiritualism is relatively new. It was invented in the late nineteenth century. Its primary aim was to contact the dead so as to provide the living with reassurance from their relatives. Spirit mediums (who were almost invariably women) organized séances at which they would communicate with the souls of the dead on behalf of members of the audience. Generally the medium would go into a trance and make contact with a spirit guide. That guide, normally someone exotic such as an American Indian chief, would then pass messages from people on 'the other side' to the audience via the spirit medium, who would deliver them in a strange dissociated voice. Sometimes the messages came through automatic writing: the medium would hold a pen over paper and then write as if her hand had become possessed. Or she might spread letter cards in a circle and have the participants sit around a table, with a glass in the middle. Everyone puts a hand on the glass and, when the medium makes contact with the other side, the glass seems to move of its own will around the cards, spelling out a simple message.

It has to be said that most of the messages from the other side that were produced in spiritualist circles were thoroughly banal. They generally took the form of Fred reassuring his left-behind loved ones that he was content. The main points were to prove that there was another realm of existence beyond the material world and that departed loved ones were happy. New Age *channelling* is different in that it takes the endurance of the self for granted and concentrates on delivering wisdom and advice. Messages from the other side tend to be philosophical, ethical, and even political.

For the Victorians and even those interested in spiritualism in the 1920s, the assumed model was rather Christian (or at least theistic). We were down here and the souls of the dear departed were over there somewhere, on the other side, in the land of God or Gods. Alice Bailey's Arcane School was built on the revelations given by her Tibetan Hidden Master. Although, as we saw with Dorothy Lewis, Bailey still has her followers, the Hidden Masters approach to channelling is now rather passé. The modern approach is to look within.

The Return of the Occult

As the shelves of any major book shop attest, magic and witchcraft are now acceptable: the occult has returned. The assumption behind the occult (which means that which is hidden) is that there are mysterious sources of power that can be accessed with the right rituals or incantations. For many people, interest in the occult is limited to divination, where what is divined is the future. Fortune-telling has long been a hobby of the working classes. On seaside holidays, young women consulted gypsies who stared into crystal balls, read tea leaves, or examined lines on their palms to tell them when they would meet a tall dark handsome stranger. A 1950 survey showed that between 41 and 51 per cent of respondents had consulted a fortune teller.[73] Quite how seriously this was taken is not obvious. I suspect many would have distanced themselves from their own actions by describing them as 'just a bit of fun' or some such, but it is worth noting that many respondents were frequent users. Of those who had ever consulted a fortune teller, 39 per cent of women and 17 per cent of men had been 'several times'.[74] One telling (because it is inadvertent) illustration of the popularity of divination is an Edwardian etiquette manual that explains:

> The hours for an 'at home' day are from 3 to 6.30 or 4 to 7. . . . On special occasions the invitations are sent out on 'at home' cards, with the date and the hours in one corner, and if there is to be any especial attraction, such as music or palmistry, this is generally mentioned on the card.[75]

So palmistry was sufficiently popular as a social entertainment for it to be one of the two 'especial attractions' that came to the etiquette expert's mind. Horoscopes have long been a popular feature of newspapers and weekly magazines, but many New Agers take divination much more seriously and either call on the *I Ching* or, as did Dorothy Lewis, have detailed astrological charts drawn for them.

The second element of the occult is the next step. With the right knowledge and rituals, you can not only know the future but arrange it. In classic voodoo-style spells, specific outcomes can be arranged by, for example, making wax effigies of one's enemies and sticking pins in them. Modern manipulation tends to be less specific. Two contemporary witches offer spells as forms of psychic defence.[76] Requiring only the power of the mind, 'visualization' promises that, if we think about the future in a certain way, we will achieve our goals. This bold promise is generally framed in such a way that a very wide variety of outcomes can be claimed as success.[77]

Romancing the Stones

New Agers are generally romantics. They suppose that, while industrialization has brought many material benefits—only a tiny number prefer a bender tent to a house with plumbing—it has cost us our souls. The manufactured and processed are bad; the natural is good. This critique is not new. In the early nineteenth century poets such as William Blake, William Wordsworth, and Samuel Taylor Coleridge, with better reason than is now the case, held that cities and factories were vile places that killed the soul and that enlightenment was to be found in remote parts of nature: the mountains, fells, and lakes of the Lake District, for example. The problem for the contemporary romantic is that there are increasingly few parts of the world that can serve as the primitive contrast with modernity. The Lake District is now so popular with tourists that the police have to close the major roads into the area on warm bank holidays. Tibet filled that role in the nineteenth and early twentieth centuries, but the Dalai Lama now appears on talk shows and the Chinese have built a railway that connects Tibet to the modern world. Native American Indians live off the sale of casino and oil-extraction licences. The world of the Australian aborigines is shrinking.

The remote past is one remaining resource for romantic imagining. The stone circles of Brodgar in Orkney, Callanish in Lewis, or Stonehenge in Wiltshire can serve as the thin base for an inverted pyramid of historical speculation. As indeed can the pyramids. A historian has noted: 'it was a great and potentially uncomfortable irony that modern Druids had arrived at Stonehenge just as archaeologists were evicting the real Druids from it'. Stonehenge dates from the Neolithic and early Bronze ages, millennia before the Iron Age in which the original Druids first appear.[78]

There is a tension in the world of New Age healing. Some pre-1960s strands (Radionics, for example, or Dianetics) claimed the authority of science, but most modern healing claims to be ancient. Despite the remarkable advance of western medicine, contemporary healers promote Chinese and Ayurvedic medicine.[79] Mistakes are often revealing because they show what people would like to believe. One spiritual seeker described Reiki as 'an ancient method of Japanese healing'; actually there is no doubt that it was invented in 1922 by Japanese Buddhist Mikao Usui, who was proud to claim authorship.[80] A puff for the Peterchurch, Hereford, Reiki Association made the same claim.[81] An advert for Bachian flower remedies said: 'Bach was merely rediscovering what folk tradition had known for centuries. Ancient cultures, from the Australian Aborigines to the Native Americans, were using flower potions aeons before antibiotics.'[82]

Wicca is accurately described by its Wikipedia entry as a 'modern pagan, witchcraft religion. It was developed in England during the first half of the 20th century and was introduced to the public in 1954 by Gerald Gardner, a retired British civil servant.'[83] But its adherents often claim its beliefs and rituals to be genuinely ancient and present them in an archaic language of thees and thous. Its key motto is 'an it harm none, do what thou wilt', which sounds more spiritual than 'do what you like so long as it hurts no one'.[84] Serious scholars of paganism, such as Ronald Hutton and Graham Harvey, are clear that almost every element is a late-nineteenth- or early twentieth-century creation, but that does not prevent a general assumption that the spiritual repertoire is ancient and, for that reason alone, virtuous.

One important strand of New Age romanticism is a spiritual environmentalism, distinguished from the secular version by the belief that we can communicate and cooperate with the spirits of plants (Dorothy Maclean of Findhorn's devas) and of the earth and by the idea that the earth is literally, rather than metaphorically, a living being who should be respected. As Peter Lemesurier says: 'it is interesting to note how many "New Age" communes and communities revolve specifically around the cultivation of a garden, or even a full-blooded "return to the earth"'.[85] The more realistic New Agers appreciate that urbanization cannot be reversed and that the twelve million residents of a city such as Rio De Janiero cannot be fed by market gardening. From the 1890s to the 1930s there were a great many utopian rural 'colonies' founded on a variety of principles, from William Booth's evangelical Christianity to Leo Tolstoy's anarchism. These were intended to solve the economic and social problems of the urban poor by settling them in supposedly self-sufficient rural communes. All were dismal failures. The urban poor were not interested in re-creating the lives of medieval cottagers; that life appealed only to left-leaning middle-class intellectuals and then only for a short time.[86] A less utopian concern for the environment concentrates on incremental steps to reduce our 'footprint'. The Findhorn Foundation's interest in renewable energy and house insulation are examples. It is noticeable that many of the associates of Hope Tod, a healer and spiritual 'channel' whose 'solar ray work' supposedly harnessed cosmic energies in Somerset in the 1960s, were active members of the Soil Association, an organization that promotes organic and low-intensity farming.[87]

Tolerance of Diversity

There are implicit limits to New Age tolerance. When New Agers say that we should all be true to our inner selves and respect our intuition, they do not expect our inner selves to be racists, Nazis, homophobes, or misogynists.[88] Just sometimes they turn out to be less than savoury. JZ Knight heads the Ramtha School of Enlightenment in Yelm, Washington State. She channels a 35,000-year-old Lemurian warrior—Lemuria is, like Atlantis, a lost civilization supposedly now under the Indian and Pacific oceans—who once conquered two-thirds of the world before spending seven years meditating and then ascended into heaven. Students captured Knight on film in a drunken rant that included saying of the Jews: 'Fuck God's chosen people! I think they have earned enough cash to have paid their way out of the godamned gas chambers by now.'[89] But most New Agers are indeed remarkably tolerant. I have rarely heard people in New Age circles argue. And, of course, they cannot. Because they reject the idea of an external authority, there is no ground for saying that someone else's truth is nonsense. Instead, they politely dismiss something on the grounds that 'it doesn't work for me'. Or, as one attender at the annual Mind, Body, Spirit Festival said after reading an advert for one session: 'Samat Kumara, Ascended Master, Planetary Logos and a Being of Great Love and Light came to this planet approximately 18 million years ago. . . I'm not doubting it but, personally, I'm having difficulty applying this.'[90]

Syncretism

Apparent competition between ideas can be resolved by syncretism. All sorts of different ideas and rituals from very different cultures are glued together by analogy. So you start with the idea borrowed from Hinduism that, in addition to the known-to-science nervous system and blood circulation systems, we also have invisible psychic energy, which is concentrated at various chakra points on the body. Now that sounds a bit like the Chinese model of anatomy that lies behind acupuncture. So you can put together Hindu Ayurvedic medicine and Chinese acupuncture. It is a short move to transfer the model from the human body to the earth, and to add Aboriginal song lines or English ley lines to Chinese Feng Shui.[91] In this way New Agers creatively combine a wide variety of ideas that seem somewhat similar. As June Marsh Lazar said in a talk to the 1993 Mind, Body, Spirit festival: 'Well, you know about chakra points? Well, the earth has its chakra points too.'[92] Healer Nicki Scully combines shamanic healing in the Native American tradition, the 'ancient truths of Egyptian religion', and Reiki.[93] The blurb on the website for Peggy Bunt's 'Fountain technique for directing healing energy' explains that 'when we concentrate on any particular quality e.g. light or love or peace we actually produce an electro-magnetic frequency which "sparks off" change'. In providing a theoretical background for the therapy, Bunt manages to name check Deepak Chopra's Ayurvedic medicine, quantum physics, paganism, the works of French Jesuit Teilhard de Chardin, the Kabbalah, R. D. Laing, and huna (a supposedly ancient Polynesian healing therapy 're-discovered' by Max Freedom Lang in the 1920s). She even uses the Aramaic word for God and thus connects to the New Testament.[94]

Holism

Such syncretism is justified by the underlying belief that everything is connected to everything else, if not in some more specific manner, then at least at the level of cosmic consciousness. As in the term 'holistic spirituality', the adjective 'holistic' is often used as a general claim to virtue. In the field of medicine, for example, holistic healing is contrasted with Western medicine's limited focus on specific ailments and body parts. My doctor attends only to the specific problem with which I present at her surgery and, if I am referred to a hospital-based specialist, he or she will work in the ear, nose, and throat department, the maxillo-facial unit, urology, and the like. In contrast, my Reiki healer attends to my entire person and body. In reality, such contrasts are almost always self-serving and inaccurate. None of the many healers who have treated me has ever spent more than fifteen minutes asking about my physical or mental health beyond the symptom with which I have presented. My general practitioner has access to detailed notes covering tests and treatments spanning thirty years, and no surgery involving a general anaesthetic has ever been preceded by less than an hour of detailed physical examination.

More often than not, the holistic claim for spiritual healing actually disguises something more interesting: the extravagant claims for the benefits of one therapy. So incautious Alexander Technique therapists will claim that all manners of ills are caused by poor posture and hence a very wide range of improvements will follow from their pet therapy. A therapist claimed that Reiki was useful for arthritis, ME, depression, eating disorders, and motor neuron disease 'to name just a few'.[95] Bio-energetic healing, which involves 'clearing blockages' by manipulating the body's magnetic aura and electrical impulses, simply by using the movement of the hands, apparently 'cures asthma and cerebral palsy'.[96] A leaflet for Bowen Therapy (a form of 'gentle and non-invasive massage') claimed it could treat asthma, hay fever, irritable bowel syndrome, constipation, diarrhoea, Crohn's disease, migraine, ME, MS, and all the unpleasant side effects of pregnancy.[97] Rena Denton (aka Mata Yogananda Matasaya Dharma) claimed her Self-Realization Centre could cure 'broken bones, muscle and tissue damage and whiplash', and she treated cancer patients. She also fraudulently extracted very large sums of money from them.[98] Transcendental Meditation (of which more in the next chapter) claimed that its Ayurvedic medicine could cure half of all diseases in three years and eventually create a disease-free society.[99]

Mainstream medicine had to abandon the dream of a panacea—a single cure for everything—before it could make significant progress. Spiritual healers bring back the dream.

THE STRUCTURE OF THE NEW AGE MILIEU

The world of New Age spirituality has some major producers that might wish to be religious sects, but they are hobbled by the consumer's assertion of individual authority. Some popular gurus (such as Sai Baba and Deepak Chopra) garnered huge followings, but even their followings do not usually turn into loyal followers. Rather people will listen, experiment, and take away what they find useful. As Dorothy Lewis did with Radionics, they will adapt what they find to suit their preferences and existing practices. Some providers try to counter this 'take-away' attitude. L. Ron Hubbard responded to his frustration over the failure of those who read his exposition of Dianetics to stick rigidly to his method by reinventing it as the revealed religion of Scientology, which was revealed only to him. As we will see in the next chapter, Transcendental Meditation has tried to retain some control over its product by creating an inner core of higher-grade adepts. The Lucis Trust, which manages the heritage of Alice Bailey, would like those who study her teachings to learn those and only those. But most New Age providers accept the logic of a realm in which each individual consumer decides what is true for him or her.

The resulting structure is a web of interlocking facilities. Where one sees the structure of the New Age milieu very clearly is in the annual Festival for Mind, Body, Spirit that occurs in London over the late May public holiday. In the main hall there are over a hundred stalls: publishers of books, cassettes, and magazines; promoters of such remedies as flower healing, massage, and iridology; representatives of organizations such as the Swedenborgians, the Theosophical Society, and the Bahais; and purveyors of royal jelly, crystals, and tarot cards. Throughout the week-long festival, New Life Promotions (which seems remarkably broad in its remit) presents a menu of lectures and workshops. One can hear Nicki Scully on 'Shamanic Journeys to the Spirit World' or Mirtha Vega on 'Becoming a Warrioress: A Celebration of Strength and Self for Women'. Apache Oh Shinnah teaches 'Prophecy and the Way of the Warrior in Times of Purification', while Richard Lawrence explains 'UFOs: Their Plan on Earth'. Many of the speakers at the festival will tour the country under the auspices of New Life. There are a large number of retreats that offer weekend or week-long courses in whatever form of enlightenment or spiritual growth might attract customers.

Equally important is what, in contrast to commercial New Age promotion, one might think of as subsistence spirituality. Much of the lattice of the cultic milieu is made up of people sharing mutual interests. For example, a couple who teach T'ai Chi in their spare time invite trainees to stay the weekend in their large house in return for a donation that covers meal costs. Some members of the T'ai Chi group also rotate weekly meditation sessions around their homes. One offers the others Reiki healing; another draws astrological chart horoscopes.

As an aside, it is important, in gauging the popularity of contemporary spirituality, to note that 'producers' have a rather different relationship with 'consumers' from what one finds in the Christian churches. As evidence of the popularity of new spiritual expressions, Linda Woodhead said:

> We did a famous research project in 2000–2002, taking the town of Kendal in Northern England, called the Kendal Project. We looked there just at what was happening; we took that town as a kind of spiritual laboratory, and we looked at how the churches were declining, but we found to our astonishment, even in 2000, this huge proliferation of alternative forms of spirituality: of mind, body, spirit care. We found 126 different practitioners in this one small town.[100]

This is profoundly misleading. The typical Christian cleric in 2005 served 165 church members, but many of the Kendal practitioners had very few clients or consumers, other than themselves and each other.[101] In subsistence spirituality, there is no clear divide between producers and consumers.

Publishing—originally books and magazines, but increasing websites—is an important resource. Although some outlets have a clear and limited set of interests (the Findhorn Press, for example), others take the view that one cannot have too much of a good thing and present an array from which the interested may pick and choose as they wish. In the same Glastonbury bookshop I found books that promoted a simple back-to-nature lifestyle alongside manuals teaching how to use magic to become successful in business.

CONCLUSION

The beliefs of a church, sect, or denomination can be readily listed. The order for the Church of England's Evensong service has the congregation reciting the Apostle's Creed, which begins 'I believe in God the Father Almighty' and works its way through fifteen propositions till it gets to 'I believe in the Holy Ghost; the holy Catholick Church; The communion of Saints; The forgiveness of sins; The resurrection of the body; And the life everlasting. Amen'.[102] Some sects specify what distinguishes them from other bodies with whom they might be mistaken. The Shorter Catechism used since the Reformation by Presbyterian churches makes clear the nature of their opposition to Roman Catholicism. Even more particular, the ordination service for ministers and elders of the Free Presbyterian Church of Ulster requires assent to propositions that codify opposition to both Romanism and liberal Protestantism. There is nothing similar for New Age spirituality precisely because the autonomy granted each individual person prevents the codification of beliefs. There is no Curia or committee of ayatollahs to decide what is required and what is forbidden. Hence the best we can do is sketch a range of interests, beliefs, and attitudes that are more or less popular within the New Age milieu: individual autonomy, the importance of intuition, the persistence of the self through reincarnation, a melding of the realms of the living and the dead, the occult, a romantic critique of industrial modern society and a preference for the natural and the ancient, tolerance of diversity, and syncretism and holism.

It is obviously hazardous to choose only one of these as the key to New Age spirituality, but brevity requires such selection, and I would offer as the keystone the importance of intuition. If we are to contrast conventional religion with new expressions of spirituality, the primary difference would be the location of authority. Traditionally the great theistic religions have supposed that we are essentially bad and become good only by subjecting ourselves to the external authority of God's will. Contemporary spirituality assumes we are essentially good, have been made bad by our experiences (either of our parents, or society, or both), and that redemption comes not from an external source but from the divine within.[103] An advert for a Nicki Scully talk 'The Path of the Warrior or Healer' said: 'the journey is about being fully in your power, strong and clear in everything you are doing. It's about honouring yourself and owning who you are, now.'[104] Although it is impossible to prove a direct causal connection between such amorphous cultural changes as the modernization of the West and the rise of the New Age, the connection seems clear. Modernization has brought with it increased individual freedom, a consumerist orientation, and the novel confidence in human faculties that David Martin called 'mastery over fate'. And it is precisely those things that we see in the New Age milieu.

NOTES

1. C. Riddell, *The Findhorn Community: Creating a Human Identity for the 21st Century* (Forres: Findhorn Press, 1997), 90.
2. Many New Agers disclaim the term, but it is usefully short, and David Spangler, arguably one of the main creators of the concept, still liked it twenty years later: 'the idea of a New Age can be a powerful inspiration' (D. Spangler, *The New Age* (Issaquah, WA: Morningtown Press, 1988), 2).

3. P. Caddy, *In Perfect Timing* (Forres: Findhorn Press, 1996). For outsider accounts of Findhorn, see S. Sutcliffe, *Children of the New Age: A History of Spiritual Practices* (London: Routledge, 2002), and 'A Colony of Seekers: Findhorn in the 1990s', *Journal of Contemporary Religion*, 15 (2000), 215–31; P. Abrams, A. McCulloch, S. Abrams, S. Gore, and P. Gore, *Communes, Sociology and Society* (Cambridge: Cambridge University Press, 1976); and A. Rigby, *Alternative Realities: A Study of Communes and their Members* (London: Routledge and Kegan Paul, 1974). For an insider account, see Riddell, *Findhorn Community*. Although Riddell was a resident, and the publication by Findhorn Press gives it the official imprimatur, she was previously a sociologist at the University of Lancaster and writes with an eye to many of the concerns that interest me.

4. R. Prince and D. Riches, *The New Age in Glastonbury* (Oxford: Berghahn Books, 2000).

5. H. Fisher, 'My Findhorn Experience' <http://www.earthwell.com.au/my-findhorn-experience/> (accessed May 2012).

6. E. Caddy and L. Hollingshead, *Flight into Freedom: The Autobiography of the Co-Founder of the Findhorn Community* (Longmead, Dorset: Element, 1988), 87.

7. Caddy and Hollingshead, *Flight*, 87.

8. P. Hawken, *The Magic of Findhorn* (London: Souvenir Press, 1975), 1.

9. Rigby, *Alternative Realities*, 150–61.

10. Hawken, *Magic*.

11. Caddy, *In Perfect Timing*, 261–2. Belief in life on other planets has been common at least since the ancient Greeks. In the 1745 edition of *Poor Richard's Almanac*, Ben Franklin wrote: 'It is the opinion of all modern philosophers and mathematicians that the planets are inhabitable worlds' (see M. J. Crowe, *The Extraterrestrial Life Debate 1750–1900* (Cambridge: Cambridge University Press, 1986)).

12. Caddy, *In Perfect Timing*, 262.

13. Caddy, *In Perfect Timing*, 262.

14. Although not specifically criticizing the Findhorn Foundation, in 1988 Spangler wrote rather critically that now 'the New Age seemed to be mainly channels, crystals, harmonic convergences, UFOs, prosperity workshops, and "self-divination" seminars' (Spangler, *New Age*, 4).

15. In 1993 the Scottish Charities Office, having received complaints concerning its use at the Findhorn Foundation, commissioned the Regius Professor of Forensic Medicine at the University of Edinburgh to investigate Breathwork. His opinions caused the Findhorn Foundation to suspend the programme.

16. For a summary, see A. Walker (ed), *The Kingdom Within: A Guide to the Spiritual Work of the Findhorn Community* (Forres: Findhorn Press, 1994).

17. Spangler was very fond of light and darkness as metaphors; see D. Spangler, 'The Role and Future of Light Centres', *One Earth*, 5 (1978), 24–9.

18. Findhorn Consultancy Service, *Organisational Development, Training, Coaching* (Forres: Findhorn Consultancy Service, 2015).

19. For US examples of corporations showing interest in New Age practices, see I. I. Mintoff and E. A. Denton, *A Spiritual Audit of Corporate America: A Hard Look at Spirituality, Religion and Values in the Workplace* (San Francisco: Jossey-Bass, 1999).

20. D. Lewis, *The Way Home: Chronicles of an Inner Journey* (Forres: Findhorn Press, 1995), 7.

21. This sort of narrative is common in certain evangelical Christian circles, where decisions are taken to the Lord in prayer and the unexpected overcoming of obstacles to a certain course of action is taken as a confirmatory 'message from the Lord'.

22. Lewis, *Way Home*, 14.

23. Lewis, *Way Home*, 17.

24. Lewis, *Way Home*, 19.

25. A. Watkins, *Early British Trackways and The Old Straight Track* (Hereford: Watkins Meter, 1922).

26. J. Mitchell, *The View Over Atlantis* (London: Sago Press, 1969). Wikipedia has a fulsome and well-referenced entry for Mitchell. He was an Old Etonian bohemian who popularized belief in UFOs and founded *The Cerealogist*, a magazine that promoted the view that crop circles were the work of alien spacecraft.

27. Lewis, *Way Home*, 22.

28. Lewis, *Way Home*, 24.

29. Lewis, *Way Home*, 25.

30. The US Food and Drugs Administration rejects all the claims made for Radionics.

31. 'Our Abrams Investigation and Our Abrams Verdict', serialized in *Scientific American* (October 1923–September 1924).

32. Lewis, *Way Home*, 26.

33. Lewis, *Way Home*, 31.

34. Bailey is a key figure in English esoterica, but many people, New Agers as much as critics, have trouble with her anti-Semitism, on which, see H. Newman, 'The Rainbow Swastika: A Report to the Jewish People about New Age Antisemitism' <https://philologos.org/__eb-trs/> (accessed May 2017).

35. Lewis, *Way Home*, 50.

36. Lewis, *Way Home*, 54.

37. I. Losada, *The Battersea Park Road to Enlightenment* (London: Bloomsbury, 2001).

38. Stasinoupolou moved to the USA, where she married Republican Congressman Michael Huffington. For a while she was a right-wing commentator. Then in the Obama years she moved to the left and founded the Huffington Post. She has continued to discover the solution to all problems, personal and planetary (see A. Huffington, *The Fourth Instinct* (London: Piatkus, 1994)) and is now a leading promoter of mindfulness; A. Robb, 'How 2014 Became the Year of Mindfulness', *New Republic* <http://www.newrepublic.com/article/120669/2014-year-mindfulness-rich> (accessed July 2015).

39. R. Wallis, 'Inside Insight', *New Humanist* 25/3 (Autumn 1979), 94. The tripping-over-itself style of the prose is intended to mimic the speaker's style. Wallis attended Insight and est, and a variety of similar trainings in the research for his *Elementary Forms of the New Religious Life* (London: Routledge and Kegan Paul, 1984).

40. Losada, *Battersea Park Road*, 51.

41. Losada, *Battersea Park Road*, 61.

42. Losada, *Battersea Park Road*, 64.

43. Losada, *Battersea Park Road*, 68.

44. Losada, *Battersea Park Road*, 114.

45. Guild for Structural Integration, *Rolfing: Structural Integration* (Boulder, CO: Guild for Structural Integration, n.d.).

46. Despite its scientific-sounding name, there is no scientific support for NLP's claims.

47. Losada, *Battersea Road*, 223.

48. In case Losada be thought unique, consider Joyce Collin-Smith, a New Ager *avant la lettre*. She began with the works of Rudolf Steiner, moved on to Frank Buchman's Oxford Movement, and then married a disciple of Ouspensky and Gurdjieff. After his death, she became a follower of the Indonesian Pak Subuh (founder of Subud). She then joined Maharishi Mahesh Yogi for eight years. When she became disillusioned with him, she set herself up in business as an astrological consultant, Tarot reader, esoteric writer, and spiritual teacher. Her obituary is in the *Daily Telegraph*, 11 February 2011.

49. A. W. Smith and W. Blake, 'And did those Feet? The Legend of Christ's Visit to Britain', *Folklore*, 100 (1989), 63–83. Some modern worshippers of the fifth-century Irish Saint Bridget or Bride also want to claim her for Glastonbury; see B. Frances, *Did Saint Bridget Visit Glastonbury?* (Glastonbury: Friends of Bride's Mound, 2008). On Goddess spirituality in Glastonbury, see M. Bowman, 'Procession and Possession in Glastonbury: Continuity, Change and the Manipulation of Tradition', *Folklore*, 115 (2004), 273–85.

50. For a detailed account of Glastonbury in the inter-war years, see T. Hopkinson-Bell, *The Rediscovery of Glastonbury: Frederick Bligh Bond Architect of the New Age* (Stroud: Sutton Publishing, 2007).

51. 'Glastonbury', Wikipedia <https://en.wikipedia.org/wiki/Glastonbury> (accessed July 2015).

52. K. E. Maltwood, *A Guide to Glastonbury's Temple of the Stars: Their Giant Effigies Described from Air Views, Maps* (London: Women's Printing Society, Ltd, 1934).

53. P. Weston, *Avalonian Aeon: From Glastonbury Festival to 2012. A Personal Occult Journal* (Glastonbury: Avalonian Aeon Publications, 2010), 22.

54. The event was filmed by Nicholas Roeg and David Putnam as *Glastonbury Fayre*.

55. The design of the pyramid stage was the work of John Mitchell. See n. 26.

56. Weston, *Avalonian Aeon*, 34.

57. Weston, *Avalonian Aeon*, 31.

58. On the early twentieth-century history of Glastonbury, see P. Benham, *The Avalonians* (Glastonbury: Gothic Image Publications, 2013).

59. R. Prince and D. Riches, *The New Age in Glastonbury* (Oxford: Berghahn Books, 2000), 64.

60. Prince and Riches, *New Age*, p. xiii.

61. Prince and Riches, *New Age*, 176–7.

62. Prince and Riches, *New Age*, 166–8.

63. W. Hanegraaff, *New Age Religion and Western Culture* (New York: State University of New York Press, 1998).

64. C. Campbell, *The Easternization of the West* (Boulder, CO: Paradigm, 2007), 54, quotes Inazo Nitobe claiming 'direct perception, feeling, sentiment, intuition, religion are the outstanding instruments of the Oriental spirit'.

65. Quoted by L. Revell, 'The Return of the Sacred', in S. Wolton (ed.), *Marxism, Mysticism and Modern Theory* (London: Macmillan, 1999), 123.

66. *Spirit and Destiny* (June 2016).

67. L. Atkins, 'Are your Resolutions Destined To Fail?', *Guardian*, 30 January 2010.

68. J. A. Ray, *Harmonious Wealth: The Secret of Attracting the Life You Want* (New York: Hyperion, 2008). See also his *The Million Dollar Mindset: How to Harness Your Internal Force to Live the Lifestyle You Deserve* (Carlsbad: SunArk Press, 2005).

69. S. Tipton, *Getting Saved from the Sixties* (Berkeley and Los Angeles: University of California Press, 1982), 214.

70. H. Tod, *The Maze and the Arc of Light* (Forres: Findhorn Press, 1989), 109.

71. T. T. Tattersall, *Journey: An Adventure of Love and Healing* (Forres: Findhorn Press, 1996). Although the Findhorn Press is as broad in its publications as the Foundation is in its teachings, that the book was published by the Press means that its content is at least minimally acceptable to a group representing one of the major New Age centres.

72. A. Smith, 'For all those who were Indian in a former life', Manataka American Indian Council Women's Circle <http://archive.manataka.org/page1113.html> (accessed May 2017).

73. Geoffrey Gorer, *Exploring English Character* (London: Cresset Press, 1955), table 100.

74. Gorer, *English Character*, table 101.

75. Anon., *Almanac and Diary 1906* (Aberdeen: Pratt and Keith, 1905).

76. J. Farrar and S. Farrar, *Spells and How They Work* (London: Robert Hale, 1990). They begin with a long warning about ethics: one should not cast spells to hurt people because it is a bad thing and anyway they will backfire. This attempt to render magic benign appears in every magic book. The problem, of course, is that the magical procurement of even apparently benign advantage will almost certainly be at a cost to someone. Spells to ensure that you do magically well in your job interview will, if they work, harm the other candidates.

77. U. Markham, *Visualisation* (Shaftesbury, Dorset: Element, 1989).

78. R. Hutton, *Blood and Mistletoe: The History of the Druids in Britain* (New Haven, CN: Yale University Press, 2009), 323.

79. It is worth noting that many New Agers are thoughtful critics of their own subculture. For example, Paul Weston, though a frequent attender at summer solstice events at Stonehenge, refers in his description of one such to 'The obligatory Hopi Indian elder' who said his piece. Weston, *Avalonian Aeon*, 39.

80. Tattersall, *Journey*, 62.

81. *Sunday Herald*, 11 June 2000.

82. W. Bristow, 'Flower Power', *Cosmopolitan* (December 1996).

83. 'Wicca', Wikipedia <https://en.wikipedia.org/wiki/Wicca> (accessed July 2015).

84. For accurate histories of paganism, see Hutton, *Blood and Mistletoe*, and G. Harvey, *Listening People, Speaking Earth: Contemporary Paganism* (London: Hurst, 2007).

85. P. Lemesurier, *This New Age Business* (Forres: Findhorn Press, 1990), 187.

86. W. H. G. Armytage, *Heavens Below: Utopian Experiments in England 1560–1960* (London: Routledge and Kegan Paul, 1961).

87. H. Tod, *The Maze and the Arc of Light* (Forres: Findhorn Press, 1989).

88. There is one obvious exception. Radovan Karadzic, the political leader of the Bosnian Serbs during the Yugoslav war and for a long time Europe's most wanted war criminal, spent a decade on the run working as

Dragan Dabic, New Age healer and author of a weekly column of spiritual guidance. It says much for the discerning power of intuition that, until the Serb government turned him over to the International Court at The Hague, apparently none of the thousands of people whom he treated and advised knew he was responsible for the massacre of thousands of Bosnian Serb men and boys.

89. T. Boggioni, 'New Age Leader Sues Ex-Students over Leaked Video of her Drunken Racist Anti-Gay Rant' <http://www.rawstory.com/2014/07/new-age-leader-sues-ex-students> (accessed July 2015). It is interesting to note how often being drunk is used in grudgingly apologetic explanations for anti-Semitic outbursts, as though hatred for the Jews was a natural condition, florid expressions of which are only inhibited by sobriety. Mel Gibson and Jean-Paul Gaultier are other examples.

90. L. M. Lim, 'Pick and Mix at the New Age Bazaar', *Herald*, 26 May 1996.

91. Weston, *Avalonian Aeon*, 24.

92. This quotation comes from my own notes of Ms Lazar's talk. Re Ayurvedic medicine, see D. Wujastyk and F. M. Smith, *Modern and Global Ayurveda: Pluralism and Paradigms* (Albany, NY: State University of New York, 2008).

93. New Life Promotions, *Nicki Scully* (London: New Life Promotions, Spring 1993).

94. P. Bunt, 'Fountain and the Quantum Field' <http://www.fountain-international.org/contributors/023.html> (accessed May 2012).

95. Anon., 'Career Profile: Gisela Stewart', *Press and Journal*, 17 July 2009.

96. S. Mansfield, 'Hands-Off Healing', *Press and Journal*, 30 June 1998.

97. Anon., *Bowen Therapy*, leaflet collected from Chelsea House Clinic, Inverurie, April 2012.

98. J. Lewis and M. Howie, 'Healer who Spirited away a Fortune', *Sunday Telegraph*, 30 January 2011, pp. 16–17.

99. *Belfast Telegraph*, 27 May 1994.

100. Linda Woodhead, 'On the New Sociology of Religion', *Social Sciences Bites* (November 2014) <http://www.socialsciencespace.com/wp-content/uploads/Linda-Woodhead-on-the-New-Sociology-of-Religion.pdf> (accessed January 2015).

101. Peter Brierley, *UK Church Statistics 2005–2015* (Tonbridge, Kent: ABCD Publishers, 2011), table 1.1.

102. *The Book of Common Prayer* (Cambridge: Cambridge University Press, 2010), 22–3.

103. For a detailed study of four healers' views of the self, see M. Birch, 'The Goddess/God Within: The Construction of Self-Identity through Alternative Health Practices', in K. Flanagan and P. Jupp (eds), *A Sociology of Spirituality* (Aldershot: Ashgate, 1996), 83–100.

104. New Life Promotions, *Nicki Scully*.

3

Yogins and Yoga

INTRODUCTION

Top of the Pops was always uncool. Disc jockey Jimmy Saville's remarkable career as an abusive sex molester was still secret, but anyone could tell, just looking at his dyed blond hair, open-chested tracksuit tops, and gold chains and medallions, that he was a creep. And most of the other DJs were as bad. But, nonetheless, *Top of the Pops* was pretty much the only pop music programme on the TV in the 1960s, and so we watched it. On 11 September 1969, the British public, familiar with platform soles, sequins, and cleavage with its pop, was treated to the remarkable sight of six Hindu monks in saffron robes. George Harrison had recorded the Radha Krishna Temple troupe for the Beatles' Apple Records and he gave them a number-12-in-the charts hit record. The lyrics were simple:

> Hare Krishna Hare Krishna
> Krishna Krishna Hare Hare
> Hare Rāma Hare Rāma
> Rāma Rama Hare Hare.

But the tune was catchy, and for weeks people who had no idea what any of this meant could be heard humming it.

This chapter will consider the fate of three Hindu-inspired new religious movements (NRMs) of the 1960s and consider the place of yoga in the popular culture.

HINDU MOVEMENTS IN THE UK

Until the 1960s, Hinduism in the UK had a rather antiquarian taste. Although contemporary distaste for imperialism has caused 'orientalism' to become a term of abuse, it is important to appreciate the important role that British orientalists played in collecting, sorting, preserving, and translating Hindu sacred texts. Prime among them was the German-born Max Muller, who held a number of chairs in Oxford, where he worked from 1850 to 1875. As is explained in the next chapter, the Theosophical Society's largely elderly membership was familiar with Hindu themes. But it was the brief flirtation of 1960s pop stars with Hinduism that brought it to a large popular audience.

Krishna Consciousness

The late 1960s saw the arrival of a number of NRMs based on or inspired by Hindu themes. One such was the International Society for Krishna Consciousness aka ISKCON or, from the mantra frequently chanted by followers, Hare Krishna. It was founded in 1966 in New York by A. C. Bhaktivedanta Swami to promote bhakti (or devotional) yoga, which aimed to direct all thoughts and actions to pleasing the Supreme Lord, Krishna.[1] As noted, the three couples sent to the UK to spread the word enjoyed considerable support from Beatle George Harrison. His recording of adherents chanting the Hare Krishna mantra was a hit single in the UK, and he also included the chant in his hit 'My Sweet Lord'. Early converts were encouraged to live in communal ashrams and to devote themselves full-time to the movement. They were required to give up all stimulants, meat, gambling, and sex. Or, to be more precise, sex was to be practised only with lifelong partners for the purposes of procreation. Despite being very well known, the movement attracted few UK adherents: a few thousand at its peak.

Bhaktivedanta Manor, the Hertfordshire mansion that was bought for the movement by Harrison and serves as the movement's head-quarters, eventually found a viable role for itself serving the ethnic Indian community that was expelled from East Africa in 1972, but in so doing it further reduced the chance that it would recruit from the native British population. It was now seen as an ethnic rather than as a universally appealing religion.[2] As part of the right-wing project to shrink the state, the Conservatives (in a coalition with Liberal Democrats from 2010 to 2015 and subsequently governing alone) offered generous start-up funding and full cost support to schools outside local government control. As a fig leaf for this ideological project, Free Schools were required to have some distinctive purpose or ethos, and, as the state already supported a large Christian school sector, bids from non-Christian religions were welcome. ISKCON set up three Hindu schools. But, again, these largely served the British-Indian community rather than recruiting white British people to the worship of Krishna.

Because their promoters provide free text and they are relatively uncontroversial, benign religious activities are the stuff of so-called news reports in local press and mass media. It is a mark of how much more tolerant the UK's culture has become that Hare Krishna now benefits from such puffery when in the 1970s it was derided as dangerous.[3] Closely examining one such bit of PR fluff gives some insight into the British reception of Hare Krishna. In 2011, the BBC's local news webpages for Norfolk featured a story which began 'A new Hare Krishna community in Norfolk is rapidly gaining members to its weekly programme of worship.' Apparently local interest had 'blossomed' since the arrival of two Latvian Hare Krishnas. 'Latvians are not new to the faith and many Bulgarians, alongside white British, Arabs and Asians, are congregating in their droves to be part of the Norfolk Hare Krishna community.' That clumsy 'congregating in droves' is entirely belied by the data given in the first paragraph. Sunday morning meetings regularly attracted thirty attendees. For a city with a population of over 200,000, thirty people are not 'droves' and if, as the reference to Bulgarians, Arabs, and Asians suggests, it appealed particularly to immigrants, Hare Krishna in Norfolk might have attracted as few as ten white British people.[4]

A better estimate of the impact on the indigenous population can be seen in Scotland, where the ethnic Hindu population is very small. An ISKCON commune was established on a run-down farm in Lesmahagow, Lanarkshire, in 1987. Its resident population rarely got above twenty and the 2001 census showed only twenty-five people in the whole of Scotland identifying as Hare Krishna.[5]

The Vital Spark

Another Hindu import has already been mentioned in the previous chapter's description of an early Glastonbury music festival. The Divine Light Mission (DLM) was an organization founded in northern India in 1960 by guru Shri Hans Ji Maharaj. DLM gained prominence in the West under the founder's youngest son, Guru Maharaj Ji

(Prem Rawat). Much was made of his youth: he was variously the 13- and then 14-year-old and so on 'perfect master'.

By 1973, DLM had thousands of followers in the West, many of them full-time residents in US ashrams, but growth was slow and the founding family split. Those in India wished to maintain the movement's original ethos. Maharaj Ji (who had married an American) determined to reorient the western DLM in the direction of the largely secular psychotherapies being taught in popular centres such as Esalen.[6] He closed the ashrams and eliminated the remaining Indian influences so that he could promote his 'teaching in a way that was free from any particular religious or cultural association'. Elan Vital, as it is now known, 'is not a religion and there are no particular rituals, sacred days, pilgrimages, sacred places, doctrines, scriptures, or . . . any other dimension associated with a religious lifestyle'.[7]

> For Elan Vital, the emphasis is on individual, subjective experience, rather than on a body of dogma. The teachings provide a kind of practical mysticism. Maharaji speaks not of God, but of the god or divinity within, the power that gives existence. He has occasionally referred to the existence of the two gods—the one created by humankind and the one which creates humankind. Although such references apparently suggest an acceptance of a creative, loving power, he distances himself and his teachings from any concept of religion . . . deliberately keeping a low profile has meant that the movement has generally managed to escape the gaze of publicity that surrounds other NRMs.[8]

The Orange Order

Rajneeshism is an eclectic world-affirming combination of Hindu meditation and spiritually oriented psychology.[9] A former philosophy professor, Shree Bhagwan Rajneesh attracted large numbers of young middle-class westerners to become what he called 'neo-sannyasins'. His adherents had to wear orange clothes. They had to wear a necklace (or mala) with a picture of the Bhagwan. And they had to practise the Bhagwan's Dynamic Meditation. Where traditional Hindu disciples renounced the world, the neo-sannyasins embraced 'life, love and laughter', and they also embraced each other. For a while sex (which Rajneesh held to be enlightening) formed a regular part of his 'Dynamic Meditation'.[10] What was 'dynamic' about it was that participants would work themselves into a froth by heavy breathing, shouting, and jumping up and down—meditation rooms were heavily padded—before settling down to the more conventional meditation. For a guru, Rajneesh was surprisingly open to the wide range of New Age interests, therapies, and revelations: 'Sannyasins from European and American therapy communes brought encounter groups, Primal Scream therapies, gestalt therapies, bioenergetics, Rolfing, everything from yoga to karate, T'ai chi to the Tarot.'[11] As Frances Fitzgerald put it, Rajneesh offered 'a spiritual garage for anyone with a method'.[12]

Rajneesh's movement was almost destroyed by his decision to move his base to the USA and by the behaviour of his senior lieutenants. From 1981 to 1987 the movement attracted thousands to rural Oregon. The local residents were not welcoming, and the Rajneeshees acted with an indifference to local interests that drifted from arrogance to criminality.

Rajneeshpuram (or 'the Ranch' as adepts called it) was built on land originally bought with subterfuge. As the land was zoned for agricultural use, the purchasers pretended they planned to create a small agricultural community. It quickly grew to a town of some 3,000 people and created the institutions of a small town: its own fire and police services, restaurants, shopping malls, townhouses, an air field, and bus system.[13] When the scale of the project became clear, locals protested, and the Rajneeshees retaliated by trying to take over the main site of opposition: the nearby town of Antelope. Both sides deployed a wide range of legal and bureaucratic weapons. The Attorney General of Oregon maintained that Rajneeshpuram was essentially part of a religious organization and so its incorporation as a city offended against the constitutionally required separation of church and state. When a series of lawsuits prevented the further expansion of 'the Ranch', followers tried to build in Antelope, which was briefly renamed Rajneesh, when sufficient numbers of Orange people registered to vote there and won a referendum on the subject.

The Bhagwan's secretary and chief executive Ma Anand Sheela (aka Sheela Silverman), the de facto leader of the commune in Rajneesh's frequent absences, was a polarizing force whose hostility to any who failed to obey her exacerbated the conflict.[14] In 1985, Sheela and a number of top aides fled the commune, and shortly after the Bhagwan publicly accused Sheela of serious crimes. It turned out that she and her cabal had been responsible for the poisoning and attempted murder of Rajneesh's physician (they feared his influence), extensive bugging within the commune, the poisoning of two public officials, and arson. Sheela was extradited from Germany and imprisoned for these crimes. The Bhagwan was arrested while trying to flee the country with $40,000 in cash and a collection of luxury watches worth $400,000. He was charged with breaking US immigration law: many of his sannyasins had entered the USA on tourist visas and then married in order to gain resident status. As part of a plea bargain, he agreed to be deported and had to face the indignity of being refused entry by country after country. He wandered the less attractive parts of the world for a number of years before returning to India and dying in his Poona ashram. The Ranch was bought by a Christian youth group.

The Rajneeshpuram project and the vast amount of publicity it garnered might suggest that Rajneeshism was popular. The population of the USA is such that almost any movement based in or recruiting largely from the USA seems successful, but a better sense of its fate can be gained from its growth in Britain. The core of full-time disciples, committed enough to live in the movement's ashrams, was never more than about 500. A resident of Medina Rajneesh, a large mansion in Suffolk that was the main British ashram, says that, while the number of residents declared to the local government planning department was 300, the actual total was closer to 450, not including the children.[15] A 'where are they now' website run by a former resident lists 461 people.[16] To get the scale right, we need note only that this is the congregation of one popular urban church.

Death seems to have enhanced rather than diminished Rajneesh. This is not unprecedented. The charismatic leader can often be difficult to manage and he can wander 'off piste'. Once dead, his loyal followers can codify his teachings and present them to the world as a finished and orderly product. Under the name of Osho, Rajneesh continues to influence New Agers who wish to combine Hindu meditational techniques with secular psychotherapies and the Poona ashram again attracts large numbers of westerners who fit a fortnight's pursuit of enlightenment into their busy lives. Although Tim Guest was extremely critical of the movement in which he grew up (his mother having been a senior figure in England and Germany), his disdain for the reformed version is clear in his description:

The [Poona] Ashram is now officially the 'Osho Meditation retreat'. . . . it soon grew from the original six acres to encompass forty acres of Koregaon Park. Visitors wore maroon during the day and white for evening meditations. There were waterfalls, gardens, an Olympic-sized swimming pool, and a cyber-café.... The website had a pop-up ad offering 'The Wellness Weekend Getaway Special'—a three-day package including a free white and free red robe. (The site quoted the British Airways in-flight magazine: 'It was the sheer beauty of the place I first fell for. Meditation was in the very air.') The Osho logo was shown as a registered trademark.[17]

Some of the ethos of the movement has survived. There are two small residential communities: in Dorset and Somerset.[18] But the greatest impact is probably the enduring commitment to various forms of alternative therapy of many of those schooled at Medina Rajneesh. A website run by a former child resident lists the occupations of 103 former pupils. The school's refusal to teach a conventional curriculum or to submit its students for formal examinations made university attendance and conventional middle-class careers difficult. Hence most former residents have had to rely on personal skills and initiative. The largest group—a third—work in some strand of the arts: musicians, graphic designers, clothes designers, and photographers. The next is construction workers and gardeners: presumably people using skills they acquired in renovating and maintaining the old Medina mansion. The third largest group are therapists: most offering some form of 'bodywork' but a few astrologers.[19] And just behind the therapists are people working in either computer software design or hardware construction and repair: a sphere of work for which, in its pioneering days, there were no formal qualifications and hence which was open to bright people from unconventional backgrounds.

As an aside, it is worth noting, for alternative religions as much as for the mainstream, the power of childhood socialization. By all accounts, the Rajneeshee children were badly neglected. Rajneesh thought there were too many people in the world. Pregnant women were pressed to abort, and it became a mark of commitment to be sterilized.[20] And yet very many of them have retained beliefs and values close to those in which they were raised.[21]

In sum, the original Rajneesh project to enlist full-time adherents in the creation of an alternative society was, like ISKCON's similar ambition, a flop. For all the noise, the movement in the UK never amounted to more than a couple of large Christian congregations. Osho's teachings continue to have some influence only because what is expected of adherents has been scaled down to allow people with mainstream occupations and families to improve their mundane lives with some of his ideas. Like Findhorn (discussed in the previous chapter), the Poona ashram is now a training centre that allows people with conventional occupations to visit for a week or a fortnight's enlightenment. The small British centres similarly survive as venues for teaching and training that fit into the general cultic milieu of New Age enlightenment and alternative medical therapy. Like much Christianity, Rajneeshism is, for most of its very small number of adherents, a leisure pursuit that has little impact on their daily lives.[22]

Transcendental Meditation

The most successful of the Hindu imports is Transcendental Meditation (or TM). It began life as a fairly conventional expression of Hinduism. Founder Maharishi Mahesh Yogi, who began teaching in 1958, tried to export it to Britain but he had little success until the Beatles and a number of other celebrities attended his Rishikesh ashram in February 1968.[23] As a world-rejecting religion, TM had few recruits but, promoted as a secular therapy, it became popular. As dissemination was based on autonomous instructors charging clients fees, it is impossible to know how many people learnt TM, but the number for the UK must be in the very large thousands.

TM's problem was an inability to turn a popular product into an enduring movement. Like Dianetics before L. Ron Hubbard recast it as Scientology, TM was appropriated by adepts who modified it as they incorporated it into their personal practice. As William Bainbridge said of TM in the USA: 'Most of the millions who had been initiated either ceased meditating or did so informally and irregularly without continuing connections to the TM Movement.'[24]

TM's secular drift is clear from the following advert, which ran in British newspapers in the 1990s:

> Transcendental Meditation is a natural and effective technique which relaxes, revitalises and recharges your energy to get more out of life. It leaves you feeling positive, alert and clear with the calmness and inner contentment to tackle life with enthusiasm. It protects you from stress and future ill-health. TM has been verified by independent scientific research and is recommended by hundreds of doctors in Britain.... it requires no belief or change in lifestyle.[25]

In case it be thought that I am making too much of one presentational text, there is ample evidence that this disavowal of the movement's religious foundations was standard practice.[26] When researching the gender breakdown of various NRMs, I emailed a number of TM instructors. In explaining why I wanted to know the relative proportions of men and women who had been taught TM, I thoughtlessly used the word 'religion'. I received the following reply from Transcendental Meditation National Enquiries Office:

> Transcendental Meditation is not a religion. It is a scientifically validated technique which does not involve holding any faith or belief, just as in the same way it doesn't conflict with any belief that a person may already have. You can see this on our website... on the home page, there is a... video by a Catholic priest who practises TM on how it enhances his religion. We also have quotes from various religious leaders, such as Jewish Rabbis, Catholic Priests, Shamans, United Reform Church and the Islamic faith, who have found Transcendental Meditation has enhanced rather than conflicted with their faith.

Although its front stage presentation was secular, TM did retain a religious back stage. The Siddhis programme of advanced meditation makes claims to supernatural power. Among other powers, its adepts can supposedly levitate. It also claimed that, if enough of them gathered to meditate in some trouble spot, then political conflicts could be resolved. That pacific potential was advertised by the Natural Law Party, which in 1992 contested 310 seats in a Westminster election and won 0.19 per cent of the vote. In the 1994 European Parliament election, it contested every seat and gained 0.63 per cent of the vote. In the 1997 election, the NLP ran 197 candidates and won 0.10 per cent of votes cast. Although the first electoral intervention could have been justified as relatively cheap publicity, repeatedly proving it was only as popular as the Monster Raving Loony party was hardly sensible. It did not contest the 2001 election and formally ended its political career two years later by de-registering from the Electoral Commission.

Aware that movements, such as ISKCON, which demanded communal living, had not been a success, TM tried to create a less demanding base by encouraging adepts to move to the Lancashire town of Skelmersdale. 'Skem', as it is locally known, was created in 1971 as a planned new town to take population from the redevelopment of the cramped slums of north-side Liverpool. In order to improve its chances of development, the planners made the deliberate decision not to provide good commuting transport links to Liverpool or Manchester. The rapid decline in the UK's manufacturing sector in the late 1970s sucked the life out of the town before it had a chance to prove itself. Though the cynic might suggest Skem needed moral uplift a lot more than most places, it is hard to imagine that anything other than very cheap property and a local council desperate for any development attracted TM to the town.

TM's Sidhaland comprised a Vedic health centre, an arts and sports centre, and a school. One former pupil acknowledged the area's general social problems:

> I lived off-site, so to speak, in an estate about ten minutes' walk from the Sidhaland. Friends from school wouldn't come as far as mine, as they were too afraid of running into the local kids. But apart from one or two incidents (no more than your average teenager), life was pretty subdued.[27]

Thirty years on, the Skem project has patently failed. To quote the website:

> Membership is currently 300. Our aim is to expand to a population that would enable 800 experts in Transcendental Meditation and the more advanced TM-Sidhi Programme, including Yogic Flying, to practise the programme together twice a day in the Maharishi Golden Dome, which forms the heart of the community. Scientific research has established that 800 people is the required number to create a significant influence of positivity and coherence throughout collective consciousness in the UK.[28]

Note that 300 people—the total number of TM followers willing to move to Skem—is the population of a single town street or a popular church congregation, and other settlement schemes have been less successful. A plan to build on the disused USAF base at Edzell, Angus, was mooted and then dropped. A grand scheme for a 'garden village' built to the 'timeless principles of Maharishi Vastu-Sthapatya Veda' in Rendlesham, Suffolk, finally amounted to a meditation hall, twenty-nine houses, and twenty-eight flats.[29] The Skelmersdale school struggled on with low numbers until in 2011 it was fortunate enough (like the ISKCON schools already mentioned) to be an accidental beneficiary of the Conservatives' Free Schools programme.[30] In addition, many celebrities, such as film producer David Lynch, have promoted the secular benefits of TM and, in a much-watered-down form, meditation has found some acceptance in British schools. A number, for example, have experimented with punctuating the school day with a 'stress-free quiet time'.[31] Note that this is a further 'secularization': a religious exercise became a secular therapy, which became 'quiet time'.

In brief, TM was very successful in promoting its meditational technique and was responsible for giving many British people their first taste of meditation, but it achieved that only once it had reconfigured its product as a secular psychotherapy.

FROM YOGINS TO YOGA

Hindu-inspired NRMs did not recruit well in Britain. One obstacle may have been a relative lack of appeal to women. Generally speaking, women are more religious than men, and so characteristics that deter women ensure less than optimal growth. The problem in explaining any gender gap in recruitment is that there are many possible causes and the statistical data are not good enough for the multi-variate analysis that might help. The best we can do is somewhat speculatively to list what may have been obstacles to recruiting women.

ISKCON was brought to Britain by three men and three women, Rajneesh welcomed powerful female lieutenants, and TM had many women trainers, but nonetheless they (and the Divine Light Mission) were all led by male gurus, and their cultural background was one in which women were very clearly secondary to men. The followings of Sai Baba, Deepak Chopra, and the like show that western women can be attracted to Indian male leaders, but the sort of women whose spiritual seeking involved feminist thought may well have been put off by the patriarchal associations of the original Indian contexts and by the sex scandals.[32]

Another obstacle, particularly in the early years, may have been the degree of sacrifice required. Those NRMs that required communal living and full-time commitment attracted fewer women than those that offered something that could be assimilated to a conventional family life. For example, women were 51 per cent of those learning the TM technique, but only 25 per cent of those who joined TM in its early communal phase.[33] We can only guess precisely what it is that women were unwilling to give up. My unstructured interviews over three decades suggest that the loss of opportunity for a normal family life was important, as was the loss of a conventional career. One has to recall that in the 1970s and 1980s women were only just beginning to break into high-status professional jobs. They may well have been reluctant to give up what they had only just acquired.

A related issue concerns the world-affirming versus world-rejecting divide. Generally speaking, women were less likely than men to be attracted to world-rejecting movements. ISKCON was that in both doctrine and organization, as were the Divine Light Mission and TM in their early days. Rajneeshism was more complex in that its doctrine was world affirming: Rajneesh believed that sex, for example, was a joy to be enjoyed as much as possible. However, core members were required to exile themselves from conventional society and to subordinate themselves entirely to the movement. They were treated like enlisted soldiers: posted here and there as the senior management decided. Tim Guest describes how his mother was shunted between British posts before being sent to the Ranch and then demoted and sent to Germany before being posted back to Suffolk. The frustration of the young child's wish to be with his mother—denied even when they were in the same place by the movement's commitment to communal child-rearing—is heart-rending. It is not difficult to imagine that many potential members were put off by the thought of being denied a normal family life.

But what these and less well-known movements did succeed in doing was popularizing (or at least making more familiar) two spiritual practices: yoga and meditation. Meditation will be discussed in the next chapter. Here I want to consider the popularity of yoga.

Positional yoga first came on the radar in the early 1960s. Apparently hundreds of students were studying yoga in evening classes organized by the local education authority in Birmingham in 1965.[34] In 1967, officials of the Inner London Education Authority approved yoga classes provided they did not involve 'treatment of the philosophy of yoga'.[35] The involvement of government officials in such decisions was not state censorship of religion. It was simply that adult education classes were subsidized by the taxpayer and thus local government officers had an interest in deciding what classes were funded. What the hippies of the late 1960s and the various NRMs that used yoga as spiritual exercise did was to popularize the 'treatment of the philosophy of yoga' that ILEA officers were keen to ensure did not sully the physical exercise classes.

The study of the English Lake District town of Kendal (described in detail in Chapter 6) found that yoga was the most popular activity in the holistic spirituality milieu, practised by an average of 128 people in a typical week. When asked, just over half of them said they thought of it as spiritual. This is probably on the high side for the population of Britain as a whole. Because the Kendal respondents were found by following links between people who were prominent in New Age activities, they were often involved in a number of such activities. That is, far more of the Kendal yoga sample were committed spiritual seekers than would be the case if one tapped those attending a weekly yoga class in any village hall. When my female farmer neighbour told me that she was going to a yoga class in the local sports centre, I expressed surprise at her interest in Hindu religion and she asked: 'What has yoga got to do with Hinduism?' She was a keen keep-fitter. She had tried Pilates and various forms of dance exercise and a decade later she owned a franchise for Curves, a women-only circuit exercise programme. To her and, one suspects, very many like her, yoga was just another weapon in the fight against the indignities of growing old.

If the stories that reach the press are at all representative, that view of yoga seems common. When a Church of England vicar denied a yoga class the use of his church hall, a British Wheel of Yoga spokesperson described his action as 'ignorant' and added: 'It's not a religion and it doesn't push any version of one.'[36] A yoga group for toddlers was banned from a Baptist church and a Church of England hall.[37] An instructor in Southampton found her hire of a Catholic Church hall cancelled because the priest did not want to promote a competing religion. The instructor said:

> I had never heard about any religious issue with yoga before but I have looked into it since and found that some other religions feel that when people meditate it could let the devil inside them. But there was never any meditation in my class—it was just exercises. . . . I tried to explain to the church that my yoga classes were not religious at all and I even offered to come and demonstrate the class. It is about calmness and relaxation.[38]

That the instructor had never noticed the religious background to yoga is unusual. That she thought her classes 'were not religious at all' is not, and attempts to interest men in yoga—such as Broga—have all taken the form of replacing residual religious elements with more strenuous exercises. One London operation has replaced all the Indian position names with English ones.[39]

Two further observations about the secularization of yoga are worth adding. First, its recasting as a physical exercise regime is not the only possible secularization. Some practitioners have found yoga valuable as a response to psychological stress. One woman, for example, took it up as a way of distracting herself from grief over the death of her father:

> I have learnt that yoga helps me cope with grief. It gives me a sense of grounding, the sandbags to shore up the watery wash of my emotions. A distraction that means I can sometimes get a sense of a bird's eye view, rather than a bug's eye view, and a way to feel my body.[40]

Second, it is quite possible, as Andrea Jain has argued, that positional yoga is a novel secular product and that to some extent its character can be explained by global social forces that encourage individualism rather than as a simple capitulation to the secularity of the West. Her case is well made, but it is an argument about nuances that is not necessary for my simpler purpose.[41] My concern is to show that the positional yoga that is practised in the West is either entirely secular or spirituality-lite. The implication is that, were it otherwise, it would be markedly less popular than it is.

REBIRTH AND COSMIC JUSTICE

Beyond the practices of meditation and yoga, the religions of the East have contributed two important notions to the general culture: reincarnation and karma. Here we have what looks like good evidence for Colin Campbell's 'easternization of the West' thesis, for both offer a holistic alternative to Christianity's radical divide of us and God and this life and the next.

For reasons I will mention in a moment, these data are highly contentious, but they are nonetheless worth noting. A 1947 survey of a London suburb had only 4 per cent of respondents saying they believed in reincarnation.[42] A large national survey of the early 1950s found only 1 per cent.[43] The 1990 European Values survey had

24 per cent assenting to: 'Do you believe in reincarnation?'[44] A 2011 poll reduced that figure to 11 per cent. The difficulty with such data is that surveys become ever less useful the more abstract and complex the question. It is possible, for example, that some people hear reincarnation as meaning the Christian model of being 'born again' in heaven. However, that ambiguity was avoided in the 2001 Scottish Attitudes survey, which asked respondents if they had lived a previous life and found that 18 per cent said they had.

That there has been an increase in the proportion of those of us who prefer some reincarnation model to the Christian version of life after death is what one would expect from experience and from socio-logic. As Christianity has declined, so its preferred model of transition to a final resting place has also declined in popularity, which has left space for alternatives, both in the sense that more people have not been raised in the Christian model and are thus potentially open to alternatives, and in the sense that the Christian churches no longer have the social power to stigmatize alternatives as dangerously deviant. At the same time, the number of people who are interested in any sort of religion has declined. The two things together would lead us to expect a growth in the popularity of reincarnation, but only small growth.

Survey questions tend to ask about reincarnation in either the abstract or the future, but most claims for reincarnation are retrospective. Many spiritual seekers claim to have lived previous lives. In an interview, a young female Country and Western singer Caitlin Rose said:

> You know how some people say they're an old soul? I think I'm a boozy old man's soul. My favourite thing when I was in high school was to go to a waffle house and sit around 60-year-old men who were smoking and reading the paper. It was one of the first places where I really felt at home—around truck drivers. I'm not a glamour queen; I'm just a boozy old man in overalls![45]

Clearly Rose is speaking tongue-in-cheek, but, irrespective of how much weight the reader (or Rose) gives to the explanation, the language of previous lives allows her to talk about her character. At the very least, that she expects magazine readers to understand the first sentence shows the extent to which the reincarnation model has become a recognized part of our cultural landscape.

The difficulty in interpreting current use of reincarnation is to know how much of it reflects thoughtful commitment to a particular model of the relationship between the human body and the self and how much is just a convenient way of talking about other things. As Rose uses it, it gives us an alternative to the Freudian 'blame it on your parents' model for talking about one's personality. It may also allow us to talk about somewhat unusual experiences such as *déjà vu*, without the speaker being entirely committed to reincarnation beyond such usage.

At first sight, any great interest in reincarnation might seem like good evidence of the easternization of the West thesis, but closer examination suggests something rather different.[46] There are, of course, very many different beliefs about the self in Hinduism and Buddhism and there are as many inconsistencies as there are in Christian notions of life after death, but the general tenor of eastern views is to stress the unimportance of the self. This causes some logical tensions with the notion of karma, but the key motif is the impermanence of the self (and everything else for that matter). Those for whom life is at least the last three of the states mentioned in Thomas Hobbes's 'solitary, poor, nasty, brutish, and short', there is consolation in the realization that all things must pass and that the proper performance of rituals due in their station will result in a better rebirth until, the final goal, they are released from the necessity of being.

In western hands reincarnation has been inverted into a belief that the self is a fixed entity that repeatedly returns to life on earth. Where Hinduism diminishes the importance of the self, the westernized version elevates it. We are simply too important to die. To put it in exaggerated contrast, in the eastern version the self vanishes; in the western version the self endures. As Colin Campbell says: 'Thus while in the Orient the great hope has always been to escape as quickly as possible from the wheel of rebirth . . . in the West the tendency is to seek to extend the process of rebirth.'[47] Or, to put it in terms of dualism versus holism, where the eastern version of reincarnation is 'holistic' in that apparently separable human selves are really just part of the single unitary cosmic consciousness, the westernized version is, like school custard, lumpy with persisting selves.

Among other things, religion provides what Max Weber called a 'theodicy': 'Religious teachings . . . serve to shelter the individual from "chaos"—from a reality that makes no sense—by providing explanations of suffering, death, tragedy and injustice.'[48] Karma offers such explanations. According to two recent surveys, around a third of the British apparently believe in it.[49] Hindus differ, but, generally speaking, karma is the spiritual principle of cause and effect where the morality of our actions influence our future. Good deeds are rewarded in this life or in a good rebirth. Bad deeds are punished in this life or in a bad rebirth. Thus what in one lifetime might look like injustice is merited over a number of lives. The same reservations as for the reincarnation data apply, but clearly the idea is more popular than once it was.

There is no doubt that the notion of a personal creator God has declined in popularity. When surveys offered only the choice of believing in God or not, the vast majority of people said they believed in God. But, as surveyors have become more sophisticated, the personal God alternative has slipped, shipping numbers first to 'higher power or life-force' and then to the wonderfully vague 'There is something there.' We now find implausible the idea of a wise old man who sees everything and sorts the sheep from the goats or the wheat from the chaff or whatever agricultural metaphor one prefers. The inherent implausibility has long been recognized by Christians; it is nowhere better expressed than in a popular country-and-western song 'Farther Along'.[50]

> Tempted and tried, we're oft made to wonder
> Why it should be thus all the day long;
> While there are others living about us
> Never molested, though in the wrong.
> Often when death has taken our loved ones
> Leaving our home so lone and so drear,
> Then do we wonder why others prosper
> Living so wicked year after year.

Those verses perfectly pose the classic question of why God allows bad things to happen to good people and vice versa. But the answer given in the repeated chorus is a remarkably unsatisfactory one:

> Farther along we'll know more about it
> Farther along we'll understand why;
> Cheer up, my brother, live in the sunshine
> We'll understand it all by and by.

So it makes no sense now but, at some unstated point in the future, God will explain all. Against that, provided one can believe in the supernatural, the idea of an impersonal moral accounting system that settles scores across rebirths may seem appealing.

In May 2008, an earthquake in Sichuan province killed some 70,000 people and left millions homeless. In a spontaneous response to a question rather unfairly posed to her while she was posing on a film premiere red carpet, the American actress Sharon Stone said:

> I'm not happy about the way the Chinese are treating the Tibetans because I don't think anyone should be unkind to anyone else. And then this earthquake and all this stuff happened, and then I thought, is that karma? When you're not nice then bad things happen to you.[51]

In an exemplification of karma, Dior immediately dropped Stone from a lucrative cosmetics contract for insulting potentially one of its largest markets.

Actually, Stone is probably one of the more thoughtful ones. This is a very difficult case to demonstrate, because it requires very detailed follow-up to a simple survey question such as 'Do you believe in karma?', but I strongly suspect that contemporary references to the idea differ in two important ways from the obvious interpretation of a popular cultural shift. Or at least there has been a shift, but it is not the obvious one.

Campbell follows Max Weber in presenting Christian dualism and eastern holism as competing alternatives, with the latter increasing in popularity as the former declines. That seems logical, but presenting them as a forced choice may not properly capture the relationship. It could well be that, insofar as people take it seriously, the causes of the decline of Christian dualism bear as heavily on the holistic alternative. Given the collapse of Christianity, that karma has not become a much more popular idea suggests that actually few of us find it stands up to much scrutiny. Its apparent popularity may, like that of reincarnation, owe a lot to karma's value as a familiar (in certain circles) shorthand for talking about extremely complex matters. My grannie always warned against presuming that we would be safe from the vast array of hazards she assumed would beset anyone who left the house by adding to any statement of intention 'if we're spared', almost as a nervous tic, like touching wood. Although 'if we're spared' might in the Calvinist Presbyterian culture in which she was raised have expressed real belief that the world (or our part in it) might end soon, her continued use of the phrase into the 1980s was probably only the equivalent of 'you never know'—a universal caution that expresses a certain personality type. My feeling is that 'that's karma for you' is a borrowing from the Orient of a particular phrase to recognize that, as it happens, someone has got what he or she deserves rather than an expression of a commitment to an oriental view of cause and effect in the universe. That is, what has been adopted by cosmopolitan westerners is not the karmic model of justice within the context of reincarnation but simply a phrase that allows us to add an 'and it is no more than he deserved' endorsement of particular events—a comment on specific past events rather than an expectation of future ones.

My point is a caution in how we interpret such popularity as reincarnation and karma appear now to possess. When a set of beliefs is deeply embedded in popular culture and most people have been socialized in them in childhood and continue to act with some regard to them, then we can reasonably assume that talk apparently predicated on those beliefs should be taken at something like face value. But, in the absence of such deep roots, it may be that what is being borrowed is just a few words and phrases that allow us to talk about perennial concerns that would once have been treated in the now-discredited Christian framework. This is not insignificant. That some British people may now say 'that's karma for you' instead of 'that's God's judgement' is a notable cultural change, but it may be a rather superficial one.

CONCLUSION

This brief examination of the fortunes of various Hindu-inspired NRMs suggests a number of important conclusions. ISKCON began as world rejecting and remained world rejecting and tiny. DLM began as world rejecting and then became world affirming and as Elan Vital blended into the New Age milieu, as did the world-affirming Rajneesh movement. TM was very briefly world rejecting before becoming world affirming. As such it was successful in marketing a meditational technique that it assured the interested was both easy and secular. But it was hardly more successful than ISKCON or Rajneeshism in creating the foundations of a viable alternative enclave. Choosing Skem as its base might explain some of that failure, but then no other similar movement (and that includes the Findhorn Foundation discussed in the previous chapter) has been any more successful.

Some people were willing to dabble; almost no one wanted to build a life around TM.

Set against the large millions lost to Christianity since the 1960s, the thousands attracted to ISKCON or TM are trivial and offer no evidence that there is a steady natural demand for religion such that, when one type of religion declines, another must rise to fill the gap. But equally important for assessing the relative merits of the change-and-decline versus the just-change models explained in Chapter 1 are the relative fortunes of our movements and their direction of change. None has been popular in the sense that disco music or dope-smoking have been popular, but the most popular have been the movements that require the least sacrifice and that can most readily be fitted into a secular life. Secondly, the movement that performed best was the one that most shifted in a secular direction.

The same case can be made for the cultural innovations associated with our Hindu-inspired movements. Although positional yoga has become popular in Britain, it has succeeded as a form of low intensity exercise and not as a technique for the pursuit of spiritual enlightenment. That reincarnation and karma are at all popular shows how the decline of Christianity has opened up space for alternatives, but nothing suggests they have become sufficiently popular to maintain the balance of the religious and the secular as it was in 1900 or 1950. In these senses, the religious activities examined in this chapter confirm the book's title: the secular beats the spiritual.

NOTES

1. The two best accounts of ISKCON are E. Burke Rochford, *Hare Krishna in America* (New Brunswick, NJ: Rutgers University Press, 1985), and *Hare Krishna Transformed* (New York: New York University Press, 2007).
2. Rochford, *Hare Krishna Transformed*, 181–200, makes the same point.
3. The *Craven Herald*, the weekly paper for the north-west corner of North Yorkshire, presented a lightweight puff of a visit from the leader of the Brahma Kumaris opposite, and in much the same tone as, a detailed report of the Hellifield Women's Institute learning Morris dancing. Just part of life's rich tapestry! *Craven Herald and Pioneer*, 29 April 2005.
4. BBC News, Hare Krishna community thriving in Norwich'. 22 February 2011 <http://www.bbc.co.uk/news/uk-england-norfolk-12537112> (accessed July 2015).

5. The farm found a new purpose in social work by offering training places to out-of-work young people. In 2004, the leader of Hare Krishna in Scotland in the 1990s William Somerville (aka Balabhadra Das) was exposed by ISKCON as having misappropriated donations to fund an extravagant lifestyle, physically abused male followers, and sexually abused female disciples. See Anon., 'GBC-EC Statement and Report Regarding Balabhadra das (formerly Bhakti Balabha Puri Maharaja)', *ISKCON News* <https://iskconnews.org/page/gbc-ec-statement-and-report-regarding-balabhadra-das-formerly-bhakti-balabha-puri-maharaja,19/> (accessed May 2017).

6. Despite the movement's prohibition on alcohol, drugs, and sex outside of marriage, Prem Rawat managed a great deal of all three. Michael Dettmers, who ran the organization in the late 1970s and early 1980s, frequently procured female adherents for Rawat's sexual pleasure. See Gail Finch in Michael Finch, *Without the Guru* (Amazon: Booksurge Publishing, 2009), 32. See also J. Kramer and D. Alstad, *The Guru Papers: Marks of Authoritarian Power* (Berkeley: North Atlantic Books, 1993).

7. R. Greaves, 'Elan Vital', in C. Partridge (ed.), *New Religions: A Guide* (Oxford: Oxford University Press, 2004), 202.

8. S. Hunt, *Alternative Religions* (Aldershot: Ashgate, 2003), 116. To place Rajneeshism in this chapter is to locate it within a tradition that its founder disdained. Rajneesh was born a Jain (a class-distinct fraction of Hinduism), but he rejected much of his background, was scornful of Gandhi and other Hindu political leaders, and regularly praised Buddha, Christ, and other great spiritual teachers. Nonetheless, writing requires ordering, and Rajneesh's use of such Hindu terms as sannyas, darshan, and ashram is justification enough for placing him here.

9. Elisabeth Puttick, 'The Osho Movement', in Partridge (ed.), *New Religions*, 191–2. The best detailed account of Rajneeshism from the position of a child whose mother was a key figure in its British activities is T. Guest, *My Life in Orange* (London: Granta, 2004).

10. There were sinister aspects to the Rajneeshees' sexual freedom. Some leaders used the idea that a possessive attitude to one's sexual partner was a failing to be overcome as a way of extending the pool of followers whom they could exploit and as an excuse for voyeurism: 'One device made popular in Teertha's groups was to sit and watch your lover have sex with someone else and feel the emotions that came up. (Any rage or jealousy you happened to feel was, of course, an excellent opportunity to practise your detachment)' (Guest, *My Life*, 42). An even more sinister aspect of their permissiveness was the exploitation of children. Tim Guest notes: 'That year, in the summer of 1984 at the Ranch, many of the Medina kids lost their virginity; boys and girls, ten years old, eight years old, in sweaty tents and A-frames, late at night and mid-afternoon,

with adults and other children. I remember some of the kids—eight, nine, ten years old—arguing about who had fucked whom, who would or wouldn't fuck them' (Guest, *My Life*, 198–9). Clearly much of this activity was statutory rape, in that, however willing the children, they were nonetheless well below the age of consent.

11. Guest, *My Life*, 39–40.
12. A. Storr, *Feet of Clay: A Study of Gurus* (London: Harper Collins, 1996), 55.
13. The population was more than doubled by the 'Share-a-home' pro-gramme, which offered accommodation to some 4,000 homeless people, who were bussed in from all over the USA.
14. A detailed account of the rise and fall of Rajneeshpuram can be found in Guest, *My Life*, and in L. F. Carter, *Charisma and Control in Rajneesh-puram* (Cambridge: Cambridge University Press, 1990).
15. Guest, *My Life*, 81.
16. 'Medina—where are we now' <http://www.sannyas.net/medina/where. html> (accessed July 2015). The site notes that some people did not want to be listed. However, others who are noted in photographs but could not be identified may have been non-Rajneeshee visitors. For the purpose of estimation we can suppose the two cancel out. Even this exaggerates the movement's popularity. If we assume that those not given a foreign ethnicity include all British residents, then at most 85% were British. The next largest group were German (at 20% of the 70 with a given non-British ethnicity) followed by Scandinavian and Irish, both at 16%. A reasonable conclusion is that the Rajneesh movement had at any one time no more than 500 committed adherents in Britain.
17. Guest, *My Life*, 286.
18. According to its website in 2015, the Dorset Osho Leela centre had ten permanent residents <http://osholeela.uk/?page_id=338> (accessed July 2015).
19. These figures are calculated from the professions listed against the names in KIDS, a website run by former Medina child resident 'Rupda' <http://www.rupda.com/network.htm> (accessed July 2015). What is clear from the longer biographies given in 'Medina—where are we now' is that many of those with mainstream jobs have maintained their alternative spirituality interests and have at times worked at least part-time to promote them.
20. Storr, *Feet of Clay*, 56.
21. Although he makes relatively light of it, the sexual abuse of minors at the Ranch is documented by Guest, *My Life*.
22. H. B. Urban, 'Osho, from Sex Guru to Guru of the Rich: The Spiritual Logic of Late Capitalism', in T. A. Forsthoefel and C. A. Humes (eds), *Gurus in America* (New York: SUNY Press, 2005), 147–68.

23. When the Beatles and their entourage visited the Maharishi Mahesh Yogi's ashram, the Yogi either made a pass at or tried to rape the American actress Mia Farrow; accounts differ. John Lennon said later: 'There was a hullabaloo about him trying to rape Mia and a few other women. The whole gang charged down to his hut and I said: "We're leaving!" He asked why and I said: "If you're so cosmic, you'll know why' (N. Webster, 'Maharishi Inspired Beatles but Died Leaving £2bn and Rape Rumours', *Daily Mirror*, 7 February 2008). Farrow put the incident down to a misunderstanding. Later another British disciple, Linda Pearce, claimed the Maharishi had seduced her when he was in his 60s. 'He was a brilliant manipulator. I just couldn't see that he was a dirty old man. We made love regularly.' Pearce's husband reports that, when years later he confronted the Maharishi, he did not deny the accusation. The Maharishi is also reported to have had a number of sexual encounters with young boys in his entourage (L. Williamson, *Transcendent in America: Hindu-Inspired Meditation Movements as New Religion* (New York: New York University Press, 2010), 92). For a detailed account of three years in an Indian ashram from the standpoint of a western seeker who was not a celebrity, see M. O'Doherty, *I was a Teenage Catholic* (Douglas, Cork: Marino, 2003).

24. W. S. Bainbridge, *The Sociology of Religious Movements* (New York: Routledge, 1997), 189. There is some evidence that, towards the end of his life, the Maharishi was pursuing the Hubbard strategy of trying to regain control over his product by, in this case, reintroducing Hindu themes; see C. A. Humes, 'Schisms within Hindu Guru Groups: The Transcendental Meditation Movement in North America', in J. R. Lewis and S. M. Lewis (eds), *Sacred Schisms: How Religions Divide.* (Cambridge: Cambridge University Press, 2009), 287–305. Bikram Choudhury has tried to maintain control over his Bikram yoga by having his postures copyrighted and by threatening to excommunicate yoga schools that do not adhere strictly to his teachings; see J. Carrette and R. King, *Selling Spirituality: The Silent Takeover of Religion* (London: Routledge, 2005), 8.

25. *Independent*, 4 February 1992.

26. For an early analysis of the secularization of TM, see E. Woodrum, 'Religious Belief Transformation: A Study of This-Worldly Religion', *Sociological Inquiry*, 55 (1985), 16–27.

27. C. Christie, *Liverpool's Failed Utopian Commune*, 2012 <http://www.vice.com/en_uk/read/liverpools-decaying-yogi-commune> (accessed 9 April 2015).

28. TM, *Sidhaland*, 2014 <http://www.maharishi-european-sidhaland.org.uk/Index.htm> (accessed 9 May 2015).

29. I do not know if this played any part in selecting the location, but Rendlesham forest is the site of one of the best-attested UFO sightings in the UK.

30. J. Harris, 'Free for all', *Guardian Weekend Magazine*, 5 January 2013, pp. 23–4.

31. A. Hannaford, 'Mantra with a Mission', *Sunday Times Magazine*, 12 December 2010, p. 69.

32. For a detailed discussion, see M. K. Trzebiatowska and S. Bruce, *Why Are Women More Religious Than Men?* (Oxford: Oxford University Press, 2012). That Hindu and Buddhist traditions have tended to regard women as second class is clear from their view that rebirth as a woman is less advantageous than rebirth as a man. On Sai Baba, see BBC, *The Secret Swami*, 2004. See also the detailed accusations made by victims of his predation in M. Brown, 'Divine Downfall', *Daily Telegraph Saturday Magazine*, 27 October 2000.

33. Trzebiatowska and Bruce, *Why Are Women?*, 40.

34. S. Newcombe, 'Stretching for Health and Well-Being: Yoga and Women in Britain, 1960–1980', *Asian Medicine*, 3 (2007), 38.

35. Newcombe, 'Stretching', 42.

36. *Press and Journal*, 2002.

37. 'Churches Ban Child Yoga Classes as "Un-Christian"', *Daily Telegraph*, 31 August 2007.

38. Daily Mail reporter, 'Is Yoga Religious?' *Daily Mail*, 26 September 2012.

39. H. Booth, 'Spirit Level: A New Generation of Teachers Is Replacing Tradition with Simplicity but Is this Still Yoga?', *Guardian G2*, 19 July 2011.

40. G. Roberts, 'The Poses that Eased my Pain', *I*, 11 June 2013. Note: until the *Independent* newspaper went web-based only in 2016, *i* was the slimmed-down version of it.

41. A. Jain, *Selling Yoga: From Counterculture to Pop Culture* (Oxford: Oxford University Press, 2013). Jain rejects the idea of yoga being changed by the imperatives of the western culture that has adopted it. Yoga 'was in fact a movement that developed in response to transnational cultural developments . . . in consumer culture' (Jain, *Selling Yoga*, 46–7). For reasons given in Chapter 7, I do not think that, even if accepted, this changes my basic argument that Hindu-inspired religious innovations cannot sustain the 'just-change' rebuttal of the secularization thesis.

42. H. Waterhouse, 'Reincarnation Belief in Britain: New Age Orientations or Mainstream Option', *Journal of Contemporary Religion*, 14 (1999), 97.

43. G. Gorer, *Death, Grief and Mourning* (London: Cresset Press, 1965), 167.

44. Waterhouse, 'Reincarnation', 97.

45. S. O'Connell, 'A Good Year for the Rose', *Uncut* (September 2103), 28.

46. C. Campbell, *The Easternization of the West* (Boulder, CO: Paradigm, 2007).

47. Campbell, *Easternization*, 338.

48. R. Wuthnow, 'Religion as Sacred Canopy', in J. D. Hunter and S. C. Ainley (eds), *Making Sense of Modern Times: Peter L. Berger and the Vision of Interpretative Sociology* (New York: Routledge and Kegan Paul, 1986), 127.

49. C. Field 'Spirituality in the Ascendant?', *British Religion in Numbers*, 18 October 2011 <http://www.brin.ac.uk/2011/spirituality-in-the-ascendant> (accessed March 2017).

50. <https://en.wikipedia.org/wiki/Farther_Along_(song)> (accessed May 2017).

51. *Sunday Telegraph*, 1 June 2008.

4

Buddhism Religious and Secular

INTRODUCTION

Buddhism encompasses a variety of beliefs and practices largely based on teachings attributed to Gautama Buddha, who lived in India sometime between the sixth and the fourth centuries before Christ. It divides into three major traditions: Theravada, Mahayana, and Vajrayana. Like the Protestant, Catholic, and Orthodox strands of Christianity, they have much in common and considerable internal variegation. Roughly speaking, Theravada Buddhism is the more intellectual, rigorous, and demanding. The Mahayana strand allows for the equivalent of Christian saints: bodhisattvas who have attained enlightenment but choose to be reborn in order to help the rest of us attain that goal. It also allows that enlightenment can be attained by lay people, as well as by monks, and can be achieved in one lifetime. The Vajrayana tradition adds to the Buddhist core a great deal of esoteric ritual. As its name (which means 'great vehicle') would suggest, the Mahayana tradition (to be found in Bangladesh, Bhutan, Nepal, China, Japan, Korea, Malaysia, Mongolia, Taiwan, and Vietnam) is the most popular, with over half of the Buddhist population. Theravada (the dominant religion in Cambodia, Laos, Myanmar, Sri Lanka, and Thailand) accounts for about a third. Vajrayana Buddhism is represented by about 6 per cent of the Buddhist population and is strongest in Tibet, where for centuries the religious leadership was also the government.

As with any faith that has existed for centuries and spread across a large number of cultures, Buddhism is not easy to summarize, but a rough idea of key points can be found in a statement agreed in 1966 by the World Buddhist Sangha Council (made up of leading monks from Theravada and Mahayana traditions).[1]

- The Buddha is our only Master.
- We take refuge in the Buddha, the Dharma (the Buddha's teachings) and the Sangha (or community of Buddhists).
- We do not believe that this world is created and ruled by a God.
- Following the example of the Buddha, who is the embodiment of Great Compassion and Great Wisdom, we consider that the purpose of life is to develop compassion for all living beings without discrimination and to work for their good, happiness, and peace; and to develop wisdom leading to the realization of Ultimate Truth.
- We accept the Four Noble Truths: suffering, the causes of suffering, the end of suffering and the path to the end of suffering; and the universal law of cause and effect (that is, karma), as taught in Dependent Origination.[2]
- We understand, according to the teaching of the Buddha, that all conditioned things are impermanent and suffering, and that all conditioned and unconditioned things are without self.
- We accept the Thirty-Seven Qualities conducive to Enlightenment (a mix of propositions about the nature of reality, moral injunctions, and instructions for training) as different aspects of the Path taught by the Buddha leading to Enlightenment.
- There are three ways of attaining Bodhi or enlightenment, according to the ability and capacity of each individual: namely as a disciple, as a self-taught enlightened being, and as a perfectly enlightened Buddha. We accept it as the highest, noblest, and most heroic to follow the career of a Bodhisattva and to become a perfectly enlightened Buddha in order to save others.

BUDDHISM IN BRITAIN

As with Hinduism, British Buddhism pre-1960s was a rather dusty affair that owed much to the British Empire and to a handful of orientalist scholars. In 1864, Thomas Rhys Davids, a young Welshman, went to Ceylon as a civil servant. He became fascinated by Sinhalese Buddhism and by ancient Pāli texts. On his return to Britain, he founded the Pāli Text Society and was eventually appointed to a chair of comparative religion at the University of Manchester. His *Buddhism: Being a Sketch of the Life and Teachings of Gautama, the Buddha* was a popular introduction. In the view of Rhys Davids, the Pāli canon showed the true Buddhism before it was corrupted by Mahayana accretions. It probably says more about his Welsh Congregationalist background than its says about Buddhism, but Rhys Davids saw his imagined pristine Buddhism as being like primitive Christianity, a pared-back ascetic religion, before it was distorted by the changes that eventually provoked the Protestant Reformation.[3]

Rhys Davids was an active orientalist. In very many ways he tried to promote Theravada Buddhism and Pāli scholarship in Britain. Whether he really believed that a better understanding of Indian religion and culture would help preserve the British Empire or was just opportunistically fund-raising is not clear, but he seems to have been genuinely committed to his belief that the 'Aryan' peoples of Britain shared a common ethnicity with the peoples of India and Ceylon. His wife Caroline Foley, as well as being a noted Pāli scholar, was a supporter of Theosophy. He was not.

The Theosophical Society was founded by Russian émigré Madame Helena Blavatsky and Colonel H. S. Olcott in New York in 1875. It was initially intended to study and explain the work of such spirit mediums as Madame Blavatsky, but it broadened its scope when the founders moved to India to pursue their growing interest in Eastern religion.[4] The Theosophical Society was just one of many Victorian organizations that, like the Masons, were structured in lodges and claimed esoteric knowledge, which was gradually revealed to members as initiation rituals and tests elevated them through grades of membership. It inspired many imitators, including the Hermetic Order of the Golden Dawn, which numbered Aleister Crowley, the founder of modern Black Magic, among its members. Another member went to Ceylon in 1898 as C. H. Allan Bennett and returned as Ananda Metteyya, the first Englishman to be ordained as a Buddhist monk in the Theravada tradition.[5]

In 1924, Christmas Humphreys, a barrister who later became a judge, formed the London Buddhist Society as a lodge within the Theosophical Society. This was the first really successful organization in Britain to provide a platform for all schools and traditions of Buddhism. A slow trickle of westerners travelled to Asia to take monastic ordination, mainly as Theravadin monks, and a few Asian monks came to live in Britain. Humphreys was responsible for inviting Ananda Bodhi (who had been born George Dawson in Canada) to head the small Buddhist centre in London, and Bodhi bought Johnstone House in remote Dumfriesshire as a meditation and retreat centre.

What helped bring Buddhism to popular attention was *The Third Eye*. Published in 1958 (against the advice of experts), this purported to be the biography of one Tuesday Lobsang Rampa and gave detailed accounts of being raised in a Tibetan lamasery, including a rather gruesome account of his having a hole drilled in his forehead to open his 'Third Eye' of perception.[6] The author was soon exposed as Cyril Hoskin, a plumber from Devon who had never left Britain, but that it was a fraud did not prevent the book becoming a global bestseller.[7]

This chapter will describe a number of Buddhist centres in the UK, assess Buddhism's impact on the general argument that religion in the UK is not declining but simply changing, and then discuss the recent marketing of a secular Buddhism as 'mindfulness'.

OF TEMPLES AND MONASTERIES

Although it was often shallow and short-lived, popular British interest in Buddhism was given a clumsy shove by the counterculture of the 1960s. Superficially Buddhism might have been created for a post-Christian world.

> Some of this is about the quest for greener fields but people also cite patriarchy, fundamentalism, sectarianism and condoning of violence among reasons for their dissatisfaction [with Christianity]. Without any knowledge of Buddhist history in Asia, where all these occur, Westerners see Buddhism in a rather idealistic light.[8]

There was certainly a period when claiming to be 'into Buddhism' was commonplace among artsy intellectuals and student wannabe artsy intellectuals. In November 1968 the Incredible String Band, very briefly one of the hippest bands in Britain, released *Wee Tam and the Big Huge*. Robin Williamson and Mike Heron had begun as a folk duo playing traditional material and by 1969 were Scientologists, but in between they produced what one critic called 'an informal exploration of alternative beliefs'.[9] Williamson's *Maya* is a marvellously evocative collation of mysterious and portentous phrases: 'All the world is but a play | Be thou the joyful player'; 'Twelve yellow willows shall fellow the shallows'; 'Ah, but every face within your face does show | Going gladly now to give himself his own'. Sung over a variety of exotic acoustic instruments, it seemed profound, though God knows what any of it meant. In similar vein was Heron's *Douglas Traherne Harding*, which borrowed chunks of prose from the seventeenth-century Christian mystic Thomas Traherne that had been used by Douglas Harding's *On Having No Head*.[10] Harding was an architect who also taught comparative religion. While walking in the Himalayas during the Second World War, he had experienced a mystic rebirth when he had a stunningly strong impression of having no head—a rather literal expression of the Buddhist notion that true enlightenment requires us to transcend not just the body but also the mind.

The upside of the hippie-era endorsement of Buddhism was that it stopped being esoteric and fusty, associated with little old ladies and antimacassars. The downside, as we will see in the case of Samye Ling, was that the freestyle of the 1960s was a temporary obstacle to the creation of a serious Buddhist culture.

Samye Ling

Tuesday Lobsang Rampa may have whetted the appetite, but an enduring Tibetan Buddhist presence was the work of two real Tibetans. Akong Tulku Rinpoche and Chogyam Trungpa Rinpoche had been raised from childhood as incarnate lamas; with the Dalai Lama and other more senior monastic leaders (who were also the government) they fled to India when in 1959 the Chinese government markedly tightened its grip on Tibet. At the receiving refugee camp in Assam, Akong and Trungpa were befriended by an English woman working for the Indian Civil Service who arranged for Trungpa to study comparative religion in Oxford. In 1963, the Tibetans arrived in London, where they were met by Bodhi and various British Buddhists and supporters of Tibet.

Helped by a BBC radio profile and the publication of *Born in Tibet*, an account of his escape, Trungpa developed a reputation that led to invitations to speak at Johnstone House, and then an offer to take over the enterprise, which had been losing money.[11] In March 1967, control was passed to the Tibetans. Like the Findhorn Foundation, Samye Ling was at times in danger of being swamped by countercultural drop-outs whose interest in Tibetan Buddhism was less than their interest in sex and drugs. The stories of celebrity interest have grown legs over the years, but certainly Leonard Cohen lived nearby for almost a year. David Bowie is reputed to have stayed and considered becoming a monk, though there is no evidence for this in any of the detailed biographies.[12] The Incredible String Band lived within easy travelling distance and may well have been visitors. John Lennon and Yoko Ono are reputed to have visited. Tim Goulding, a member of the Irish folk band Dr Strangely Strange, stayed for some months and was married by Akong.[13]

Part of the early chaos resulted from Trungpa's growing fondness for alcohol and sex with young followers; when he moved to the USA, Akong was able to set the centre on a firm organizational footing.[14] As with Findhorn, the key was to create clearly distinct categories of belonging (where the final say rested with the monastery and not with the applicant) and to have clear routes through various forms of association all the way from casual visitor (the Tibetan Tearoom does a fine line in home bakes) to trainee monks and nuns serving almost four years of isolated contemplation.

Tibetan Buddhism (part of the Vajrayana tradition) is exotic. The temple is decorated with hundreds of ornate statues representing all the previous incarnate llamas in the lineage that links Samye Ling to the original Buddha. One of the Englishmen who helped build the temple complex ruefully described the décor as being 'over the top and then some; it makes an Indian restaurant seem dowdy'. One building contains prayer wheels: large tubes inscribed with prayers that are sent up to the Gods when the wheels are turned by an electric motor. At the entrance there is a very large white stupa that contains important relics. There is a garden of healing herbs, and trees are decorated with prayer flags. The main reason why Samye Ling has preserved a great deal of Tibetan culture is that its founders, quite rightly, believed that the Chinese would do their best to incorporate Tibet into China and, along the way, strip it of the distinctive culture that might form the basis for rebellion. Building a stupa, temple, and herb garden in southern Scotland may not be much, but it is something.

As we will see shortly, Samye Ling associates have been in the forefront of promoting a secular Buddhism, which is somewhat ironic given that the parent institution makes no bones about the supernatural basis of its religion. For example, the official history ascribes miracles to the Karmapa (the equivalent for the Black Hat tradition to which Samye Ling belongs of the Dalai Lama in the Yellow Hat or Gelugpa tradition). Religious rituals are held to have supernatural power. And prayers are not just internal conversations that make us better people: they are requests made to the Gods that will be answered. At the end of every prayer session in the temple, a clerk notes how many rounds of prayer were said by each participant. The more prayers, the greater the merit earned in that session.

Throssel Hole Abbey

My acquaintance with the UK's main Soto Zen Buddhist institution came by accident while researching the decline of Christianity in the Allendale area of Northumberland. In the nineteenth century Allendale had a number of successful lead mines that employed over 400 people, and most of those miners were Methodists, as were many of the smaller tenant farmers of the dale.[15] Of twenty-two chapels in a small dale, two had been opened in the eighteenth century, eleven were founded in the first half of the nineteenth century, and a further eleven in the second half.[16] Half of those chapels were Wesleyan Methodist, the older, more staid and respectable branch of the Methodist movement. The others were 'Primitive' Methodists—not a description of their lifestyles but an insult that was turned into a claim for virtue and incorporated in the formal title of the movement. The Prims split because they felt the Wesleyans had become too formalistic in their worship and had compromised many of the ascetic demands initially associated with Methodism. Although the match was never perfect, it was roughly the case that the Wesleyans recruited a 'better class' of member than the Prims. In Durham colliery villages, for example, the Wesleyan chapel was often at the end of the village where the foreman and overseers lived and was markedly better built than the Prim chapel located at the rougher end of the village.

Many of the Allendale chapels were small. Those located in the main villages had seating for between 200 and 300, but nine of the others averaged 136 sittings. Methodists were expected to have been converted, to attend weekday evening meetings as well as Sunday services, and to maintain an exemplary 'walk with the Lord', and membership was not asked for or given lightly. Hence the common phenomenon in the nineteenth century of attendance being at least twice the membership. The Wesleyan chapel in remote High Keenley Fell had only twelve members in 1915, but more than thirty people regularly attended its services.

Chapel membership declined steadily over the twentieth century, first with the decline in population as the lead mines closed and the mechanization of farming reduced the need for labour—population fell from a peak of 6,383 in 1851 to 2,221 in 1900 and 1,704 in 1961— and then more quickly as those who remained in the dale failed to pass on their faith to their children. In 1900, there were 626 Methodist members in the dale; by the end of the century there were just 100. And the penumbra of attenders fell even faster. In 1900, attendance was between two and three times that of membership. By 2000, not all members attended.[17]

Some villages had both Wesleyan and Prim chapels, and the merger of Wesleyans and Prims in 1932 immediately made one of each pair redundant. The improvement of roads and the availability of cars also made many chapels pointless, but most members are intensely loyal to their building, and there is always great reluctance to rationalize the plant. But, even if the remaining handful of members did not mind meeting in a chapel that had once housed large crowds, their resilience was eventually broken by maintenance costs and by the difficulty of finding preachers. Every circuit of Methodist chapels has a full-time clergy superintendent who can preach at two chapels on a Sunday, but the rest are served by lay preachers who rotate on 'the plan'—preaching at different chapels in the circuit each week. As the number of lay preachers is a fairly stable proportion of the membership (and was thus declining), finding enough to fill the plan gradually became impossible, and chapels were closed. Of the twenty chapels still in business in 1900, two had closed by the reunion in 1932, half had closed by 1949, and by the end of the century there were only seven left.

Two things drew me to the Limestone Brae chapel: the name of its location and its design. Any place called Throssel Hole had to be interesting (throssel, I discovered, meant thrush), and the building was a fine example of a chapel with the door at the side rather than at the end.[18] By the time I photographed it, it had been sold and converted into a private house. I was parked outside the chapel, on a quiet road in a silent dale, taking photographs when a man in purple Buddhist monk robes and sandals walked by me. For cold and remote Northumberland, that would have been a surprise under any circumstance, but, because I was locating and photographing disused chapels, my mind was very much in the world of Methodist lead miners, and a Buddhist monk was so far off the scale of likely intrusions that for a moment I wondered if this was some sort of cosmic joke. Looking around I realized that just next to the chapel was an entrance with a sign saying 'Throssel Hole Buddhist Abbey'.

Like Samye Ling, the large farmhouse at Throssel Hole had for a short time been a hippie commune. Both the hippies and the Zen Buddhists were attracted by very cheap property in a rural area too sparsely populated for complaints from the locals. But there is something poignant in its proximity to a former Methodist chapel. The population decline that had drastically reduced one expression of religious sentiment had created the opportunity for another to move in.

The abbey was founded in 1972 by Roshi Jiyu Kennett, an Englishwoman who returned from a career that had seen her work in a Japanese temple before moving to San Francisco. Her continued role in the San Francisco work slowed the growth of Throssel Hole, but eventually modern accommodation blocks were constructed, and by the end of the twentieth century the abbey was firmly established.

An interesting account of life at Throssel Hole is provided by a model who stayed there for eleven months after the failure of a relationship left her feeling suicidal. Life was spartan.[19] All possessions had to fit alongside a folding mattress in a large locker in the temple; trainees slept side by side on the temple floor, with men and women divided by a curtain. Talk was discouraged. Communal meals were eaten in silence. Trainees spent two to five hours each day sitting cross-legged and meditating: 'thinking non-thinking'.

> I was left to tame my emotional life without interference. Sometimes in the private spiritual counselling sessions I would howl in pain, while the attending monk sat and gazed at me, or told me I'd got the wrong end of the stick.... Sitting cross-legged is painful... the mental pain was worse... When I finally decided not to give in to distraction, the feelings I was left with almost overwhelmed me. Sadness grew into grief, irritation into rage. After four months of sitting I was very close to getting up, hollering wild profanities and bashing someone just so I'd have to leave.[20]

She persisted and gradually she gained a clearer sense of a shared purpose: 'I trusted people more by living and working with them quietly over time that I ever had in a romantic relationship.'[21] But she knew she was not cut out to be a nun and eventually she returned to the world of modelling and wine bars, considerably happier and better balanced. She continued to meditate.

Chithurst Forest Sangha

The Theravada strand of Buddhism is represented by the Thai Forest tradition-influenced Chithurst Sangha, established in a semi-derelict Victorian Sussex mansion in 1979 and eventually spawning five outposts. When Christmas Humphreys died, the Chithurst leader, Ajahn Sumedho, was invited to become honorary president of the Buddhist Society, a move that was described as the end of 'intellectual Buddhism' and the beginning of more committed study and practice.[22]

The Chithurst day begins and ends with *pujas*—ceremonies of devotion to the Buddha that include chanting, offering incense, and bowing. It usually also involves at least two hours of meditation, an unusual feature of the Forest tradition being to meditate while 'walking in the woods'. One feature of the Thai tradition that was quickly abandoned was alms-begging. In Thailand, lay people support monks by putting food in their bowls as they walk slowly around the neighbourhood—not a technique that works well in a largely secular society with busy roads and foul weather. Another contentious issue of adaptation is the language of chanting. All British Buddhist institutions have had to choose between continuing to chant in the original languages or chanting in English. As with the arguments in Protestantism over Bible translations after the 1611 King James Version, and in Anglicanism and Catholicism over modern liturgies, the tension is comprehensibility versus heritage. The argument against change is that, while the original language might act as an initial obstacle to understanding, it adds solemnity and reminds both speaker and listener of the movement's origins and history. The argument in favour is that the original chants were written in the language of the people who chanted them, not in a foreign language or a version of the language four centuries old. The Catholic Tridentine Mass was in Latin, not because the authors wanted to make life difficult but because in the Middle Ages Latin was the language of educated people across Christendom. Chithurst plumped for the compromise of using both Pāli and English.

The Scale of Institutional Buddhism

These and all the other UK Buddhist centres are small. Throssel Hole, for example, has a resident population of around twenty, and Chithurst is similar. The Aruna Ratanagiri Monastery—a converted farmworker's cottage and small barn in rural Northumberland—has perhaps ten residents and visitors at any one time. Hartridge, a sanctuary in rural Devon in the Forest tradition, normally has around ten monks. Taken together, they involve only a few thousand people at any one time. However, around them is a penumbra of lay supporters and ex-monks and nuns.[23] The opening of the temple building at Amarvati (a Chithurst offshoot) was attended by some 2,500 lay visitors, and the *Forest Sangha Newsletter* is sent to 1,500 people, 'which seems a reasonable estimate of committed supporters'.[24]

There is a vastly greater number of visitors—often people who regard themselves as Buddhists and stay in such centres for periodic 'top ups'. The website for Hartridge, for example, says: 'Guests can stay for a few days or longer, taking the opportunity to deepen their understanding of Buddhism and themselves in an environment that encourages peaceful reflection.'[25] Such guests are expected to observe the Eight Precepts . . . and to join in community activities. Newcomers to meditation are encouraged to plan their visit to coincide with one of the monthly mediation worships.[26]

In addition to the visitors to residential centres, we must figure in the large thousands of people who regularly attend classes in Buddhism in centres in cities and major towns.

One way of estimating the scale of conversion to Buddhism is to work from the 2001 Census. It showed 149,000 people or 0.3 per cent of the population describing themselves as Buddhist (or, to be more precise, being described as such by the person who filled in the census form for the household). Of those, more than half were born outside the UK: Thailand, Japan, Vietnam, and Hong Kong lead the lists. Hence the *Sri Lankan* Buddhist Vihara in West London and the *Burmese* Buddhist Vihara in Birmingham. Many of the 67,000 British-born Buddhists are the children of Asians. So a reasonable guess for the number of native British people who have converted to Buddhism may be about 40,000. Because the Scottish census asked both for current religion and religion of upbringing, it is possible to approach the same question from a slightly different angle. In 2001, 53 per cent of those who then identified as Buddhist had not been raised as such. This is a higher conversion rate than the one arrived at for England and Wales by using place of birth, but that reflects the fact that Scotland has proportionately far fewer immigrants.

Although it is not as powerful a sign of secularization as that discussed in the next section, it is worth noting that the three most popular Buddhist movements among native Britons are all so far from the mainstream that their legitimacy is denied by many Buddhists. Although originally Tibetan, the New Kadampa Tradition (or NKT) describes itself as Mahayana, rather than Vajrayana, in order to distinguish what its teacher, Geshe Kelsang Gyatso, considers the core elements of his lineage's teaching from Tibetan culture and the Tibetan Buddhist state. The largest NKT Centre is the Manjushri Institute in Cumbria, but there are around thirty other centres in the UK, and many groups.

After its defeat in the Second World War, Japan saw an explosion of interest in a variety of new movements catering for lay people, many of which were vaguely Buddhist in their orientation. The largest of these, Soka Gakkai, is also one of the largest Buddhist movements in the UK, claiming several thousand adherents. It derives from the Nichiren tradition of Japanese Buddhism, which has historically had a difficult, some would say inherently problematic, relationship with other forms of Buddhism. Practice is based around the chanting of *nam myo ho renge kyo*, which is an invocation of the Lotus Sutra. What makes it suspect in the eyes of many mainstream Buddhists is the way in which it has shortened the relationship between right action and material rewards. In the conventional model (as in all the main world's religions) one behaves in a certain manner because that is what is required by God, Gods, or karma, and one hopes (one cannot presume) that the divine will reward moral behaviour and religious observance with this-worldly and postmortem benefits. Soka Gakkai claims that chanting its mantra while thinking of one's needs will result in those needs being met. Adepts talk of 'chanting for' this or that material gain.[27]

In 2010, the Friends of the Western Buddhist Order (FWBO) changed its name to the Triratna Buddhist Order to reflect the fact that its Indian membership had grown to outnumber that of the West.[28] FWBO had been founded by Sangharakshita (aka Dennis Lingwood) in London in 1967. With some thirty urban and retreat centres, the Triratna order can claim to be one of the biggest British Buddhist organizations. Three features, all in various ways a product of the period in which it was founded, make it markedly more secular than Samye Ling, Chithurst, or Throssel Hole. First, it declines to establish legitimacy in the conventional Buddhist manner by claiming that its founder is descended by pupillage and ordination from the Buddha by an unbroken line of accepted Buddhist teachers. Whether Lingwood was making a conscious decision to appear modern by rejecting the notion that lineage established authority or simply had never been close enough to any of the great teachers under whom he supposedly studied during his twenty years in India plausibly to claim lineage is not clear, but, whatever its cause, the rejection of an inheritance line was an important break with tradition. So too was Lingwood's stress on the value of modern culture (the high arts especially). Finally, there was Lingwood's support for gay rights long before it was an acceptable cause. Lingwood's view that single-sex activities were spiritually beneficial probably owed more to his homosexuality than to the traditional Buddhist emphasis on chastity, but his championing of gay rights put the FWBO at odds with much of the Buddhist world.[29]

Whether there are 40,000 or 70,000 converts to Buddhism in the UK, we are still talking about a small corner of the religious picture.[30] However, that there are, relatively speaking, far more converted Buddhists than Hindus raises an interesting question about the relative appeal of alternatives to Christianity.

Although it is Indian in origin, Buddhism spread sufficiently far across Asia for it not to be handicapped by a strong association with the caste system, and its ethnic associations can be overlooked by those who study it at one remove from Buddhist institutions, which do usually have ethnic associations. In addition, most strands of Buddhism lack the theism that many find unappealing about Hinduism (and for that matter Christianity). With careful selection, one can find a Buddhism that is largely philosophical and ethical and requires little or nothing that looks like devotion. But possibly its greatest appeal is its malleability. We will return to this in the next chapter, but here it is enough to note that, like Quakerism for Christians, Buddhism is flexible enough to allow people of diverse interests to find some version that suits.

MINDFULNESS

Holy Isle (sometimes called Holy Island) is a rock off Arran in the Firth of Clyde, about 1 kilometre long and 3 kilometres wide. In modern times, apart from providing some very rough grazing, its main purpose has been as a base for a lighthouse that warns ships off what otherwise would be a major hazard on the way to the Clyde estuary and the port of Glasgow. In ancient times, it was a site of pilgrimage, with a healing spring and a cave said to have been inhabited by the sixth-century monk Saint Molaise. In 1992, the owner, a pious Catholic, sold the island to Samye Ling below market price on the instructions of the Virgin Mary, who had told her she wanted it to be used for spiritual purposes. The lighthouse accommodation was renovated, and several 'ecologically sensitive' buildings added. Although Samye Ling uses it as a location for trainee monks and nuns to live in seclusion for three years, three months, and three days, the renovations have deliberately been austere and plain and, apart from a few stupas, eschew Samye Ling's bling housestyle. A fund-raising flyer from the 1990s stresses the ecumenical nature of the retreat. In addition to housing long-term monastic retreats, the island would provide a place where 'Buddhists, Christians and those of any faith may seek spiritual regeneration. Others might come simply for a period of quiet reflection.'[31] A decade later that 'quiet reflection' had morphed into mindfulness. And, if Holy Island is a little too severe, you could get away from it all with 'a walking and mindfulness' holiday in Cumbria.

> Your base is the Hassness Country House hotel on the shores of Lake Buttermere. There's no phone signal or TV just fabulous views and plenty of Cumbrian hospitality. After a hearty cooked breakfast, you set off into the hills, breaking off for lunch at a local inn before returning to the hotel for dinner.[32]

And you can attend classes in mindfulness. Which you might want to because you have read *Sane New World: Taming the Mind* by comedian and journalist Ruby Wax or, like novelist Julie Myerson, had it recommended to you by your doctor.[33] You can now study for diplomas in mindfulness at British universities, and many medical training programmes include short taster courses in which it is presented as a non-invasive solution to the milder and more common psychiatric conditions.

Some authors present mindfulness as the pristine original Buddhism.[34] One can argue that the Buddha did not aim to found a religion. Instead he identified the source of suffering in this life and presented a solution. The worship of the Buddha and the creation of the institutions that now embody the core of Buddhism were the work of his disciples. In its academic and health contexts, mindfulness is presented as an entirely secular therapy. According to the University of Aberdeen's advertisement for its postgraduate courses in the topic, mindfulness

> is an innate capacity of the mind to be aware of the present moment in a non-judgemental way. It promotes a way of being that helps us to take better care of ourselves and lead healthier lives. It also enables us to access inner resources for coping effectively with stress, difficulty and illness. This training in mindfulness is entirely secular and is available as a blended learning opportunity, combining e-learning and face to face teaching. Participants study part-time at a distance while staying in post in their own professional setting. An important part of the programme is that participants develop a daily mindfulness practice.[35]

Yet that 'entirely secular' is somewhat compromised. Its religious origins are clear from the contents of publications, from the biographies of the people who promote it, and from its locations. The Aberdeen programme, for example, says: 'in each of the first three Mindfulness-based courses students are expected to attend 2 weekends at Samye Ling and a week long retreat on the Holy Island is part of the experience in each of the first 2 years of the programme'.[36] An article on the benefits of mindfulness for mental health on the NHS website does not mention religion in its main text, but when the final paragraph lists 'formal mindfulness practices', it offers only meditation, yoga, and tai-chi, all originally religious.[37] An article in *Psychology Today* offers a largely secular promotion of mindfulness but it mentions the Buddha twice and in giving instructions says: 'If you like, you can make a small altar of some kind and decorate it with pictures or photos or sacred objects from your tradition.'[38] Of the twenty tutors listed on the 2012 website of the Mindfulness Association, the religious backgrounds of eight are not clear (though they may well be Buddhists), two identify as Buddhists, and ten both identify as Buddhists and mention links with Samye Ling.[39] Many British mindfulness trainers have been inspired by the Vietnamese Buddhist monk (now based in France) Thich Nhat Hanh.[40] The director of the Aberdeen University mindfulness programme administered a questionnaire to three cohorts of students enrolling between 2010 and 2012. The most popular religious affiliation was 'none' (with 44 per cent). Buddhism was second, with the grossly disproportionate 33 per cent. No other identification was claimed by more than two or three students, and most of them were obviously nominal (as in 'brought up as Church of Scotland' or the lovely 'Church of Scotland-ish').

That many of those who take part in group mindful sessions have long histories of involvement in a wide variety of New Age activities means that there is often seepage across the spiritual/secular divide. For example, one of the women who took part in what was billed as 'an introduction to the secular practice of mindfulness' in my village hall placed a large bowl of beach-combed smooth stones in the middle of our circle of chairs, with a ring of stones around it, and, before the trainer began the session, she lit a large candle in the bowl. Whatever the precise significance to her of these artefacts, they certainly nodded towards some sort of shamanic background.

Exactly how mindfulness 'promotes a way of being that helps us to take better care of ourselves and lead healthier lives' is complex. Few practitioners would put it as bluntly as this, but it begins with the assumption that most of the problems that beset us are actually beyond solution (by any of us, at least). As we cannot change things, we should change our attitude to things. We do this by becoming more 'present-centred': instead of allowing our minds to cycle anxiously and fretfully through endless list of obligations, fearful challenges, and memories that either catalogue our failures or make our successes ironic by suggesting they may soon be reversed, we learn to experience fully our bodies and our immediate environments. Concentrating on some part of the anatomy (the mindfulness 'body scans' I have experienced have all started with the big toe) allows us either to stop our minds wandering or to observe and appreciate that they are wandering without feeling bad about that fact. As one trainer put it: 'We actually have an immense power to control our thoughts.' Later she added: 'OK so odd thoughts keep getting in the way but that's ok. Just accept that. Let it go.' But becoming mindful is not just a fatalistic acceptance of things-as-they-are. By learning to be more 'in the moment' and by responding in a non-judgemental way to our sense experience, we can become more compassionate towards ourselves and others and become more effective actors in the world. Being mindful is not a substitute for right action but is a necessary precondition for it. And learning to be 'self-compassionate' is not an invitation to selfishness, though it often seems to encourage self-absorption.

Because it shows the limits to the popularity of mindfulness, it is worth noting the to-date-narrow section of society that is interested. The following are unrepresentative in that those who wish to acquire credentials are a distinct subset of those interested in the phenomenon. Nonetheless, they are not that far out of line with the impressions I have gained through extensive acquaintance of mindfulness groups. Aberdeen University's mindfulness students were overwhelmingly middle class. The most popular occupation was 'counsellor or psychotherapist' (15 of 63), followed by 'manager' (11), teacher (10), nurse (6), and 'business/life coach' (also 6). The rest included FE and HE lecturers, yoga teachers, consultants, social workers, psychologists, arts performers, martial arts instructors, and charity workers. Women easily outnumbered men (about two to one), and the modal age was in the band 46–50.[41] At the starter day in my village hall, all the thirty-one participants other than me and my daughter's boyfriend (and we were press-ganged by our partners) were women, and twenty-five were middle class. Three young women accompanied their mothers; for the rest the modal age was clearly above 50. Insofar as I could ascertain occupation, there were two farmers (this was rural Aberdeenshire!) and two housewives, and the rest mirrored the Aberdeen University list: teacher, child psychiatrist, psychologist, personal trainer, nurse, speech therapist, physiotherapist. In brief, the caring professions predominated. I will return to this in Chapter 6.

The Next Secularization

If mindfulness is the secularization of Buddhism, 'calm' is the popular reduction of mindfulness. In schools, mindfulness is reduced to a timetabled 'quiet time'. The John Lewis instore magazine *Edition* for Spring 2016 uses various mindfulness buzz words to advertise everything from furniture to electrical goods to swimwear (the upper-case letters in the following are in the original):

> Tap into this season's CALM mood by combining minimal design and neutral palettes with DISCREET technology . . . CONTEMPLATE. Although the idea of 'switching off' is at the core of this trend, it doesn't mean turning

your back on the technological advances of 21st century living . . . these can help you zone out and relax.

The 'Spring hot list' promises 'New ways to re-energise your cool, calm and creative side this season' and item 8 on that list are three phone apps 'to help you get started' on your mindfulness. But the serious spiritual seeker is not entirely neglected. The magazine puffs a 'relaxed retreat' at a hotel in Vietnam sufficiently 'luxe' for every room to have a private pool. Guests can 'wake up to sunrise yoga on the beach or meditation under the Lady Buddha, a 67-metre high effigy. Then you might visit a Buddhist orphanage or learn tai chi on Marble Mountain. Or simply kick back in the spa.' The author added her personal endorsement: 'I rocked up here an exhausted, empty shell. But, with 24/7 pampering, daily yoga and meditation, plus delicious food, I'd reached peak Zen within a week.'[42] Clearly the now enlightened guest had not thought how 24/7 pampering, delicious food, and the revealing bikini advertised as a suitable accessory for the trip might be squared with the asceticism of Buddhism's eight precepts, but one of Britain's major department stores thinks it has the finger on the cultural pulse.

Finally, we can note an interesting parallel with the Findhorn Foundation's marketing of its services to major capitalist corporations. Mathieu Ricard, a Buddhist monk billed as 'the world's happiest person', attends the annual World Economic Forum meeting of leading capitalists and politicians at Davos, where he 'leads meditation sessions for captains of industry, Nobel-prize winning academics, and heads of state before they start their deliberations'.[43]

CONCLUSION

The decline of Christianity has been accompanied by the rise of alternatives. In the 1950s the number of Buddhists in the UK would have been in the small thousands. At the 2011 Census, 178,453 people in England and Wales ticked the Buddhist box, of whom 59,040 chose as their ethnicity 'white British'. In Scotland, 12,795 people (0.2 per cent of the population) were listed as Buddhist and 46 per cent of them gave their ethnicity as 'white'. This tells us that Buddhism has had far more success than Islam or Hinduism in converting the indigenous British, but, in the context of the millions lost to Christianity, these figures are far too small to support the general claims that religion in the UK has changed rather than declined or that all people are inherently religious. The attempt to deny the reality of secularization is further confounded by the fact that the most popular Buddhist organizations are the least orthodox and even the orthodox traditions are now involved in marketing the secular psychotherapy of mindfulness: Buddhism without the religion.

None of this is intended to diminish the experiences of those who have benefited either from Buddhism or from mindfulness. My concern here is not to judge individual experience but to see what can be inferred about the nature of Britain's religious culture from the numbers of people enjoying those experiences. Nothing in the fact or scale of British Buddhism suggests either that the description of the UK as largely secular needs any modification or that there is something about the human condition that causes us to need religion.

NOTES

1. This comes from 'Basic points of Buddhism' <http://www.religionfacts.com/basic-points-of-buddhism> (accessed June 2016). In what follows I have also drawn on my rather dim memories of my Buddhism courses at the University of Stirling in the 1970s, for which I have always been extremely grateful to my teacher Glyn Richards, who had been raised in the Welsh chapels but found eastern religion vastly more congenial.

2. The Wiki article on Dependent Origination (Wiki, 'Pratītyasamutpāda' <https://en.wikipedia.org/wiki/Prat%C4%ABtyasamutp%C4%81da> (accessed June 2016)) says that Peter Harvey 'highlights the Buddhist notion that all apparently substantial entities within the world are in fact wrongly perceived. We live under the illusion that terms such as "I", self, mountain, tree, etc. denote permanent and stable things. The doctrine teaches this is not so.' The Wiki article draws heavily on P. Harvey, *Buddhism* (London: Bloomsbury Academic, 2001), esp. 242–4.

3. There are obvious parallels between the intercessory role of the Virgin Mary and the Saints in Catholicism and the role of such figures subsidiary to the Buddha as Amida and other Bodhisattvas. Essentially an ascetic lifestyle and esoteric philosophy is replaced for the common people by a pattern of supporting the religious professionals to acquire religious merit on their behalf and of allowing the long process of improving reincarnations to be replaced by a fast exit aided by divine and semi-divine figures.

4. For an introductory history, see B. F. Campbell, *Ancient Wisdom Revisited: A History of the Theosophical Movement* (Berkeley and Los Angeles: University of California Press, 1980).

5. I. P. Oliver, *Buddhism in Britain* (London: Rider, 1979), 49.

6. T. Lobsang Rampa, *The Third Eye* (London: Secker and Warburg, 1956). Frederic Warburg bought the book in good faith and feared the fraud would destroy his nascent company. It actually did very good business.

7. There is an interesting Ph.D. for someone in the subject of why being plausibly criticized for fraud and plagiarism should do nothing to prevent certain books becoming enduringly popular. The works of Carlos Castaneda are a good example, as is the career of Helena Blavatsky, who was plausibly accused of cheating in her displays of magic; see Campbell, *Ancient Wisdom*.

8. A. Skilton, 'Why is Buddhism hip?', *BBC Religion and Ethics* <http://www.bbc.co.uk/religion/0/27039902> (accessed June 2015).

9. D. Kidman, 'A Song Cycle', in A. Whitaker (ed.), *The Incredible String Band Compendium* (London: Helter Skelter Publications, 2003), 106–15.

10. D. Harding, *On Having No Head: Zen and the Rediscovery of the Obvious* (London: Buddhist Society, 1961).

11. C. Trungpa, *Born in Tibet* (London: George Allen and Unwin, 1966).

12. That Bowie had some interest in Buddhism is vouchsafed by Chime Rinpoche, who also fled Tibet in 1965. While teaching in a north London Buddhist centre, he was approached by Bowie, who said he wanted to become a monk. Chime asked, 'What is your talent?' and, on being told 'music', said that Bowie should stick to the music. *The Week* (June 2016).

13. I am grateful to Tim Goulding, formerly of the Irish hippie-folk band Dr Strangely Strange, for personal communications concerning this period.

14. Trungpa married Diana Pybus, an impressionable 16-year-old who had heard him speak in London. Akong persuaded them to migrate to the USA, where Trungpa's private life seems to have better fitted the hippie ethos: the Shambala movement that he founded became extremely successfully. In her published autobiography, Pybus says that she was just over the age of consent when she and Trungpa first had sex (D. Mukpo and C. R. Gimian, *Dragon Thunder: My Life with Chogyam Trungpa* (Boston: Shambala Publications, 2006), 17). However, in an interview with a sympathetic magazine, she admitted that their affair had begun while she was minor (S. Silberman, 'Married to the Guru', *Shambala Sun* (November 2006), 44). Trungpa thus managed to break his monastic vows and the law of the land, and, after his marriage to Pybus, he continued to take advantage of his guru status to enjoy a number of extramarital affairs. Worse was the behaviour the man Trungpa nominated to succeed him. Ösel Tendzin (aka Thomas Rich) not only continued the tradition of

having sex with students but continued to do so after he had been diagnosed as HIV+; see Wikipedia entry for Tendzin <https://en.wikipedia.org/wiki/%C3%96sel_Tendzin> (accessed November 2016).

15. G. Dickinson, *Allendale and Whitfield: Historical Notices of the Two Parishes* (Newcastle: Andrew Reid, 1903). Occupation data for 1881 come from the Allendale CP entry in Vision of Britain <http://www.visionofbritain.org.uk/place/8673/units> (accessed July 2015).

16. These and subsequent figures come from my original research on Methodism in the northern dales. I am grateful to the staff of the Hexham Public Library and the Northumberland Archives at Woodhorn for allowing me access to the records of the chapels of the Allendale circuits.

17. The population data are from the Allendale CP entry in *Vision of Britain* <http://www.visionofbritain.org.uk/place/8673/units> (accessed July 2015).

18. The Wesleyan Methodist chapel at Forest-in-Teesdale and the Eggleston, Teesdale, Baptist chapels are further examples.

19. The sign at the entrance says 'Abbey'. Many sources refer to 'Priory'. Presumably the changes reflect the status of the person in charge.

20. M. Hansson, 'First Person', *Guardian Magazine*, 8 January 2010.

21. Hansson, 'First Person'.

22. R. Bluck, *British Buddhism: Teachings, Practice and Development* (London: Routledge, 2006), 26.

23. Figures for growth of such institutions should always make an allowance for monks and nuns who 'disrobe'. This more often reflects a wish to pursue romantic relationships than any disagreement with Buddhist teachings, and such people often remain strong lay supporters of their former institutions.

24. Bluck, *British Buddhism*, 27.

25. Hartridge Buddhist Monastery, 'Coming to stay' <http://www.hartridgemonastery.org/> (accessed January 2015).

26. The eight precepts are refraining from destroying living creatures; taking that which is not given; sexual activity; incorrect speech; intoxicating drinks and drugs that lead to carelessness; eating at the forbidden time (i.e. after noon); dancing, singing, music, going to see entertainments, wearing garlands, using perfumes, and beautifying the body with cosmetics and lying on a high or luxurious sleeping place.

27. B. R. Wilson and K. Dobbelaere, *A Time to Chant: Soka Gakkai Buddhists in Britain* (Oxford: Oxford University Press, 1994).

28. As of 2016, the FWBO name was still being used in Scotland.

29. There is also good evidence that at least some of Lingwood's relationships were exploitative. Because it shows the way in which religious commitment can be used to manipulate, it is worth quoting one young male lover at length:

from the perspective I now have, looking back on the sexual relationship I had with Sangharakshita 27 years ago, I feel deeply unhappy.
Firstly, having read the interview posted on his website a few months
ago entitled 'Conversations with Bhante, August 2009' I feel angry
and disappointed at what I perceive to be a lack of honesty on his part
towards me regarding his sexual preference. I believed, at the time
that I was involved with him, that we were both making a sacrifice
'giving up our natural attraction towards women for the sake of the
Dharma'. I believed that, in doing this, I was doing what he had done
before me many years ago. I also received encouragement from him to
make this sacrifice. At no time in the 6 or so years that I was close to
him did he tell me that his sexual preference was for males. His
memoirs, which I thought were an honest account of his life, also
didn't convey his preference. Now I discover that what for me was a
sacrifice, was for him a preference, and I have a sense of disgust and of
being used. From my side, I consider that I wasn't free to be able to
make my own choice regarding my behaviour in this important area
of my life, because I didn't have all the facts available to me.

Lingwood later defended his actions by claiming that he had believed his
sexual relationships to have been consensual and that, if not, he was very
sorry. For a detailed rebuttal of some of the criticism of the FWBO, see
Dharmachari Vishvapani, 'Perceptions of the FWBO in British Buddhism', *Western Buddhist Review* 3 <http://www.westernbuddhistreview.
com/vol3/Perceptions.htm> (accessed February 2016).

30. For histories of all the British movements mentioned in this chapter, see
Bluck, *British Buddhism*, chs 6–9.
31. Samye Ling, 'Help us to buy Holy Island as a place of prayer and retreat',
undated flyer *c.*1992 collected at the Findhorn Foundation.
32. *The Week* (April 2015).
33. R. Wax, *Sane New World: Taming the Mind* (London: Hodder and
Stoughton, 2013). J. Myerson, 'How Mindfulness Based Cognitive
Therapy Changed My Life', *Guardian*, 11 January 2014.
34. For example, S. Batchelor, *Buddhism without Beliefs* (London: Bloomsbury, 1997).
35. Anon., 'Programmes in Mindfulness', Aberdeen: University of Aberdeen
2015.
36. Anon., 'Mindfulness'.
37. NHS, 'Mindfulness' <http://www.nhs.uk/conditions/stress-anxiety-
depression/pages/mindfulness.aspx> (accessed May 2015).
38. K. K. Wegela, 'How to Practice Mindfulness meditation', *Psychology
Today* <https://www.psychologytoday.com/blog/the-courage-be-present/
201001/how-practice-mindfulness-meditation> (accessed May 2017).

39. Unfortunately that website has now been revamped. The 2016 version <http://www.mindfulnessassociation.org/About.aspx> (accessed November 2016) does not have a separate tutor listing, though it is much more open about its links with Samye Ling and with Buddhism more generally.

40. For a short guide to his teaching, see Thich Nhat Hanh, *The Miracle of Mindfulness* (London: Rider, 2008).

41. G. Nixon, D. McMurty, L. Craig, A. Nevejan, and H. Regan-Addis, 'Studies in Mindfulness: Widening the Field for all Involved In Pastoral Care', *Pastoral Care in Education*, 34 (2016), 167–83. I am grateful to Graeme Nixon for clarifying some data.

42. John Lewis, *Edition* (Spring 2016), 118.

43. R. Biddulph, 'What would you Pay to be Happy?', *Observer Magazine*, 10 May 2015, p. 25.

5

Islam: The Unpillaged Eastern Religion

INTRODUCTION

In 1971, the albums that female students were most likely to possess were Cat Stevens's *Tea for the Tillerman* and *Teaser and the Firecat.* Bob Dylan had temporarily deprived professional songwriters of work by popularizing the role of singer-songwriter—the artiste whose success depends more on his or her ability to express authentic feelings than on the performer's ability to interpret the skilful work of the composer. A whole host of other poets with acoustic guitars (or occasionally pianos) followed. Donovan, James Taylor, Paul Simon, Carly Simon (no relation), Janis Ian, and Al Stewart are a few examples. Cat Stevens (born Steven Demetre Georgiou) had one pop hit in 1967 before catching the cultural trend by stripping back the instrumentation, bringing his voice forward in the mix, and emoting. In December 1977, five years after his *Catch Bull at Four* album (the title is a reference to one of ten stages of progress to enlightenment in Zen Buddhism), Stevens converted to Islam, changed his name to Yusuf Islam, and retired from the music business to work full-time for Muslim schools. Another convert to Islam was Richard Thompson, one of the founders of the long-lived British folk-rock band Fairport Convention. Unlike Stevens he did not give up music completely, but his faith caused problems. Fellow musician John Kirkpatrick was embarrassed: 'The most spectacular thing was that every couple of hours, he'd get out his prayer mat and dive down. After a [recording] take, he'd be on his knees, and you didn't know quite what to do.... We'd look at each other and say "Are we supposed to join in?"'[1] The sleeve of Richard and Linda Thompson's album *Pour Down Like Silver* had both of them in Arabic costume, but, to such of an audience as Richard Thompson enjoyed, his conversion could be largely overlooked. Many of his songs of this period used Arabic poetry as the basis for their lyrics, but, like Christian devotional works, the object of the singer's love can readily be heard as another person rather than as God.

What is significant about Stevens and Thompson is that they pretty well exhaust the list of British celebrities who became Muslims. Islam has, of course, had a considerable influence on British religious culture because of the presence of Muslims and because of the reactions that presence has provoked. But it has had nothing like the influence on new religious movements or on the cultic milieu of contemporary spirituality of Hinduism and Buddhism, and the one branch of Islam that has attracted some followers is the least central: some westerners have been attracted to Sufism. This strand of Islam—regarded by many Sunni and Shia Muslims as close to heretical—replaces the focus on the Quran and correct or 'halal' living with the opportunity for direct contact with God through spiritual exercises. Music—banned by some Sunni and Shia traditions—plays an important part in Sufism. It is probably best known to the West through the devotional Quwalli music of performers such as the Pakistani Nusrat Fateh Ali Khan. Though Sufis in the Muslim world probably do not see this contrast, they are taken by many westerners to differ from the Muslim mainstream in being peace-loving and tolerant.

In contrast to Hinduism and Buddhism, Islam has inspired only one NRM and that only partly: Subud. According to Wikipedia:

> Subud is an international spiritual movement that began in Indonesia in the 1920s, founded by Muhammad Subuh Sumohadiwidjojo. The basis of Subud is a spiritual exercise commonly referred to as the latihan kejiwaan, which was said by Muhammad Subuh to represent guidance from 'the Power of God' or 'the Great Life Force'. He claimed that Subud was not a new teaching or religion. He recommended that Subud members practise a religion but left them to make their own choice of religion. Some members have converted to Islam, but others have found their faith in and practice of Christianity and Judaism, for example, have deepened after practising the latihan. There are now Subud groups in about 83 countries, with a worldwide membership of about 10,000.[2]

Dorothy Lessing was a follower and friend of Idries Shah, the movement's principal figure in Britain, but I can think of no other well-known adherents, and Subud has had very few British followers.[3] Shah's books sold well, but, like Zen Buddhism and Judaism, Sufism was reduced to a series of thought-provoking and witty instructive stories.

WHY IS ISLAM NOT PILLAGED?

All of this raises the question of why it is that the 'easternization of the West' has made little use of Islam, and answers to that question are useful in allowing us to see the necessary conditions for the West's appropriation of themes from foreign religious cultures.

Answers must begin with Islam's unpopularity among non-Muslim Britons. Surveys that ask about 'feelings of warmth towards' regularly put Islam below other faiths.[4] By the Pew Forum's rankings, Islam was rated unfavourably over the decade 2004–14 by a mean of 20 per cent.[5] The war in Palestine, the enduring conflict between Pakistan and India, the wars in Afghanistan, the chaos in most Middle Eastern countries, and terror attacks in western capitals all combine to create the impression that, despite what most Muslims say, Islam encourages violence. The political scientist can readily distinguish between the actions of a nation state that just happens to be Islamic and the political consequences of Islam, but the general public does not.[6] One can certainly see why. That probably explains why, when Yusuf Islam returned to the music business in the post 9/11 world, he dropped the second part of his name, and by 2016 his tour posters said 'Cat Stevens' in large upper-case letters with 'Yusuf' superimposed in a fainter italic script.

However, we can hardly explain attitudes towards Islam in the early 1970s by views common thirty years later. The Iranian Revolution of 1979—when American embassy officials were taken hostage—would have been for many the first hint of a 'clash of civilizations'.[7] For others it was the Ayatollah Khomeini's *fatwa* on the author Salman Rushdie in 1989 that first alerted them to the possibility that Islam was incompatible with western values. So we have at least a decade from the late 1960s in which Islam could, like Hinduism and Buddhism, have been treated as a repository of exotic spiritual resources, but it rarely was.

Furthermore, insofar as there was a consistent pre-1979 British attitude towards Islam, it was positive. Edward Fitzgerald's translation of *The Rubáiyát of Omar Khayyám* (originally written in Persian in the early twelfth century) was extremely popular with British readers. Sir Richard Burton (1821–80) was an explorer, geographer, translator, writer, soldier, and diplomat. His translation of *One Thousand and One Nights* (or *The Arabian Nights*) ran to sixteen volumes and because of that (and its sexual content) it was only privately circulated, but during the first half of the twentieth century numerous short selections were published and became bestsellers. Two generations of Britons were raised on the romance of *The Seven Pillars of Wisdom*. T. E. Lawrence's account of mobilizing Arab forces against the Ottoman Empire during the First World War was a bestseller in the 1930s, and Peter O'Toole's performance as Lawrence in David Lean's 1962 film ensured a second generation of admirers.

Edward Said's famous *Orientalism* is now known for the general argument that, as a consequence of, and a justification for, western domination of the East, western scholars systematically caricatured the mystic Orient. Because it is now read in the light of George W. Bush's disastrous 'war on terror', *Orientalism* is assumed to be arguing that the West demonized Islam by extending the jihadi attitudes of the very few to the many, but the original case was rather different and more interesting.[8] Said concluded that 'Western knowledge of the Eastern world, i.e. Orientalism, fictionally depicts the Orient as an irrational, weak, and feminized non-European Other, which is negatively contrasted with the rational, strong, and masculine West'.[9] Put in slightly more positive terms, one might have thought that 'irrational, weak and feminized' would have been very attractive to the hippie counterculture of the late 1960s, with its 'make love not war' slogan and its preference for intuition over rationality.

The Wrong Sort of Religion

One obvious difference between Islam, on the one hand, and Hinduism and Buddhism, on the other, is that, like Christianity, Islam has a single creator God who is to be worshipped and a foundational text that allows its officials to be dogmatic and doctrinaire about precisely how that worship is to be conducted.[10] One way of seeing the point is to imagine conversion. The New Ager may change her or his life many times. Give up meat, give up dairy, or, in the case of the Breatharians inspired by Australian charlatan Ellen Greve, give up all food and drink.[11] Sit in Zen meditation or stand in the poses of Qi Gong.

Chant with Nichiren Shoshu or wear Orange and a picture of Shree Bhagwan Rajneesh. In such spiritual seeking, it is the convert who decides what sort of life change is required by her or his new interest. The convert to mainstream Islam chooses to convert, but, having made that decision, does not determine the consequences. Of course, foot-dragging and back-sliding are always possible, but, for a western audience, what it means to be a Muslim is determined by communities of Muslims to a far greater extent than is the case with being Hindu or Buddhist.

In this respect, Islam is precisely the sort of religion that the denizens of the New Age milieu reject. One of the defining characteristics of New Age epistemology is that the believer determines his or her truth. An American spiritual seeker made the point forcefully when she described her sources of spiritual growth:

> I do follow by a lot of different spiritual paths. I don't consider myself— I call myself a witch but I'm not Wiccan. I study tantric techniques, but I'm not a tantric Buddhist. Uh, I do dream work techniques, but I don't really follow that original path. Um, I look into Native American studies and at what they have, but I don't consider that my path. I'm very eclectic—I like this idea of pulling from all different sources to find what works for me . . . diversity is the key. Whatever works for you is great as long as you don't hurt anybody else. I think it's fair. It's about the only creed that I expect everyone to follow—don't fuck with anybody else's business, you know. That's why I have a problem with a lot of the mainstream religions, because they're fucking with other people's business.[12]

Requiring What is Right and Forbidding What is Wrong

A second difference is that, for all its internal divisions, Islam is far more coherent and consistent in demanding a certain way of life than the more variegated Hinduism and Buddhism. While much of Hindu and Buddhist religious life is concerned with rituals that can be performed in private, much of Islam rests on a particular way of life. There are rules that have to be followed, and, as we saw with Richard Thompson's recording sessions, some of them have to be followed in public. And both of those elements—conformity and public display—are unpopular with the followers of holistic spirituality.

Furthermore, what most Muslims assert Islam requires is generally conservative. Whether the patriarchal attitudes that segregate the sexes, require women to hobble themselves to prevent men becoming sexually aroused, discourage women from working outside the home, and oppose gay rights are Islamic or are the accidentally associated mores of the conservative societies from which most British Muslims come is neither here nor there for our purposes. Whatever their origins, the conservative attitudes of most Muslims in the 1980s or 1990s would have been enough to discourage cultural borrowing.

An Islamic Presence

The first two points concern putative features of a religion as a set of ideas. Those ideas become most significant when they are embodied by people and organizations. Which brings us to the third difference: Britain possesses relatively large Muslim communities. Of the non-Christian religions in Britain, Hindus make up 1.3 per cent and Buddhists 0.4 per cent. These are small numbers, and they are widely distributed. Muslims are 4.4 per cent of the population, but they are concentrated so that in the East End of London they are over one-third of the population, as they are in Burnley in Lancashire. And young male Muslims are not backward in coming forward to defend their faith. The protests against Rushdie's *Satanic Verses* have already been mentioned. Of course, there has been nothing in the UK to match the violent attacks by ISIS on populations that they regard as apostate or heretical, but there has been at least one widely reported murder. In March 2016 Glasgow shopkeeper Asad Shah was murdered by a Bradford Muslim after he had posted on his Facebook page 'Good Friday and a very happy Easter, especially to my beloved Christian nation'. Shah was an Ahmadiyya, a minority community banned by the constitution of Pakistan from referring to themselves as Muslims. That Islam is represented by a large number of actual Muslims (rather than, as is the case for Buddhism, being known mostly as a set of texts and traditions) means that cultural pillage, even if it were desired, would be difficult.

The easy way to see the point is to consider some florid cases of appropriation and invention.

FENG SHUI, NATIVE AMERICAN INDIANS, AND CELTIC WARRIORS

In the 1980s one of the most popular topics on the list of New Age publisher Element was feng shui. Lillian Too was the author of eighty-four books, including *Illustrated Encyclopedia of Feng Sui*, *Creating Abundance with Feng Shui*, *Lillian Too's Practical Feng Shui*, and *The Complete Illustrated Guide to Feng Shui*. Feng shui is a Chinese philosophical system for harmonizing everyone and everything with Qi (pronounced 'chi'): the invisible spirit force that unites the universe, earth, and all of humanity, including the dead. In ancient China this was a serious business. In the modern West, it has either been reduced to the obvious or fluffed up with a series of unrelated New Age claims.

As a good example of the reduction to the obvious, consider these seven tips to feng shui your bedroom.[13] First, exclude TV, computer, and exercise equipment. 'In addition to creating high EMFs, they also bring the energy of work, stress and are mainly distractions and bad news for a good relationship (with yourself or your loved one).' Second, 'Open the windows often . . . You cannot have good feng shui in your bedroom if the air you breathe in is stale and full of pollutants.' Third, have your bed approachable from both sides. 'Have two bedside tables (one on each side).' Now this is indeed ancient wisdom: one can only imagine the numbers who without it would have put both bedside tables on the same side. Fourth, when decorating, know that feng shui bedroom décor is a 'balanced décor that provides the best flow of energy for restorative sleep, as well as sexual healing'. Fifth, choose one's bedroom art wisely, 'as images carry powerful energy . . . Unless you enjoy being sad and lonely, do not use sad and lonely images in your bedroom.' Sixth, have several levels of lighting in your bedroom. 'Candles are the best feng shui bedroom lighting, as they not only clean the energy, but also create a very intimate, warm and healing atmosphere.' They also create a very intimate fire hazard. Finally, keep all bedroom doors closed at night. 'This will allow for the best and most nourishing flow of energy.'

Thus is ancient Chinese geomancy and philosophy reduced to five banalities and one fire hazard. Many more examples of such bastard-ization could be added, but I will confine myself to one fine piece of opportunistic marketing. In April 2006, Motorola filed a patent application for a feng shui mobile phone.

When you want to carry out Feng Shui analysis of particular building or location you just have to take some pictures of the surrounding area, point the phone to the main wall of the house and press the button. The phone will do everything else.

Determine the directions which the main wall faces and deduct points if the direction is west or add points if the wall faces east, etc. Evaluate if the colors around you are favorable or undesirable, balanced or not. Analyze the noise level of the surroundings, measure magnetic fields and calculate chi values for all the parameters to give you results. The results can be displayed as a summary indicating positive, neutral, or negative chi, or you can get detailed report about the chi rating for every parameter measured.[14]

The alternative to banality is New Age bricolage. New Yorker Eleni Santoo supposedly combines American Indian sacred knowledge with Chinese energy principles to remove negative vibes from buildings by 'smudging'. This technique employs

> Tibetan bells, a status of Ganesh—the Hindu God of prudence and sagacity—an antique Chinese bell, an African necklace of yellow, red and green beads and a silver bowl containing three limes [which]... have the capacity to absorb negative energy. There is also a small bronze bowl into which Santoo places a jade-green powder, High John the Conqueror incense, specially ordered from the House of Hermetic in California.[15]

Santoo also uses a pack of angel cards from which she (or more precisely the angels) selects three which represent light, release, and humour. While playing cassettes of appropriate New Age music, Santoo carries first the incense and then the Chinese bell and a Druidic bell and a lime around the corners of the room. The range of Santoo's cultural borrowings seems extreme, but one can hire smudgers in London, and smudging incense sticks are readily available in New Age shops. One British practitioner wrote:

> I was introduced to smudging at a workshop by the wonderful Denise Linn. The scent of the burning bundle of herbs sent tingles through my body and I could feel how the energy of the room instantly shifted as the smoke was wafted through it. Smudging is a powerful cleansing technique from the Native American tradition. It calls on the spirits of sacred plants to drive away negative energies and put you back into a state of balance. Think of it as the psychic equivalent of washing your hands or scrubbing the bath. How does it work? Who knows? But variations of it have been used for thousands of years in indigenous

cultures around the world and I'm pretty sure that, one day, quantum physicists will show how the energy of certain plants can affect our bodies and our environment. After all, we're all made of energy.[16]

The Celts are not eastern, but their contemporary use helps illustrate the theme of this section. New Agers use the premodern inhabitants of Ireland and the west of Britain for a wide variety of purposes. The young man mentioned in Chapter 2 was told by his channelling diviner that he and his intended lover had been 'Celt warriors' in a previous life. A Canadian shaman and healer describes himself as 'a neo-Celtic practitioner reviving the ancestor-based spirituality of his own Gaelic heritage'.[17] He had moved on from borrowing American Indian rituals to imputing ancient wisdom to the Picts and Celts of Argyll (he gets them mixed up) after an experience during a Sun Dance revealed that his task in life was to 'remember' the ways of his ancient Scottish ancestors. This was something he could do because he believed, against the consensus of evolutionary biologists, that detailed knowledge of cultures could be passed down through many generations of carriers who were entirely unaware of the putative heritage they transmitted through their DNA. Celtic spirituality is often invoked as ancient legitimation for various invented wedding rituals involving jumping over broomsticks and tying knots.[18]

As with the 1950s interest in Shangri-La, the more remote the culture, the easier the appropriation. Tuesday Lobsang Rampa could peddle his romanticized fiction of Tibet because few people knew any better. Almost anything can be claimed to be ancient Native American wisdom, and so little is known about the religion of the ancient Celts that anything can be anachronistically imputed to what is taken to have been more congenial to the modern mind than the Latin Christianity that displaced it.[19] For example, one contributor to the debate on the virtues of ordaining woman as bishops asserted that the Celtic church had female leaders.[20]

As noted in Chapter 2, the claims of modern pagans to be lineal descendants of the original Druids are undermined (for those who wish to investigate such claims) by the work of archaeologists and historians. One way to avoid such inconvenience is to locate ancient wisdom in an entirely fictional place. That anyone now believes in the supposedly lost island of Atlantis is the result of a simple inability to understand allegory. In order to show the superiority of his own model state, Plato invented a powerful civilization that, having defeated most other powers, failed to conquer Athens and was drowned by the Gods, and he placed it some ten centuries before his own time.[21] That would have been the end of the matter had nineteenth-century US Congressman and author Ignatious Donnelly not mistaken Plato for a historian and worked Atlantis into a narrative acceptable to American Christians by having it destroyed in the biblical Flood.[22] As there is no real Atlantis to constrain fantasy, many implausible characteristics—for example, the ability to produce large amounts of electricity from crystals—have been imputed to it.

My analytical point is that such trivialization, distortion, or wholesale invention is possible because in western Europe there is no significant Chinese community (and the largest faith bloc of British Chinese is Christian), there is no American Indian community, the prehistoric Celts (or were they Picts?) are safely prehistoric, and the only extant Atlanteans are double-decker buses of that name. In contrast, Islam is alive and well and is represented by a large community of Muslims, some of whom are highly vocal in protecting and projecting their faith. Textile World (a chain of big warehouse stores selling curtains and settee coverings) held a 'Feng Shui' weekend and no one blinked an eye. Were a DIY store to mount a 'The Prophet's Guidance on Conservatories' weekend, the Muslim Council of Great Britain would be up in arms, and angry young men would be picketing the store.

CONCLUSION

Britain once had very close ties with Muslim countries. When the Transjordanian Arab League army attacked Israel in 1948, it was led by Sir John Bagot Glubb, whose honours—KCB, CMG, DSO, OBE, and MC—show his place at the heart of the British establishment. We no longer command the armed forces of Middle Eastern countries, but we still train their officers. Muslims form the largest block of non-Christians in Britain. And, if Said is right about western orientalist stereotypes before the current concern with terrorism displaced an earlier preoccupation with the soft, feminized, and languid version, Islam should have been popular with the countercultural 1960s. One might have supposed that all of this would make the appropriation of Islam an important element in the easternization of the West.

That it has not been shows two important features of our contemporary cultural appropriation. First, those people who have abandoned Christianity because it is doctrinaire and dogmatic are not interested in another doctrinaire and dogmatic religion, especially when many of its adherents maintain premodern attitudes to gender relations and sexuality. Second, actual presence is an obstacle to the imaginative reworking at the heart of cultural pillage. The less we really know of something, the easier it is to mould it to our interests and purposes. In the business of cultural borrowing, ignorance is indeed bliss.

NOTES

1. P. Humphries, *Richard Thompson: Strange Affair* (London: Virgin, 1996), 165.
2. Wikipedia, 'Subud' <https://en.wikipedia.org/wiki/Subud> (accessed June 2016). See also C. Partridge, 'Subud', in his *New Religions: A Guide* (Oxford: Oxford University Press, 2004), 140–1.
3. J. Diski, *Ingratitude* (London: Bloomsbury, 2015), 86–7, 183, 221.
4. See, e.g., the 2008 British Social Attitudes data available from the UK Data Archive at the University of Essex.
5. C. Field, 'Islam and Other Themes', BRIN, 17 May 2014 <http://www.brin.ac.uk/news> (accessed April 2016).
6. For a very detailed summary of what recent surveys tell us about British attitudes to Islam, see C. Field, 'Islamophobia in Contemporary Britain: The Evidence of the Opinion Polls 1988–2006', *Islam and Christian-Muslim Relations*, 18 (2007), 447–77.
7. S. Huntington, *The Clash of Civilizations and the Re-Making of the World Order* (London: Simon and Schuster, 1966).
8. Said himself developed the violence theme in *Covering Islam* (Harmondsworth: Penguin, 1997).
9. E. Said, *Orientalism* (New York: Vintage, 1979), 65–6.
10. As noted in the previous chapter, the idea that Buddhism is free of contaminating association with ethnic identity, state power, and violence is largely wishful thinking, but what matters in explaining social behaviour is what those whose behaviour is being explained think.
11. Ellen Greve (aka Jasmuheen) teaches that enlightened people can live without food or water. Her attempt to prove this on film was ended after four days because the doctor advising *60 Minutes* believed that she was endangering her health. At least three people have died trying to live on what Greve calls 'pranic nourishment'. The previous best-known

advocate of Breatharianism, American Wiley Brooks, claimed he had not eaten for nineteen years, but was caught scoffing a chicken pie in 1983 (T. Leonard, 'How Michelle Pfeiffer was Seduced by a Deadly Cult that Says you can Live on Air Alone', *Daily Mail*, 16 November 2013). See <http://rationalwiki.org/wiki/Breatharianism> (accessed May 2017).

12. J. P. Bloch, 'Individualism and Community in Alternative Spiritual "Magic"', *Journal for the Scientific Study of Religion*, 37 (1988), 295.

13. R. Tchi, 'How to Feng Shui your Bedroom' <http://fengshui.about.com/od/glossaryofterms/ss/What-is-Feng-Shui.htm> (accessed July 2015).

14. S. Bielinis, 'Motorola's Feng Shui Phone', *Unwired View*, 28 April <http://www.unwiredview.com/2006/04/28/motorolas-feng-shui-phone/> (accessed July 2015).

15. D. Fowler, 'Positive Vibrations', *Independent Saturday Magazine*, 6 December 1997.

16. J. Alexander, 'Smudging—Clear Your Home, Your Aura, Your Life', 2 April 2015 <https://brutallyfrank.wordpress.com/2015/02/04/smudging-clear-your-home-your-aura-your-life> (accessed July 2015).

17. S. Bruce, *Scottish Gods: Religion in Modern Scotland, 1900–2012* (Edinburgh: Edinburgh University Press, 2014), 189.

18. R. Probert, 'Chinese Whispers and Welsh Weddings', *Continuity and Change*, 20 (2005), 211–28, and M. Bowman, 'Reinventing the Celts', *Religion*, 23 (1993), 147–56. Some Scots have taken the invention as far as to create a 'Celtic Church in Scotland' with its own ordained priests and bishops; see K. Mann, 'A Celtic Wedding Is a Tie that Really Binds', *Sunday Post*, 29 April 2007, p. 23.

19. Until the Synod of Whitby in the seventh century, a form of Christianity promoted by Irish monks associated with Columbus and Iona had coexisted in Britain with a Latin Christianity resulting from direct evangelism from Rome. At the Synod, the King of Northumbria opted for the Latin version, and this conveniently marks the British church being brought into line with the Roman church on such matters as the dating of Easter.

20. I noted this from a discussion on the internet site *Ship of Fools* around 2014. Unfortunately I have lost my note of the details. The conflict between nationalists and unionists in first Ireland and then Northern Ireland has added something to the romantic view of 'Celtic' Ireland. 'Ireland' is white-washed cottages, peat fires in beautiful scenery, and 'craic' in homely pubs; 'Ulster' is grim-faced Orangemen in bowler hats, hectoring evangelical religion, and heavy industry.

21. Plato, *Timaeus and Critias* (Harmondsworth: Penguin, 2008).

22. I. Donnelly, *Atlantis: The Antediluvian World* (New York: Harper and Brothers, 1882).

6

Counting the Spiritual

INTRODUCTION

One common caricature of the secularization thesis is that it predicts the imminent and complete death of religion; this allows any religious innovation, irrespective of popularity or nature, to be presented as refutation. A more reasonable approach is to think how well any novel expression of religious or spiritual interest fills the gap left by the decline of Christianity and then consider the nature of those innovations. If the innovations are both popular enough to compensate for the decline of the churches, and religious, the secularization thesis is refuted. If the innovations attract few of the unchurched people or if the most popular innovations are also the least religious, the secularization thesis stands.

As will be clear by now, our new expressions of spiritual interest differ from conventional religion in ways that make it extremely difficult to count adherents. Not all nineteenth-century Methodists, for example, understood and were committed to the movement's key principles, but Methodism generally had an agenda that distinguished it from other Christian churches and that was understood by most members. To become a member one had to pass tests of doctrinal knowledge and one had to be able to articulate, at least roughly, experience of particular psychological states associated with the key beliefs. Even those who never applied for membership but attended regularly could reasonably be assumed to be familiar with distinguishing beliefs. Scottish Presbyterians sat through hour-long expositions of key beliefs, and they discussed the sermons they heard. The liturgies of the Church of England included 'call-and-response' presentations of its faith. And popular hymns clearly expressed such beliefs. In a time when basic religious knowledge was commonplace, one could not repeatedly sing the opening lines

> The Church's one foundation
> Is Jesus Christ her Lord
> She is His new creation
> By water and the Word

without appreciating the importance of Baptism (the water) and the reading and preaching of the Bible (the Word). Although they are much more than this, Christian churches, denominations, and sects are ideological organizations, distinguished from the secular world and from each other by propositions with which very many adherents would be familiar. If in no other way, we know this because they regularly split over them! And those adherents could at least roughly be counted, because, for almost all, such adherence—membership, attendance at worship, taking communion—was a public commitment. All of the above characteristics stem ultimately from the fact that such ideological organizations claimed the authority to determine what was required of those who claimed in various ways to support them. The precise location of that authority varied from the single office of the Curia for the Catholic Church to the consensus of believers for Protestant sects, but it was generally accepted that a Christian church defined the truth for its adherents and not the other way round.

The cultic milieu of alternative or holistic spirituality could hardly be more different. The term 'consumer' is used for the denizen of this world not to trivialize interest but to draw attention to the individual's right to decide what he or she will believe, and with what consequences. Rather than committing to a lifetime's loyalty to one particular teacher or organization, people will engage with a wide variety of rituals, beliefs, and practices, either sequentially or simultaneously: Dorothy Lewis and Isobel Losada (discussed in Chapter 2) are good examples. And such engagement may have few visible consequences. One might have to know someone extremely well to discover that he or she was a Nichiren Shoshu chanter or a TM meditator.

All of this means that it is difficult to estimate the popularity of new expressions of spiritual interest. But we have to try, because, if it is true, as is often suggested, that we cannot know whether people are religious, spiritual, or neither, then we must entirely give up talking about the popularity of religion or spirituality. This bears equally well on both sides of the great debate. One cannot, if one is honest, use data scepticism as a reason for denying secularization while still making vague claims about the growing attraction of novel forms of religious expression.[1]

There is no doubt that the innovative spiritual themes and practices discussed in the previous chapters have achieved considerable cultural currency and to varying degrees are now an important part of the lives of large thousands of people beyond those who formally associate with, affiliate to, or identify with any particular organizational embodiment of those innovations. This chapter will attempt to estimate the scale of that phenomenon.

CELEBRITY FROTH

A brief flirtation with Buddhism was common among the literate young in the late 1960s. Van Morrison's song about working as a window cleaner in west Belfast mentions reading 'Christmas Humphrey's book on Zen' in his lunchbreak, and his experience was commonplace. I must confess to turning my undergraduate study of Buddhism into a lifestyle statement: I gave up cigarettes, coffee, meat and recreational drugs, replaced my chairs with hard cushions on the floor, and affected a faraway stare intended to suggest a mind fixed on higher things.[2] That lasted about three weeks.

It is almost de rigueur for celebrities in the arts to claim some eastern-inspired spiritual interest. For a few years in the late 1990s and early 2000s, a number of the colour supplement magazines included with Saturday broadsheet newspapers featured brief philosophically oriented interviews with famous people. As an entirely unscientific data-collection exercise, I clipped all those (and it is around half) that mentioned a religious or spiritual theme. More than half of those referenced some eastern belief or practice. For example, a famous Italian clothes designer follows breakfast with 'an hour and a quarter swimming and 25 minutes doing Tibetan yoga'.[3] The architect who designed the Shard (an enormous glass building in central London) included a meditation room on the very top floor, which was, as he described it, 'an almost metaphysical space'.[4] The celebrity hypnotist and self-improvement author Paul McKenna usually meditates in the afternoon: 'I am currently practising a technique called Big Mind, which was developed by my friend Genpo Roshi, who is a Zen Master.'[5] It tells us a lot about the combination of insecurity and arrogance that drives many celebrities that McKenna should want to rule out the possibility that he follows a meditational technique developed by someone who was neither a Master nor a personal acquaintance. Chrissie Hynde, a pop star, said: 'My favourite book is the Bhagavad Gita. It's a 700-verse Hindu scripture and I love the verse that says your mind can be your best friend or your worst enemy. You can either pull yourself down or lift yourself up.'[6] The underwear model Rosie Huntington-Whitely says: 'People always tell me I have an old soul.'[7] Without the distancing 'People always tell me', the same claim is made by dress designer Victoria Beckham on behalf of her husband David and her friend the famously potty-mouthed chef Gordon Ramsay.[8] More grandly, the actor Michael Caine has not only claimed that he and his friends are old souls, but he has divined a previously unknown principle of reincarnation: 'Dull people don't come back. All my friends are what I call "old souls". They've been here before; they know stuff other people don't know.'[9] An interior designer collected crystals: her daughter 'got me into crystals after she learnt about them on a recent trip to India. My favourite... gives off a fantastic energy.'[10] Patsy Kensit (a TV soap actress) tried a form of mediation known as the 'Tibetan Singing Bowl' on holiday in the Maldives and announced: 'The retreat put me in the most incredible place. I have seen Utopia and it is beautiful. I have started following the Dalai Lama on Twitter.'[11] Doubtless his Holiness was impressed. The comedian, social activist, and briefly husband of Katy Perry Russell Brand has been associated with various forms of ancient wisdom, as has actress Gwyneth Paltrow, whose lifestyle blog Gloop became a veritable cornucopia of New Age nostrums.[12]

Kabbalah, a modern form of Jewish mysticism, is apparently popular with luvvies. Madonna, Gwyneth Paltrow, Demi Moore, and Princess Eugenie are supposedly devotees, and Naomi Campbell, David Beckham, Stella McCartney, Mariah Carey, Zinedine Zidane, Lindsay Lohan, and Prince Edward have all been photographed wearing Kabbalah's red thread bracelet.[13] One could dismiss this as insubstantial froth, but it does tells us two things about the zeitgeist. First, there is very little similar Christian froth. Only two of the interviews in my cuttings reference Christian themes, but they are tangential to Christian belief. Cressida Connolly, a writer who said

'I'm not a Roman Catholic but I very much like the trappings of Catholicism, the incense, the status, relics', collected Virgin Mary statuettes, as did Pearl Lowe, an interior designer.[14] Second, eastern themes have become popular badges of depth and profundity that can pre-empt the accusation that success and wealth bring shallowness.

PERVADING THE CULTURE

Divination has long figured in British popular culture. The prophecies of Nostradamus have been popular since the sixteenth century, and *Old Moore's Almanac* (which combined prophecies concerning major world events with such mundane information as tide tables) has been constantly in print since the early eighteenth century.[15] Fortune tellers have been a fixture of fairground and seaside entertainment since the early nineteenth century.[16] Working-class newspapers have long carried horoscopes, and since the 1970s these have also appeared in the magazines published by such serious papers as the *Daily Telegraph*. Since the 1980s tabloid papers have carried spiritualist 'agony aunt' columns, which combine astrological prediction with advice for the living based on communications with the spirits of their dear departed. And their pets: the exceptional British fondness for cats and dogs continues into the afterlife.

Once the hostility to the new religious movements of the late 1960s passed, New Age spirituality themes became commonplace in British popular culture, particularly when associated with alternative medicine.

It is not obvious what to make of this. We should certainly be cautious about reading off popular demand from the presence of New Age themes in the mass media, because some of that presence might reflect supply rather than demand factors. Puff articles on the 'White Witch shop' in a small Scottish town, which can supply crystals and candles and all your 'Spelling Requirements', and a long listing of alternative therapies, are, like a two-page spread on 'How to Feng Shui your House', cheap to produce and harmlessly fill column inches, which is no small matter when papers are shedding professional journalistic staff to cut costs.[17] And when such cheap copy can be accompanied by an interesting photograph—as in the regular reports of Kevin Carlyon (the self-styled High Priest of British

White Witches) performing a ritual to protect the Loch Ness monster—its appeal to a cash-strapped press is obvious.[18]

However, even if the presence of New Age material in contemporary print reflects 'supply' rather than evidenced demand, it does tell us one important thing: there is no longer any stigma attached to ideas and practices that the Christian churches in the early twentieth century would have condemned and condemned effectively. In 2001, Carlyon was the subject of affectionate reports in Aberdeen's *Press and Journal* of his Loch Ness-monster-protecting spell-casting. The attitude of nineteenth-century Presbyterian Scotland to pagans is neatly expressed in one of the papers that merged to form the *Press and Journal*. In 1876, the editor took the highly unusual step of writing a savagely critical obituary of a local man associated with spiritualism, which concluded by condemning him to hell: 'Wretched man. By this time he will be in no doubt as to the true character of the spirits with which he was so familiar.'[19]

The same point about acceptance can be made about more formal and structured involvement in formerly deviant religious and spiritual practices. Paganism is now accepted by many social institutions (the armed forces, for example) as a legitimate religious identity. But the growth of religious toleration may reflect, not growing fondness for previously stigmatized faiths, but growing indifference to all and any. We can permit pagan sailors their solstice ceremonies because we have no greater interest in Catholic sailors taking Mass or Methodist sailors singing their hymns. All are equally alien.[20] The massive extension of the repertoire of religious and spiritual themes may reflect the declining importance of religion rather than its popularity.

Possible indicators of interest are the sales, circulation, and readership figures (which are not the same thing) for New Age magazines. In order to provide intending advertisers with some reasonably independent measure of what they would be getting for their money, the Audit Bureau of Circulation (ABC) monitors circulation (and now associated website hits) for 422 magazines. Not surprisingly, the most popular are those given away either free in store or with membership of some large organization. In 2015, the top three were the National Trust and Asda and Tesco magazines (with respectively 2.16, 2.00, and 1.96 million copies). Next come three TV listing magazines: *TV Choice*, *What's on TV*, and the *Radio Times* (with 1.27, 0.98 and 0.73 million). Only one New Age magazine—*Spirit and Destiny,* which combines horoscopes, spirit guidance, alternative science, and alternative medicine—appears in the lists, and it has an audited circulation of 36,279 copies. That puts it in the company of *Classic Bike, BBC Music Magazine, Horse and Hounds,* and *Airliner World* and well behind the mean of 70,000 copies for the ten most popular 'secular' health titles.

Such data may well be incomplete, because there is little incentive for low-circulation and highly specialized periodicals to be audited by the ABC (though many are). We can identify five extant British New Age titles: *Caduceus, Kindred Spirit, Resurgence, Soul and Spirit,* and *One Earth.* Three make circulation claims on their websites. *Caduceus* claims a circulation of 70,000 for its paper version and 60,000 hits per month for its website. *Kindred Spirit* claims a circulation of 35,000.[21] *Resurgence* claims a readership of 30,000, but it has a print run of only 14,000 and only 7,500 UK subscribers.[22] So it is optimistically assuming that casual sales are twice subscriptions and that every copy is read by four people. *One Earth* is the Findhorn Foundation house magazine; its website gives no circulation or advertising information. Similar to *Spirit and Destiny* in both content and format is *Soul and Spirit* (the well-known down-market astrologer Russell Grant features), but it offers no circulation claims. If we suppose that claimed readership figures are inflated, that subscriptions offer a better comparison, and that the ratio of subscribers to inflated readership claim is the same for all, then *Caduceus* would have fewer than 20,000 subscribers and *Kindred Spirit* fewer than 9,000, and we know *Resurgence* to have 7,500 subscribers. That would put the *Caduceus* about level with *Cross Stitcher, Kindred Spirit* level with *Fly Fishing and Fly-Tying,* and *Resurgence* just above *Boxing News* in the ABC lists. The total of 36,500 subscribers for the three most popular New Age magazines is less than the audited sales of *Railway Magazine.* Unfortunately, we do not have time-series data to show how such sales have changed over recent decades; all we can say is that there is a market for such periodicals, but, relative to secular special interests, it is apparently a very small one.

There is no doubt that yoga and meditation are popular. In 2015, the British Wheel of Yoga claimed 4,000 teachers holding 9,000 classes.[23] Quite how one turns that into a number of people practising yoga is not obvious. If we assume every class has 20 participants, we get 180,000 doing yoga in any given year. If we further assume that, of those, three-quarters are new during the year and the others are experienced (that is, they started in some previous year), we have 135,000 starting yoga in any given year, or 1,350,000 over a decade. That seems too high an estimate: as yoga is probably done by few people younger than 25 or older than 64, the British Wheel of Yoga's claims would mean that about 1 in 20 adults had taken yoga classes. And, as it is far more popular with women than with men, a better estimate would be around 1 in 12 women. Were those people doing yoga in the same way that Indian Prime Minister Narendra Modi does yoga, we would have a significant expression of spiritual interest, but we can be confident that the British Wheel of Yoga's spokesperson is right in supposing that for most people yoga is simply an exercise programme.

It is not possible to guess a similar figure for meditation because there are so many possible sources and no central organizing body that parallels the British Wheel of Yoga. We know that in 2016 the smartphone meditation aid app *Headspace* claimed over 700,000 subscribers, but, as with the yoga classes, we have no idea of turnover.[24] Nonetheless, we can be confident that most British people are now familiar with meditation and that millions have tried it, if only briefly. As with yoga, the issue of numbers is compounded by the purpose of the activity. TM may initially have been opportunistic (and even deceitful) in presenting its meditation technique as a secular therapy but, as we saw with the growth of mindfulness, a thoroughly secular view of meditation is clearly possible.

So, in addition to knowing how many people practise yoga or meditation, we need to have some idea of what they think they are doing. Are they spiritual seekers or are they engaged in activities intended to promote physical and psychological wellbeing?

MEASURING SERIOUS INTEREST

In attempting to estimate the scale of what Paul Heelas and Linda Woodhead have called *The Spiritual Revolution*, detailed ethnographic studies of New Age groups, however interesting in their own right, are of no help. Tanya Luhrmann's account of a Wiccan group in London is fascinating in its description of the members and the coven's activities, but it makes no claims to being representative of

Wiccans, and it gives no indication of how popular are such activities.[25] Given that intense interest from the residents of Glastonbury may well be more than matched by the utter indifference of most residents of Guisborough and Gosforth, we need nationally representative information, and, as there are no large membership organizations to which spiritual people typically belong, such information must come either from field studies of reasonably typical places or from representative sample surveys.

Until the 1980s, the word 'spiritual' would probably have been taken by most people to mean Christian piety. Its New Age usage is relatively recent and for that reason we do not have long series of data on the popularity of spiritual as a self-description. Table 6.1 shows responses to recent poll questions that offered various degrees of spirituality, compressed into spiritual and not spiritual.

The average of eight surveys gives us 43 per cent of respondents describing themselves as spiritual, but the range of responses (between a third and a half of respondents), which may be due to differences in sampling, in question wording, or in question order, should cause us to be cautious of making too much of these data. It is also likely that reducing the range of options to a spiritual/not-spiritual choice distorts the picture. Given that churchgoing religious people could reasonably describe themselves as spiritual, there may be more value in a question that offers religious and spiritual as alternatives.

Table 6.1. Self-assessed spirituality of adults, Great Britain, 2004–2015 (%)

Date	Spiritual	Not spiritual
2004	53	46
2007	43	55
2007	50	49
2007	36	62
2008	31	54
2009–10	51	47
September 2011	35	60
April 2015	41	54
Mean	43	57

Source: C. Field, 'Secularising Selfhood: What Can Polling Data on the Personal Saliency of Religion Tell us about the Scale and Chronology of Secularisation in Modern Britain?', *Journal of Beliefs and Values*, 36 (2015), 318.

EXCURSUS: ON THE OBSOLESCENCE
OF RESPECTABILITY

A pioneering study of working-class culture in the northern town of Hunslet from the 1920s to the 1950s noted that many working-class people, despite never attending church, insisted that they were Christian.[26] Indeed, some went so far as to assert that they were really Christian while churchgoers were hypocrites who were no better than they should be.

> you can get as close to God on your own as do those who are 'always running after' the vicar or minister: 'there's good in all sorts', and you do not need to go to chapel to be a Christian. 'I'm as good a Christian, though I don't go to church,' they say. With that often goes the implied reversal: 'You're as bad as I am, even though y'do go to church.'[27]

Religion was a guide to living: 'doing good', 'common decency' 'helping lame dogs', 'being kind' . . . 'decent living'.[28] And what counted as decent living was decided by the community. Life was hard for working people, and most would like to do better, but you could not expect too much and you did your best to rub along. 'Christian' in this context seems to have meant decent, moral, and respectable (in the sense that your neighbours might actually respect you rather than in the sense of pretending to 'be something you're not').

Contemporary claims to spirituality seem to be doing something similar, but—and this is sociologically significant—the pollution that is being avoided has changed. What mattered to the faux Christians of Hunslet was their neighbours' judgement that they were 'decent living'. In our increasingly individualistic world—where the separation of place of work and residence reduces the possibility of us facing a single 'significant other' that can judge us—the fear that is being implicitly addressed concerns personality more than behaviour and two elements in particular: our sensitivity to the feelings of others and our ability to have suitably deep feelings.

Many of those who in recent surveys describe themselves as spiritual will be serious seekers after self-improvement and enlightenment. But it is probable that more simply want to be thought soulful, deep, profound, and authentic.

As is clear in Table 6.2, adding 'religious' as an option drastically reduces the numbers self-describing as spiritual. There are three rather different reasons for this. The first is purely statistical. Unless

Table 6.2. Religious, spiritual or neither, Great Britain, 2000–2013 (%)

Survey description	2000	2001	2013
Religious	27	34	10
Religious and spiritual	n.a.	n.a.	10
Spiritual	31	16	11
Neither	42	50	69
Total	100	100	100

Note: The 2000 survey was conducted by ORB, the 2001 survey is the Scottish Social Attitudes survey, and the 2013 survey is YouGov. It should be noted that YouGov surveys tend to give lower figures for religious or spirituality questions than those of other polling organization. This may be a result of its unique sampling method.
Source: Field, 'Secularising Selfhood'.

the added category is extremely unpopular, any addition of alternatives reduces the numbers left in the original boxes and thus changes the impression. The second reason is that, when the only alternative is 'not spiritual', 'spiritual' will capture many people who are conventionally religious. The third is more subtle. Survey questions that ask for simple matters of fact—how many children do you have?—are readily understood and, unless we can think of good reasons why people would agree to complete a survey but then give false answers, so are the responses. Attitude and belief questions are always more difficult. One well-supported principle is that, the more a particular matter is the subject of prior thought, the more stable and reliable are the answers. Given that most British people are religiously indifferent and show little sign of thinking much about religion in their day-to-day lives, survey answers on religious topics are unusually liable to be affected by such technical matters as question wording and placement, because the thought that such questions prompt is for many a novel activity. They are also liable to be shaped by the context. Adding 'religious' to the options 'spiritual' and 'not spiritual' may well be changing considerably what is heard by the respondent. The simple choice of 'Are you spiritual? Yes or No?' allows 'spiritual' to be interpreted in a rather secular way: as referring to one's sensitivity. Adding 'religious' to the options puts the question in a very different realm. It now very clearly frames 'spiritual' as an adjunct of 'religious', and that may well explain some of the considerable difference between the data in Tables 6.1 and 6.2.

In what follows I will describe in some detail the results of two studies that aim, in very different ways, to resolve the sorts of technical problems just described. The second is a much more detailed survey.

The first is an ethnographic study of the holistic spirituality milieu in one locale.

The Kendal Project

From 2001 to 2003, Paul Heelas and Linda Woodhead from Lancaster University investigated the scale and variety of religious and spiritual practice in the small Lake District town of Kendal and its environs.[29] I will describe their method in some detail because sadly the Kendal study remains the only attempt to enumerate all the putatively New Age activity in one particular place. Kendal, being surrounded by sparsely populated areas and being some considerable distance from the next major town or city, was suitable because the researchers could assume that few of its residents would travel elsewhere to engage regularly in what interested them. So, if Kendal people were, for example, learning positional yoga, almost all of them would be doing it in Kendal. Is Kendal representative of small-town England? In one respect not: the Lake District attracts many retirees, and its Romantic literature associations mean it probably has more than its fair share of people interested, for example, in finding a sense of the sacred in nature. But overall Kendal's social-class profile is not that far from the English norm. The one respect in which it does differ from many English towns (though not those of Wales or Scotland) is that it has few residents who are not ethnically 'white British' or who are members of some non-Christian faith community.

The Kendal study examined two types of activity: conventional churchgoing in what researchers call the 'congregational domain' and the alternative spirituality witnessed in the 'holistic milieu'. Within these categories, they compiled an inventory of all the churches and chapels, or the groups and individual practitioners active in the area. They then attempted to count the number of people involved in each during a typical week. Finally, they conducted surveys of participants and also carried out case studies of selected congregations and groups.

The conclusions for churchgoing were consistent with findings from national censuses: some 7.9 per cent of people were in church on a typical Sunday. The findings for the holistic milieu were that some 1.6 per cent of the population took part in one or more relevant activities each week. Heelas and Woodhead maintain that alternative spirituality has been growing rapidly, that this growth can be expected to continue, and that one might reasonably expect the holistic milieu to overtake the congregational domain. I have little argument with the possibility that New Age spirituality may some day become nearly as popular as churchgoing. What is at issue is whether either will be in any conventional sense of the word 'popular'.[30]

Three steps were important in arriving at an estimate of the number of people active in alternative spirituality in and around Kendal. First, it was necessary to arrive at an average weekly head-count for participation in each of sixty-three groups and a further sixty-three kinds of one-to-one treatment regarded by the organizers or practitioners as having a spiritual dimension. Second, the extent of overlap between different activities had to be estimated so that acts of participation could be translated into number of participants. Third, the investigators had to discover what proportion of the participants (as opposed to the practitioners) saw their activities as spiritual.

Researchers observed all group activities during one particular week and obtained counts of the numbers attending. Enumerating the clients of therapists was more difficult; as the authors comment, 'one person might say, "up to five people a day, three days a week"; another might say, "about 20 or 30 at any one time"; another, "about 20 a month"; still others, "it's too difficult to estimate" or "about 200–300 on my books"'.[31] The investigators used their knowledge and judgement to arrive at conservative estimates of the number of clients seen in a typical week by the various practitioners. Taking these figures together with attendance at group events, they concluded that there were 840 attendances in a typical week and that, allowing for some people attending more than one event or client session, this should be taken to represent 600 attenders.

In coming to their overall estimate of the size of the holistic milieu, Heelas and Woodhead counted participation in any group or one-to-one activity that the group leaders or service providers considered to have a spiritual dimension. It does not necessarily follow, of course, that ordinary participants or clients shared that judgement. Here the survey becomes relevant. Respondents were asked whether they had tried each practice and if so whether it had a spiritual dimension for them. In relation to the most important activity that they had pursued in the past seven days, they were asked to rank the reasons that originally induced them to try it and those that they currently found salient, where 'spiritual growth' was one of the options.

Given that completed questionnaires covered fewer than half the acts of participation, we have to consider the possibility of bias. There are good reasons to suppose that those who returned the survey were unrepresentative. People who completed it (and it ran to sixteen pages) were probably those most interested in or committed to the activity, and such people might also be especially likely to see it as spiritual. Further reason for suspecting that the survey respondents may not be typical of participants generally is that the ninety-five professional practitioners were asked by the researchers to complete the questionnaire. They might well have been more likely to respond than lay participants, partly because they were approached directly by the project team and partly because they are unusually interested in the topic. Unless the proportion of the questionnaires coming from practitioners (as distinct from their clients) corresponds to the proportion of those groups in the holistic milieu, the sample will be biased. By design, all the practitioners would describe their activities as spiritual, and hence the potential impact on this particular issue could be significant.

We can test the hypothesis that multiple attenders are more 'spiritual' than others. Fewer than half of those who listed a single activity from the previous week identified it as having a spiritual dimension, while 71 per cent of the multiple attenders found spirituality in one or more of their activities. Similarly, 45 per cent of the latter group listed 'looking for spiritual growth' as one of their top three reasons for participating, as against 34 per cent among those having done just one activity. Thus, if multiple attenders are over-represented (as the authors believe), it follows that the estimates of the spiritual significance of these activities are too high. To the extent that those responding to the survey are more committed than average, even if involved in only a single practice, the bias may be yet greater.

Table 6.3 shows the distribution of activities examined in the Kendal study. Reading down the list, it is hard not to be struck by how few activities listed are clearly spiritual. More than half of involvement is in what could easily be a secular activity: yoga, T'ai Chi, dance, singing, and art. Add in the personal pampering (massage, bodywork), and we have covered nearly two-thirds. Furthermore, the inclusion of some groups is questionable. For example, CancerCare (a winner of the Queen's Jubilee Award for Voluntary Service in the Community) is one of the larger 'healing and complementary health groups', but its ethos and activities are largely secular.

Table 6.3. Acts of participation in the holistic milieu (%)

Yoga and T'ai Chi	45.5
Massage, bodywork	13.9
Healing and complementary health groups	11.2
Reiki or spiritual healing	6.1
Dancing, singing, art, and craft	5.6
Specialized spiritual/religious groups	5.6
Miscellaneous one-to-one	5.0
Homeopathy	3.6
Counselling	3.5
	100.0

One of the main 'specialized spiritual/religious groups' is Sea of Faith, the mission of which is 'to explore and promote religious faith as a human creation'—that is, to preserve something of religion while attenuating claims to its supernatural origins. Most of its members would have been liberal Christians rather than New Agers. The same could be said of the Taizé singing group. It is thus likely that some of those presented as engaging in 'holistic spirituality milieu activity' are already appearing in the count of the congregational world and are thus being counted twice.

Even among the 237 participants and practitioners who completed the survey—a sample that, for the reasons above, is biased in favour of 'spiritual' interpretations of these activities—only a quarter chose 'spiritual growth' as the main reason for their involvement. Fewer than half said that their participation had anything whatsoever to do with spiritual growth. This brings us to the Kendal researchers' conclusion: that just less than 1 per cent of the population engaged in some vaguely New Age activity for spiritual reasons in a typical week, and for the technical reasons explained here that almost certainly flatters the New Age. Nonetheless, it is a nice round figure, and we can use it provided we remember that it represents the top end of the plausible range.

Scottish Social Attitudes Survey

At the same time as the Kendal project was being planned, a large module of religion and spirituality questions was designed for inclusion in the annual Scottish Social Attitudes survey.[32]

Two standard questions were included. Respondents were asked to describe themselves as 'religious, spiritual, or neither' and responded 34, 16, and 50 per cent respectively. They were also asked 'Which of [these] statements... comes closest to your beliefs?' and offered 'There is a personal God', 'There is some sort of spirit or life force', 'There is something there', 'I don't really know what to think', and 'I don't really think there is any sort of God, spirit or life force' as options.[33] Respondents divided much as they now do in other surveys: roughly a quarter went for each of the first three options and for the agnostic and atheistic responses combined.

Taking a cue from the Lancaster researchers, we asked if people had ever felt a pattern to life events 'as if they were meant to happen', a feeling of being in actual contact with the dead, a sense of having lived a previous life, a sense of the sacred in another person, and a sense of the sacred in nature. As we see in Table 6.4, half of the respondents thought there was some sort of foreordained pattern to life, a figure repeated in a detailed 2000 Nottingham survey.[34] It is worth remembering that these figures include the conventionally religious, who presumably had some divine ordination in mind: sensing the sacred in nature, for example, was more popular with regular churchgoers than with those who had never attended church regularly or had once done so and given it up. And it is possible that some respondents had in mind an entirely secular sense of the world being ordered. Many varieties of Marxist would assert that our lives and events are structured by class relationships. Conspiracy thinkers could suppose the world ordered by the wealthy individuals who meet at Davos every year, or a cabal of Jews, or the US government, or the European Union. Nonetheless, it is interesting that so many people feel themselves to inhabit an ordered universe.

In order to match the Kendal study's search for spiritual seekers, the Scottish survey asked a series of 'funnelling' questions about degrees of

Table 6.4. Arguably spiritual beliefs, Scottish Social Attitudes survey, 2001 (%)

	Yes	No	Can't choose
A pattern to life events as if they were meant to happen	50	42	8
A feeling of being in contact with the dead	22	71	7
A sense of having lived a previous life	18	76	6
An awareness of a sacred presence in another person	18	69	13
An awareness of the sacred in nature	25	61	14

interest and involvement in activities that might be taken to represent core holistic spirituality.[35] For example, the divination strand began with: 'And, leaving aside horoscopes in newspapers or magazines, how often, if at all, have you tried tarot, fortune telling or astrology?' If the answer was positive, it was followed by 'Have you ever paid for a consultation with a tarot card reader, fortune teller or astrologer?' The interviewer read the following warm-up: 'Some people find things such as yoga, meditation, fortune-telling, astrology and alternative medicine important at times in their life, while others just try these things and do not find them so important. Taking your answer from this card, can you tell me how important these have been to you in your life.' That divination question was followed by a similar set of questions for yoga and meditation, and for 'alternative or complementary medicine such as herbal remedies, homeopathy or aromatherapy'.

The overall figures can be summarized as follows. Most respondents had not tried divination (70 per cent) or yoga or meditation (78 per cent). Only alternative medicine was at all familiar: 45 per cent had tried some. Only 6 per cent of respondents thought their interest in divination was important and only 10 per cent thought that of their yoga or meditation practice. Again alternative medicine was the exception: 20 per cent of respondents thought it important.

It is a weakness of the Kendal research method that it does not eliminate conventional Christians from its count of involvement in the holistic spirituality milieu. Given that many churchgoers will also be users of alternative medicine and some may well meditate and go to yoga classes, we need additional filters to distinguish a core plausibly New Age population. When we look at how involvement in alternative practices combines with seeing oneself as spiritual rather than religious, we find that only a quarter of those who have used types of divination and found them important describe themselves as spiritual. And only 30 per cent of the divination users chose the 'spirit or life force' option to describe their view (if any) of God. If we look only at those people who had 'tried and found important' both divination and either alternative medicine or yoga/meditation, we find that almost half of them describe themselves as spiritual and over half chose the 'spirit or life force' option. That triangulation method led to the following summary conclusion: '15 per cent of Scots might describe themselves as spiritual (not religious) and one half of that group have engaged in some form of alternative practice which they have considered to have been of personal significance to them at some point in their lives.'[36] The proportion fell to 2 per cent when it was limited to those who had tried and found important alternative practices from both the well-being group (yoga and meditation) and the divination group.

Thus by a very different method we end up in much the same area as the Kendal study. We can argue a few percentage points in either direction, but if we are trying to gauge the size of the New Age spirituality population defined in much the same way as we would define and gauge active Christians, our bottom line is that it ranges between a possible high of about 7 per cent and low of about 1 per cent, with the actual figure being more likely to be near the bottom than the top of the range.

Further Sources

There are many reasons why people who could not tick one of the printed options in the 2011 census for England and Wales would have omitted to use the write-in option, but it is still worth considering the data that exercise generated. Taken together (in order of popularity) Pagan, Wicca, Witchcraft, New Age, Shamanism, and Occult were the choice of 71,512 people or 0.13 per cent of the population— considerably fewer than those who wrote in Jedi Knight.[37]

A 2013 survey designed by Woodhead has the virtue that it includes questions more rigorous than the usual self-description or assent-to-propositions items. She found that 15 per cent of respondents said they were spiritual (as compared with 8 per cent saying they were religious, 10 per cent saying they were both, and 48 per cent saying they were neither). But when asked 'which, if any, of the following would you say currently have an influence on you?', only 5 per cent chose 'An alternative form of spirituality—e.g. holistic spirituality, paganism' compared with the 9 per cent who chose Christianity and the 44 per cent who said 'None'. Woodhead also asked if people 'currently engage in any religious or spiritual practices with other people'. Only 15 per cent gave an affirmative answer. They were further asked about the 'group or community you are involved with'. While 67 per cent said their group was some form of Christian and 19 per cent identified a conventional non-Christian religion, only 4 per cent chose 'an alternative form of spirituality'. That 4 per cent represents just 32 people out of a total sample of 4,437 or less than 1 per cent.[38]

Finally, it is worth repeating the conclusion of the Time Use Diary study mentioned in Chapter 1. It showed that in a typical week only 8.3 per cent of people engaged in any religious activity lasting more than ten minutes and almost all of that activity lasted more than fifty minutes, was done in the company of others, outside the home, on a Sunday morning. That is, it was churchgoing. Less than 1.5 per cent of diarists recorded any solitary religious activity. As all religious or spiritual activity was coded as religious, that 1.5 per cent will include conventional Christians praying or reading the Bible as well as practitioners of TM meditating, Buddhists 'sitting', and Nichiren Shoshu adepts chanting.

In summary, the Kendal field study, the Scottish survey, the Time Use study, and various other surveys all point to the number of those whose behaviour might be taken as novel expressions of religious or spiritual interest as being somewhere near 1 per cent of the population.

PROJECTIONS AND TRENDS

Heelas and Woodhead called their study of Kendal *The Spiritual Revolution*. Less than 1 per cent of the population hardly sounds like a revolution, and they justify their title by taking recent past growth in interest in spirituality and projecting a logarithmic continuation of that trend. There is an alternative. It could be that interest in holistic spirituality is a 'cohort effect' or fashion—something that appealed to only one generation.

There is actually little or nothing in the Kendal study to support hope of future growth. One general constraint is the current narrow social base for holistic spirituality, and, given that the Findhorn Foundation was born in the 1960s, we can take the failure to break out of its social limits as an enduring rather than a temporary feature. Some 80 per cent of participants were female.[39] Very few New Agers are working class. As a very rough class index we can use regional presence. In 2015, Triratna Buddhist centres were distributed as follows: Scotland and Wales had eight; the Midlands and north of England had two, and there were twenty-nine in south of England. That is, 75 per cent of such centres (but only a third of the population) were in the affluent part of Britain. The failure of Samye Ling and the Findhorn Foundation to recruit locally has already been mentioned. Such class bias is often explained by cost. Certainly, healer Chris Dorman's *Spiritual Journey to Peru* tour (which in 2005 required a deposit of £2,700) would be beyond manual and routine clerical workers, but the Findhorn Foundation Experience Week costs between £480 and £760 depending on one's means, and that lower figure is much the same as a week at Ayr Butlins holiday camp.[40] And much New Age activity is organized on a subsistence and barter basis; it takes time but not much money. More likely explanations can be found in the style and underlying politics of most New Age activities. The style issues are, first, a willingness to talk to strangers about one's psychological problems and relationships and, secondly, a willingness to show emotion: crying is a common feature of much New Age group work. That sort of self-disclosure and intimacy is something much more common among the middle classes than in any other class. The political issue is autonomous individualism's neglect of socio-structural barriers to social mobility. Of course, there are sufficient opportunities, even in a society as class-bound as modern Britain, for a few talented and highly motived people to transcend the constraints of their upbringing and situation, but it is fatuous to suppose that some est training or Past-Life Regression will remedy the poor education, limited work opportunities, and dire housing that are the lot of most working-class families in Britain's rust towns. Actually it is worse than fatuous: it is insulting, because it makes the poor and dispossessed the authors of misfortune for which they bear almost no responsibility. It is no surprise that large parts of the population have no wish to be thus insulted.

As an aside, it is worth noting that, even at the level of micro-management, New Age 'positivity' can be oppressive. The founder of a private and very expensive New York club said: 'You're not going to find an unhappy person in the Core Club. If someone on the staff is having a bad day, an off day, we tell them to stay home.'[41] I suspect such people will not be getting paid for the off day. Obviously a gurning and complaining front-line workforce will not help any service industry, and the Core Club will be a commendable employer if it pays its workers well enough for them to be genuinely happy in their work, but such talk always carries the implicit threat that the workers had better pretend to be happy or else! Peter Lemesurier, a sympathetic commentator whose work was published by Findhorn Press, noted the same point more generally:

there can be a price to pay for affirming that the world is as one wants it to be, especially if that is not the way it is. Ignoring the seamier side of life—pretending for example, that pain and illness do not exist—is all very well, but disaster can all too easily result.[42]

This survey of the narrow social reach of holistic spirituality can be completed with the observation that there also very few spiritual seekers from minority ethnic backgrounds. Failure to appeal to the working class, to members of minority ethnic populations, to residents of the north of England, Scotland, and Wales, and to men is obviously not fatal: the manual working class is disappearing, the south of England is far more densely populated than the north or Scotland, ethnic minorities are indeed minorities, and men are under half the population. But such limits do inhibit future growth.

We should also note the age of the Kendal New Agers. Only three people under the age of 30 responded to the Kendal survey, and 83 per cent of respondents were aged 40 or over. This is important, because age is closely related to any interest in religion or spirituality. Two-thirds of respondents in the Kendal survey described themselves as 'spiritual'; three-quarters as either spiritual or religious or both. In the population at large, people under the age of 40, however, predominantly describe themselves as neither.[43] This suggests that the generation following that which dominates the Kendal study is less, not more, interested in holistic spirituality.[44]

That is true even for the offspring of the Kendal New Agers. Asked if their children were interested in their activity, two-thirds of the respondents with offspring said 'no'. Heelas is impressed by the fact that 32 per cent said 'yes', but this level of family transmission is disastrous.[45] In a society where parents have fewer than two children on average, replacing the dead requires 100 per cent of the next generation to be socialized into a practice for it to survive in the long term. Intergenerational transmission of Christian affiliation, attendance, and belief currently stands at about 50 per cent, and that rate is associated with dramatic decline.[46]

The Kendal researchers assert that interest in spirituality is not compensation for an unhappy home or work life. Most of their survey respondents rated their lives highly in these respects. However, it does seem that their respondents have not had success (if they sought it) in the conventional relationships that are most likely to support the family transmission of values. Like the Caddys of the Findhorn Foundation or Dorothy Lewis (whom we met in Chapter 2), their current satisfaction may come, not from their objective circumstances, but from their spiritual interests allowing a positive reinterpretation of what others would describe as interpersonal failure.[47] Of female Kendal respondents aged 35–49, only a third were living with husbands, the rest being equally divided between unmarried partnerships, lone parenthood, and living alone. Only half of female respondents of childbearing age have children living at home. Notwithstanding the rising age of maternity, it seems likely that a high proportion of spiritual women will not have children at all.

The above is not said in judgement but in recognition of the importance of family socialization in the transmission of religious beliefs. Most people believe the things they believe because they were raised so to do by their parents, and adult conversion is rare.[48] In the Scottish Social Attitudes survey, only 5 per cent of people who said they were raised with no religion had acquired one in adult life. If it is the case that New Agers are less likely than the rest of us to have stable family lives and to produce at least two children, then the reproduction of the holistic spirituality milieu will depend on adults coming to spirituality without any preparatory socialization, and that is an unpromising basis for future growth.

Almost all of those described in a study of small groups in Nottingham noted that they had been raised in church backgrounds, and, though they had rejected Christianity (for narrow-mindedness and intolerance), many retained a fondness for warm services and nice clergy and liked to sit in small country churches when there was no service.[49] One person had been a non-resident member of ISKCON for seventeen years. She quit partly because she preferred silent meditation to chanting but also because she resented being made to feel guilty about her levels of involvement.[50] In the Kendal study, almost three-quarters of respondents had received a religious upbringing either at home or at church.

It might be that some religious socialization in childhood is a common feature of the biography of many New Agers simply because it was a common feature of the childhoods of many middle-class women of a certain age—that is, the actual causes of both the religious background and the interest in holistic spirituality are age, class, and gender. The Scottish Social Attitudes survey gives us reason to think otherwise, because it allows us to be more precise about the role of background religious socialization. It divided beliefs into the conventional (belief in the existence of God; belief in Jesus Christ as the son of God; belief in life after death; getting an answer to prayer; an awareness of the presence of God) and the unconventional (a pattern to life events as if they were meant to happen; a feeling of being in contact with the dead; a sense of having lived a previous life; an awareness of a sacred presence in another person; a belief in astrology, tarot, or fortune telling as important). We can then see to what extent these are associated with various patterns of previous churchgoing. The survey asked not just how often people went to church but also if they had ever attended church regularly and then stopped going. Because we sensed that it represented an important difference in attitudes to religion, we further divided the 'once attended then stopped' category into those who were sure they would not return and those who might return at some point in the future.

One element of Figure 6.1's display of the relationship between previous churchgoing and the two sorts of belief is obvious. Attending church and holding conventional religious beliefs is strongly correlated.

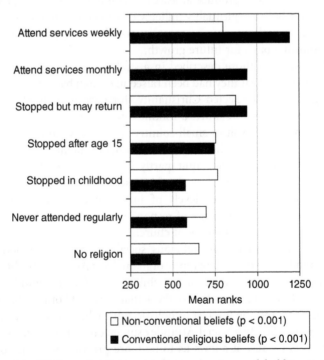

Figure 6.1. Lifetime attendance at religious services and holding conventional or non-conventional beliefs, Scottish Social Attitudes survey, 2001.

Why would it be otherwise? But what is highly significant for estimating the future of New Age spirituality is the relationship between church-going and holding unconventional beliefs. The people who are most sympathetic to unconventional beliefs are those who attended church regularly in childhood and stopped attending but might consider going back. We can see why. These are people who learnt in childhood to be sympathetic to religious ideas and for some reason gave up on Chris-tianity but did not become committed atheists.[51] This is the pool from which spirituality has recruited, and, as the churches decline, it is drying up.[52] Put very simply, 'alternative spirituality', as it is sometimes called, is not an alternative to religious indifference. It is an alternative to con-ventional religion, and, as the proportion of people with any childhood religious socialization declines, so too does the pool from which spiritu-ality recruits.

SPIRITUALITY OR BAD SCIENCE?

One clear finding of both the Kendal and the Scottish Social Attitudes study is that much of what could be taken to be new expressions of religious interest is actually an interest in physical and psychological well-being. That alternative or complementary medicine is the most popular part of the New Age milieu raises a question that few commentators have addressed: to what extent should those spiritual beliefs and practices that we take to be novel expressions of religious interest more accurately be seen as bad science? Many of the activ-ities, products, and devices described in Chapter 2 are presented by their promoters as legitimated by science. For example, Gwyneth Paltrow's lifestyle blog *Goop* puffed Dr Emoto's research. Emoto poured pure water into vials labelled with negative phrases like 'I hate you' and 'fear'. After twenty-four hours the water was frozen and microscopic examination showed grey misshapen clumps instead of beautiful crystals. Emoto then took vials of polluted water, labelled it with positive messages such as 'I love you', left it for twenty-four hours, and then froze it. Those vials produced 'gleaming perfect hexagonal crystals'.[53] Thus we can conclude that attitudes change physical realities, which, Paltrow believes, proves that Norman Vincent Peale radically underestimated the human mind when he confined the benefits of his *Power of Positive Thinking* to relationships and role performance. If our minds can pollute and purify water, healing the body should be a doddle. Because the scientifically educated among us know that water cannot read, we know that Emoto's work cannot be sound science. So we suppose that those who accept it and the very many similar cases made in the world of complementary medicine must be making a 'spiritual' judgement—a supposition that is reinforced by the variable patterns of acceptance. It is self-avowedly spiritual people such as Paltrow who promote this kind of faux science.

Some in the holistic spirituality milieu adopt 'alternative' medicine precisely because it is an alternative to the mainstream medical science they reject in favour of ancient wisdom. But it may well be that many of those who use such therapies (and who are counted in the Kendal study as engaging in spirituality activities) mistakenly believe they are doing science.[54] It is certainly the case that many forms of healing are presented by their practitioners as scientifically validated. Biographies of Deepak Chopra always mention his conventional medical qualifications, and many healers who lack such education nonetheless list strings of initials after their names. Vague references to quantum physics are a regular feature of the justifications for many forms of healing. One does not have to be too sceptical to see those, or the use of dial-laden boxes (such as those that feature in Radionics), as a way for practitioners to claim the mantle of science. The remarkable thing is that many influential opinion leaders such as broadsheet newspapers uncritically advertise panacea therapies as though they were the real thing. To give just one example from the hundreds I have collected: the *Independent's* health page published a long article on workplace stress that uncritically advertised as effective responses TM, shiatsu massage, and the possession of crystals. With not the least hint that this is not accepted medical physics, the article, somewhat ungrammatically, says: 'The crystals absorb all bad energies like a magnet and filter it back out as good energy.'[55] There is usually nothing in such puffery to warn the unwary, and hence it is always possible that consumers take broadsheet coverage as vouchsafing the scientific validity of what is actually nonsense.

Thus some of the popularity of forms of healing that observers regard as 'spiritual' may stem, not from a positive commitment to alternatives to conventional science and medicine, but from a poor understanding of science and conventional medicine among parts of the general public. The UK is certainly unusual in its poor record of science teaching and in allowing school pupils to drop science subjects at an early stage.[56] We currently lack the evidence to take this further at the moment because most surveys that touch on religion, spirituality, and healing confine their questions about respondents' education to level. We know, for example, that reading magazine horoscopes is more popular among women with low levels of education, while more sophisticated forms of divination are more popular with female graduates. But we do not know what subjects were taken to what level at school. Hence we cannot compare those with a good science background with those who dropped science subjects at the earliest possible age. We have some hint of a connection in data on occupations: primary school teachers, carers, and social workers are more common among the avowedly spiritual than research scientists and engineers, but greater confidence must await further research.

The observation is far from conclusive, but there is enough to suggest we need to be cautious of taking as signs of spiritual interest what may, for the promoters and consumers of various therapies, albeit mistakenly be regarded as science.

CONCLUSION

Let us return to the numbers. It is a strange consequence of social science that in researching some phenomenon we almost always exaggerate its importance. Simply to study New Age spirituality is to give it a degree of significance that is hardly deflated by any numerical estimate of its popularity. Even when we say, as the Kendal study concludes, that less than 1 per cent of the British people engage in some holistic milieu activity in a typical week for spiritual reasons, because it is the product of two years of research and is described in a book, it still seems like something important. It is not. A better estimation would be conveyed if we said 'Almost all British people have no interest in holistic spirituality' and left it there. Or put it this way: if we were asked to list the things that the British people *are* interested in, contemporary spirituality would struggle to make it into the top fifty items.

Second, let us consider exactly what sorts of activities the Kendal study discovered. Remember that it was designed by a self-confessed pro-spirituality partisan and located in a place more likely than

Blackburn or Burnley to attract other partisans.[57] There is almost no mention of Atlantean crystals, angels, channelled wisdom from Hidden Masters, or anything occult. Apart from yoga (and half its practitioners thought it was an exercise class), there is very little that looks like what one of the Kendal authors has called 'deep spiritual seeking'.[58] On this account, the gap left by the decline of Christianity is being filled with massage, posture improvement, singing, dance, and art. Which looks pretty much like secularization.

Third, we need to be mindful of an important consideration that is overlooked by Heelas and Woodhead in the logic of their discovery of a spiritual revolution. It is indeed the case that there is something new in the prevalence of the procedural themes of individual autonomy and personal preference in the origins of religious and spiritual commitments. But in substance many New Age interests have historic parallels. This matters because those who believe that contemporary spirituality is a novel replacement for the declining Christian churches make their case by implying that everything they find that fits the bill is unprecedented. The eastern-inspired elements are indeed new to Britain, but many are just new expressions of an enduring interest. Consider divination. It may seem notable that many twenty-first-century citizens of advanced industrial economies are interested in astrological horoscopes, tarot cards, or the I Ching, but in total there was probably more interest in divination in any previous era than there is today. Given the very different methods used in their design, one obviously has to be careful in comparing the results of Geoffrey Gorer's 1950 survey with more recent evidence, but it is still worth noting that 44 per cent of Gorer's respondents said they had visited a fortune teller and 71 per cent said they read their horoscopes in a newspaper or magazine 'regularly' or 'occasionally'.[59] Very few people now visit fortune tellers (or their modern equivalents), and recent surveys suggest that only some 22 per cent of us believe in horoscopes.[60]

Or consider that almost half the respondents to the 2001 Scottish survey said they believed there was 'a pattern to life events as if they were meant to happen'. This may seem like a very large number. But we need to remember that, as with the above data on reading horoscopes, this includes the conventionally religious, and its distribution is strongly correlated with churchgoing: it was a view approved by only 39 per cent of those who were not raised in any religion but by 55 per cent of those who had ever attended church regularly. Given that association, it seems highly likely that some version of provi-dence was vastly more popular in 1851 or earlier than it is now.[61]

The same point can be made about many of the general beliefs and attitudes that are taken now as symptoms of novel expressions of spiritual interest: parallel phenomena were almost certainly far more common in Britain when it was more conventionally religious than they are now.

Finally, I argued that the failure to discover a spiritual revolution cannot be remedied with projections of future growth. The two studies discussed here confirm and quantify what is often more impressionistically noted elsewhere: a large proportion of those who now describe themselves as spiritual rather than religious, who assent to unconventional beliefs, and who take part in New Age activities, were raised in conventionally religious families. They attended church as children. Their willingness to believe in some 'spirit or life force' derives from now finding the idea of a personal creator God implausible, not from frustration with religious indif-ference. The spiritual is an escape from the religious, not from the secular. Hence the future of spirituality is somewhat dependent on the size of the pool of the disaffectedly religious and that will shrink as the number of people with any religious socialization declines. With 'None' now being the most popular religion among young British people, there is no reason at all to imagine that the spiritual elements (as distinct from the bad science and quack medicine) of the holistic spirituality milieu will grow markedly in popularity.

NOTES

1. Those on the other side of the argument may experience the reverse. I can only report that on every occasion when I have presented data on secularization to a Religious Studies seminar, at least one person in the audience has rebutted my evidence of decline with the contradictory assertions that (*a*) we cannot really know how many people are religious or spiritual and (*b*) we can be sure the number is not going down!

2. The reference to the faraway stare is not flippant. A skim through the flyers produced by New Life Promotions shows that the typical male purveyor of New Age wisdom or therapy has a wrinkled but congenial face with eyes set on some far horizon—as though being able to see further than the rest of us vouchsafes an ability to see deeper into our souls.

3. S. De Rosée, 'The World of Brunello Cucinelli', *Telegraph Magazine*, 3 March 2012.

4. S. Marsh, 'The Man who Built the Shard', *The Times Luxx Magazine*, 19 May 2012.

5. S. De Roseé, 'The World of Paul McKenna: Hypnotist and Self-Improvement Author', *Telegraph Magazine*, 21 January 2012.

6. C. Pires, 'This Much I Know: Chrissie Hynde', *Observer Magazine*, 14 September 2014. Even leaving aside the rest of the *Mahabharata* (of which it forms part), the *Bhagavad Gita* is a substantial and philosophically difficult work of some 700 verses. Yet it is now cited as inspiration by a number of celebrities. For example, Canadian comedian Tom Stade said: 'I'm a spiritual person. When I went to Mumbai in 2010 we were partying with some Indian dudes and they gave me a copy of the Bhagavad Gita, which is about every war that has ever gone on in your mind. Before I met them I was a mess; show business has a way of messing with your mind' (E. Muff, 'The World of Tom Stade, Comedian', *Telegraph Magazine*, 8 August 2015).

7. F. Wilson, 'What I've Learnt: Rosie Huntington-Whiteley', *The Times Magazine*, 18 October 2014.

8. *The Week*, 6 December 2008.

9. *The Week*, 17 November 2007, p. 10, quoting an interview with E. Lipworth in the *Mail on Sunday*.

10. S. De Roseé, 'The World of Kelly Hoppen, Interior Designer', *Telegraph Magazine*, 27 August 2010.

11. *Press and Journal*, 10 April 2015.

12. M. Archibald, 'Still Jung at heart! Russell Brand Looks to the Skies after Emerging from Spiritual Cleansing Session', *Daily Mail*, 14 October 2012 <http://www.dailymail.co.uk/tvshowbiz/article-2217646/Russell-Brand-looks-skies-emerging-spiritual-cleansing-session.html> (accessed January 2013).

13. H. Sherwood, 'Preaching to the Converted', *Guardian*, 27 October 2015.

14. S. De Roseé, 'The World of Cressida Connolly, Writer', *Telegraph Magazine*, 23 July 2011; E. Pithers, 'The World of Pearl Lowe, designer', *Telegraph Magazine*, 5 May 2013.

15. N. Campion, *A History of Western Astrology*, ii, *The Medieval and Modern Worlds* (London: Continuum, 2009), 216.

16. Gorer has a thoughtful analysis of the popularity of horoscopes in the early 1950s; G. Gorer, *Explaining English Character* (London: Cresset Press, 1955), 266–70. On seaside fortune tellers, see D. Jarratt, 'A Socio-Cultural Analysis of the Traditional Seaside Resort and its Contemporary Meaning to Tourists with Specific Reference to Morecambe, U.K.', Ph.D. thesis, University of Central Lancashire, Preston, 2013.

17. As someone who has been an avid reader of print journalism for forty years, I note that, as broadsheet newspapers have responded to the loss of advertising income and readers to the Internet by drastically cutting the number of journalists they employ, the space given to health, well-being, and spirituality articles has grown proportionately. For a blatant example of uncritical puffery of a quack healer, see L. Macintyre, 'Destined to Work with her Hands', *Herald*, 6 March 1997.

18. D. Ross, 'The Witch, the Scientist, the Monster and the Media', *Herald*, 25 April 2001, p. 11.

19. *Aberdeen Journal*, 19 April 1876.

20. This is not hyperbole. The majority of the population has never attended a Christian church service and has no familiarity whatsoever with Christian beliefs.

21. <http://www.responsesource.com/bulletin/interviews/focus-on-kindred-spirit-with-editor-tania-ahsan/> (accessed June 2016).

22. *Resurgence* data are from the magazine's website: <http://www.resurgence.org/magazine/advertise.html> (accessed November 2016).

23. 'Third Leader', *The Times*, 30 May 2015.

24. R. Booth, 'Mindfulness Study to Track Impact of Meditation on 7,000 Teenagers', *Guardian*, 17 July 2015.

25. T. Luhrmann, *Persuasions of the Witch's Craft: Ritual Magic in Contemporary England* (Oxford: Blackwell, 1989).

26. This section title is chosen to parallel the discussion of modernity's erosion of honour in P. L. Berger, B. Berger, and H. Kellner, *The Homeless Mind* (Harmondsworth: Penguin, 1974), 78–89.

27. R. Hoggart, *The Uses of Literacy* (London: Chatto and Windus, 1957), 99.

28. Hoggart, *Literacy*, 98.

29. Although I skate over them here, I am deeply indebted to David Voas for an understanding of the technical problems involved in interpreting the Kendal statistics. We discuss them at length in D. Voas and S. Bruce, 'The Spiritual Revolution: Another False Dawn for the Sacred', in K. Flanagan and P. Jupp (eds), *A Sociology of Spirituality* (Aldershot: Ashgate, 2007), 43–62.

30. P. Heelas and L. Woodhead, *The Spiritual Revolution: Why Religion is Giving Way to Spirituality* (Oxford: Blackwell, 2005), 48. Heelas was primarily responsible for the holistic milieu work; Woodhead for the work on the congregational domain.

31. Heelas and Woodhead, *Spiritual Revolution*, 39.

32. S. Bruce and A. Glendinning, 'Religious Beliefs and Differences', in C. Bromley, J. Curtice, K. Hinds, and A. Park (eds), *Devolution—Scottish Answers to Scottish Questions* (Edinburgh: Edinburgh University Press, 2003), 86–115.

33. It should be noted that this array of possibilities combines two rather different things: the content of beliefs and the certainty and constancy with which they are held. We stuck with this format because we wanted to maintain comparability with the very many previous surveys that had used it.

34. D. Hay and K. Hunt, *Understanding the Spirituality of People Who Do Not Go to Church* (Nottingham: Centre for the Study of Human Relations, University of Nottingham, 2000), 13.

35. The questionnaire is available from the UK Data Service, as are the data <http://doc.ukdataservice.ac.uk/doc/4804/mrdoc/pdf/4804userguide.pdf> (accessed April 2006).

36. T. Glendinning and S. Bruce, 'New Ways of Believing or Belonging: Is Religion Giving Way to Spirituality?', *British Journal of Sociology*, 57 (2006), 412.

37. '2011 Census England and Wales' <visual.ons.gov.uk/2011-census-religion> (accessed June 2016).

38. YouGov, 'YouGov University of Lancaster results' <https//d25d2506stb94s.cloudfront.net/cumulus_uploads/documents/mm7go89rhi/YouGov-University%20of%Lancaster-Survey-Results-Faith-Matters-120130.pdf> (accessed November 2016).

39. Discussed at length in M. Trzebiatowska and S. Bruce, *Why Are Women More Religious Than Men?* (Oxford: Oxford University Press, 2012), 62–77.

40. *Press and Journal*, advert, 8 August 2004.

41. G. Trebay, 'Money Talks', *Independent Magazine*, 16 July 2011.

42. P. Lemesurier, *This New Age Business* (Forres: Findhorn Press, 1990), 199.

43. D. Voas, 'Intermarriage and the Demographics of Secularization', *British Journal of Sociology*, 54 (2003), 83–108.

44. Three sweeps of the World Values Survey show the scores for 'Post-Christian Spirituality' in Great Britain increase from 1981 to 1990 but then fall back for 2000; D. Houtman and S. Aupers, 'The Spiritual Turn and the Decline of Religion', *Journal for the Scientific Study of Religion*, 46 (2007), 305–20.

45. P. Heelas and B. Seel, 'An Ageing New Age?', in G. Davie, P. Heelas, and L. Woodhead (eds), *Predicting Religion: Christian, Secular and Alternative Futures* (Aldershot: Ashgate, 2003), 234.

46. A. Crockett and D. Voas, 'Generations of Decline: Religious Change in Twentieth-Century Britain', *Journal for the Scientific Study of Religion*, 45 (2006), 567–84.

47. Doreen Virtue, a popular North American advocate of the importance of angels, was on her fifth marriage at the age of 57. Elizabeth Prophet, founder of the leading US New Age body Church Universal and Triumphant, had four husbands. Many more examples could be added.

48. The importance of conversion for evangelical Protestants might seem to belie this proposition. The explanation is that very many evangelical Christians who become 'born again' have actually been raised in evangelical Christian families. Their conversion is actually a point of consciously internalizing what is already very familiar. By conversion here I mean the radical change involved in a Christian becoming a Muslim, a Mormon, or a Moonie or a non-believer becoming a Christian.

49. M. Wood, *Possession, Power and the New Age* (Aldershot: Ashgate, 2007), 97.

50. Wood, *Possession*, 132.

51. It is worth noting that the backgrounds of the young people who joined the Moonies in the 1970s was similar; E. Barker, *The Making of a Moonie* (Oxford: Blackwell, 1984), 212.

52. This conclusion is accidentally supported by two sympathetic studies of New Age spirituality. In the Prince and Riches account of the failure of some Glastonbury residents to organize a regular Sunday meeting, the participants discussed the extent to which their current interests were a reaction to conventional religious upbringings; R. Prince and D. Riches, *The New Age in Glastonbury* (Oxford: Berghahn, 2000), 176–7. The same observation can be found in a study of Nottingham New Agers; see Wood, *Possession*, 133.

53. *The Week*, 14 May 2014, p. 22.

54. On the relationship between science and pseudo-science, see the contributions to R. Wallis (ed.), *On the Margins of Science: The Social Construction of Rejected Knowledge* (Keele: Sociological Review Monographs, 1979), and R. Wallis and P. Morley (eds), *Marginal Medicine* (London: Peter Owen, 1976). I should be clear that my description of most complementary medicine as pseudo-science does not suppose that modern scientific knowledge is complete. It rests on two things. First, the extraordinary success of conventional medicine—let us just mention the eradication of polio and the now routine heart bypass surgery—is itself confirmation of the conventional understanding of human anatomy (which has no need for the always vague notions of 'energy' and 'aura' that permeate spiritual healing). Second, scientific medicine has advanced slowly but systematically through experimentation and double-blind testing; spiritual healing deliberately avoids those two techniques and instead relies solely on unverifiable anecdotal claims to efficacy. If Radionics was subjected to the same methods of evaluation and passed those tests, I would be happy to see it shifted from the 'snake oil' category to the category of science.

55. L. Bestie, 'Take it Easy, it's Only a Job', *Independent*, 22 July 1999, p. 9.

56. The UK's poor science education record is documented in OFSTED, *Maintaining Curiosity: A Survey into Science Education in Schools* (London: OFSTED, 2013). Girls are particularly likely to drop science

subjects early. In England in 2014, boys were 79% of those taking A Level Physics, 72% of those taking Further Maths, 61% of those taking Maths, and 52% of those taking Chemistry. Only in Biology did girls (at 59%) lead boys. According to the campaigning organization Women in Science and Engineering, women made up only 13% of the workforce in science, technology, engineering, and maths (the so-called STEM) occupations. See G. Arnett, 'How Well Are Women Represented in UK Science?', *Guardian*, 13 June 2015.

57. P. Heelas, 'Preface', in *Spiritualities of Life: New Age Romanticism and Consumptive Capitalism* (Oxford: Blackwell, 2008). Here Heelas describes himself as having been 'extremely fortunate to have been born in 1946. This has meant that I have...in measure experienced, the unfolding of Spiritualities of life from the time I came of age during that great "inner era" known as the sixties.'

58. L. Woodhead, 'Why So Many Women in Holistic Spirituality?', in K. Flanagan and P. Jupp (eds), *A Sociology of Spirituality* (Aldershot: Ashgate, 2007), 117.

59. G. Gorer, *Exploring English Character* (London: Cresset Press, 1955), table 104f. On seaside fortune tellers, see K. Ferry, *The British Seaside Holiday* (Botley, Oxfordshire: Shire Publications, 2009), 78, 114, and J. K. Walton, *The British Seaside: Holidays and Resorts in the Twentieth Century* (Manchester: Manchester University Press, 2000), 148.

60. The average of positive responses to the question 'Have you ever had your fortune told?' in five surveys from 1993 to 2007 was 22%. The positive responses to 'Do you believe in fortune telling/tarot'? in a 1951 survey were 20 and in 1968 33%. For three twenty-first-century surveys they were 13, 18, and 15%. That is, there is probably now less, not more, interest. A large number of survey results are reported on the *British Religion in Numbers* website: <www.brin.ac.uk/figures/belief-in-britain-1939-2009/alternative-religious-belief> (accessed November 2016).

61. T. Glendinning and S. Bruce, 'New Ways of Believing or Belonging: Is Religion Giving Way to Spirituality?', *British Journal of Sociology*, 57 (2006), table V.

7

The Secular Beats the Spiritual

INTRODUCTION

Yoga classes in Yorkshire, mindfulness training in Middlesex, Goddess workshops in Godalming; in their own right, such activities are fascinating, but here they serve to help us address one simple but profoundly important question: how is Britain's religious culture (and, by extension, that of similar western societies) changing?

Like all theorizing, this simplifies enormously, but we have two clearly competing alternatives. On the one side: the growth of religious freedom and the shift from a shared religion embedded in our major social institutions to an individualist culture of choice cause interest in the religious and the spiritual to decline. On the other side, the demand for religion is stable: 'Christianity thrives probably as much as ever it did, at least since compulsion and the threat of hell were lifted.'[1] Few scholars would make that case for Christianity, but it is commonly made for religion viewed most broadly.[2] People are still religious, but they now express their religious sentiments and interests in a variety of novel and idiosyncratic ways.

This concluding chapter will estimate the size of the gap left by the decline of the Christian churches. It will then demonstrate the rapid growth in the number of people who are self-consciously non-religious or patently religiously indifferent. It will consider the argument that the changes documented repeatedly in previous chapters are of no great import, because such attenuation of religious commitment is commonplace: part of a regular cycle that has been seen many times before. Finally, it will argue that the shift from toleration of diverse religions to religious and spiritual relativism makes any reversal of secularization extremely unlikely. But first I will address two matters that are somewhat tangential to my concerns but may none-theless be seen as alternative views.

ASIDE ONE: SECULARITY OR CAPITALISM

As my main concern is the extent to which the various innovations discussed in previous chapters represent the survival (or even revival) of religious and spiritual sentiment, I have not, beyond Chapter 1's sketchy explanation of a general secularizing trend, directly addressed what drives secularization. In general my explanation rests on the capacity of intrinsic features of religious innovations to *resist* the secular. I assume that the dominant culture of the West is now largely secular and that religions differ in their ability to protect their adherents from its siren calls. That is, we can tell the story simply in terms of minority versus majority. Any minority culture requires collective action (particularly at the stage of childhood socialization) to resist being swamped by the mainstream. The religious and the spiritual are now deviant attitudes that will survive only with considerable social effort (and with such accidental characteristics as being located in geographical peripheries that have relatively little contact with cosmopolitan culture). Such survival is imperilled by a characteristic of modernity that is also a key feature of most recent religious innovations: individualism. The assertion that lies at the heart of the New Age—that each of us has the right (indeed the obligation) to decide what is true for us and to what extent and in what manner we will commit to it—weakens the ability of contemporary religious and spiritual movements to resist the secular.[3]

Although it is not necessarily a competing explanation, it is common for the secular drift of religious innovations to be explained as capitulation to capitalism.[4] I invited such an explanation when I noted in Chapter 2 that the Findhorn Foundation has gone from promoting a revolutionary countercultural communalism to selling management training to major corporations and again in Chapter 6 when I noted that underlying much New Age philosophy was an individualism that denied the existence of structural obstacles to social mobility and wealth. As a florid example, I quote Bruce Gyngell, a successful TV executive and long-time meditator: 'I talk to people about taking their power back and explain that no one has power over you unless you are prepared to give it to them.'[5] However, though the capitulation-to-capitalism explanation seems intuitively plausible, there is a practical problem with testing it: the lack of any contrast. Since the collapse of the Soviet Union there have been so few modern non-capitalist economies—Cuba, North Korea, and to an extent China—that we have no point of comparison to allow us to separate economy from society. The economy that underlies the culture of all secular modern societies is capitalist, and it is thus difficult to distinguish which drivers of the hijack of religion are the effects of capitalist ideology and which are the results of social causes that we can imagine separate from any particular economic system.[6]

The waters are further muddied by the fact that to a certain extent capitalism and modernity share a common feature: individualism. Critics of capitalism will immediately baulk and respond that the individualism of capitalism is a sham. The idea that the free market coordinates individual preferences is a fraud designed to allow cartels and monopolies to manipulate us into thinking we are 'maximizing our utility' through personal choices in consumption when we are actually being led by the nose.

I have a lot of sympathy for that view, but, if given too much weight, it underestimates the cultural indifference of capitalism. One of the problems of left-wing denunciations of the amorality of capitalism is that they do not go far enough. Rupert Murdoch's media interests, for example, single-mindedly pursue gain. They have with equanimity supported communist China and capitalist America. They fund the rabidly right-wing Fox News and the deeply subversive Simpsons cartoon. It seems obvious to me that the interests of capitalists can be served equally well by a religious and by a secular society. The Christendom of the Middle Ages, with the Church claiming the right to determine appropriate patterns of consumption for different classes and to set 'just' prices, might cramp capitalist interests, but I cannot help but think that Andrew Carnegie or Rupert Murdoch would still have turned a groat or two. Certainly there is little in the religion of the eighteenth or nineteenth century that seriously hindered capitalism. Pious manufacturers had no difficulty squaring their Sabbath-keeping consciences with seven-day production. Pious householders kept their Lord's Day holy by keeping some servants working while they attended church. In brief, while it is practically the case that the mainstream culture to which religious innovations have largely capitulated rests on a capitalist economy,

I do not see that capitalism *requires* such capitulation, because it has been centuries since organized religion has offered any great threat to capitalist interests.

In the absence of any non-capitalist modern societies that would allow systematic comparison, we can take this argument forward only by comparing more and less capitalist economies. To do this properly would require book-length treatment, but we can at least mention the difference between Scandinavian, British, and US economies. The sceptic will say they are all the same, but the informed social scientist knows that, though the differences are eroding, those three types of society represent an array of social democratic state constraints on capital. And, within Britain, there is a distinct difference between the privatizing Blair, Brown, Cameron, and May governments that have ruled England since 1997 and the Labour and SNP governments in Scotland that, within the limits of their devolved powers, have resisted the privatization of education, the health services, and social welfare. If it was the case that the primary driver of the corruption of religion and spirituality is capitalism, we would expect the process to be more advanced in the USA than in Britain than in Scandinavia and, within Britain, more advanced in England than in Scotland. In practice, I see little difference.[7]

The idea that capitalism drives the secular drift in contemporary spirituality does have much to recommend it. TM, Insight, est, and Esalen claim, as their headline selling point, that they will help people improve their lives, and often the advertised improvement is greater capacity to succeed in the competitive world of business. Their secondary purpose is to help people become reconciled to their current circumstances. Arguably either of those purposes serves the interest of capitalism (though I can imagine est seminars fitting perfectly well with the apparatchik Communist Party culture of, say, East Germany or Bulgaria in 1960).

In sum, my first disagreement is that capitalist enterprise will flourish irrespective of the religious culture of a society and so actually has no dog in this particular race. My second is that, in practice, whatever causal weight we might wish to give capitalism as a background consideration, the foreground driver of the secular drift in religious innovations is not the interests of any particular economic system but the difficulty any minority culture (minority languages, for example) has in resisting the mainstream. The preservation of a distinctive minority culture requires insulation from the surrounding society. The Old Order Amish in the USA isolate themselves with a minority language, communal property ownership, insistence on marrying within the community, and the shunning of defectors. They sustain such deviant social practices by collectively indoctrinating their children to believe them to be required of God. In the language that is explained shortly, the Amish has a *sectarian* view of its religious culture. That does not guarantee erosion: the Amish do lose members.[8] But it offers better protection against the mainstream than does the individualism of New Age spirituality.

ASIDE TWO: WESTERNIZATION OR GLOBALIZATION?

A second tangential theoretical concern is the precise cause of what I have, somewhat flippantly, called the westernization of the easternization of the West. I have repeatedly drawn attention to the ways in which eastern religious themes (such as reincarnation) have been adapted as they have been adopted.[9] There is a plausible alternative to this characterization: what looks like westernization is actually part of a much larger and international force.[10] For example, it is said of yoga in the West:

> that these yoga systems did not develop in response to transplantation or as a result of 'cultural negotiations' between a static Indian culture and a static Western one. It was, in fact, a movement that developed in response to transnational cultural developments, namely developments in consumer culture.[11]

I am not sure that the repeated 'static' in that quotation is terribly relevant. The westernization story would work perfectly well if both East and West were changing, provided the ways in which Oriental themes and practices changed on being taken up by Westerners was in the direction of the mainstream of western culture.

It is certainly true that cultural practices change in complex ways as they spread. We have seen that, when British local education authorities supported evening classes in yoga, they classified them as physical exercise. Now Indian Prime Minister Narendra Modi—a Hindu nationalist—has established an International Yoga Day and provided a vivid photo opportunity by leading a mass synchronized postural yoga event.[12] In so doing, Modi announced that yoga was a fantastic form of exercise suitable for peoples of every culture and thus continued the process of stripping it of its spiritual associations. At the same time, he presented yoga as India's gift to the world and by that he clearly meant *Hindu* India's gift to the world. So the spiritual is downplayed but the political is emphasized in a way that fits the Hindu nationalist project of asserting the Hindu past as the core of the identity of modern India while reducing those elements of the Hindu past that hinder modernization.[13] All of which tells us that cultural exchange is complicated.

But it does not fundamentally challenge the westernization explanation. What might actually do that are changes in eastern religion that make it look more western but that have identifiable independent causes. If we imagine for a moment that the map west of Suez was a blank, would it still have been the case that yoga in India became increasingly freed from its religious background? Possibly, but this seems like a debate that has more to do with local pride than with social science theory: 'westernization' is ethnocentric but 'globalization' respects the East. It is significant that the growth of consumer culture—the shift from social class-based production to individualistic consumption as the primary source of identity—which Jain describes as an *alternative* to the westernization view, is almost precisely the account I would have given of the modernization of the West. Not only are the same changes identified but the very same sociological authorities are cited. And, given that no one doubts that the West modernized before the East and exported its culture (both directly by imposition and commercial penetration and indirectly by presenting something to be desired and emulated), there seems little value in arguing the toss.

I am quite happy to agree that some elements of eastern religion were 'westernized' in their homeland before the export process reinforced that direction of change. While the founders of what came to the West as the Divine Light Mission were determined to keep all the native Hindu elements of their faith, Maharishi Mahesh Yogi, for example, and Shree Bhagwan Rajneesh seem to have been willing to change their product to make it more attractive to a non-Indian audience *in anticipation* of recruiting in the West. I am also happy to recognize that the modernization of eastern societies can be seen as them working through the same changes as the West underwent from the late eighteenth century and need not necessarily be described in terms of the global north imposing its economy, society, and cult (though in practice that is what happened). If the East is modernizi autonomously rather than under the direction of the West, then can expect its religious culture to change. But none of this challeng my main point. It can be accommodated within this rephrasing. addition to saying that the easternization of the West has bee accompanied by subtle but effective changes to what has been bor rowed, we add 'unless such changes have already been made becaus the East is modernizing in much the same way as the West did'.

This digression has been made to pre-empt likely but misplaced criticism of the core argument of this book. All that matters for my thesis is that the eastern-inspired religious innovations (which might be claimed as proof that the demand for religion in the West is as high as ever it was) are actually quite secular.

THE SIZE OF THE GAP

If we are to argue that new religious and spiritual expressions have replaced traditional Christian church adherence, we should begin with some sense of just how much novelty is needed to fill the gap left by the decline of the Christian churches. Clearly the estimate of the gap will depend on which dates and measures of religious interest are chosen for the comparison. Because little reliable statistical information is available for any earlier period, I take the span of the twentieth century as my time period, and, rather than trying to arrive at a single figure for the secularization gap, I offer a range of estimates based on different criteria.

Church attendance can serve as the most rigorous measure of Christian interest. An extensive review of early twentieth-century attendance counts shows considerable variation but concludes: 'it is likely that the national average . . . was roughly one-quarter of adults on any given Sunday'. Clive Field adds 'two-fifths of Edwardians probably went to a place of worship at least monthly'.[14] A variety of sources put typical Sunday church attendance in 2001 between 6 and 8 per cent.[15] From British Social Attitudes survey data we can estimate 'at least monthly' attendance for 2001 as around 19 per cent.[16] These two sources of data give us an attendance gap of 19 per cent on typical Sunday attendance and 21 per cent on attending once a month or more often. For ease of calculation we can average the two and take 20 per cent as the gap in church attendance between 1900 and 2000.

For less severe measures, we can use Field's 'active involvement' (essentially membership or equivalent) or claimed affiliation. How those changed over the twentieth century is shown in Table 7.1. As we see in the top row, the difference in Field's Active figure between 1914 and 2000 is 41 per cent of the adult population. The difference in the total Christian community defined most broadly (that is, the row 3 summation of Active and Nominal) is similar at 45 per cent.

Although it is not crucial for my argument, there is something interesting in row 2: the proportion of Nominals grows before falling back. This is actually what we would expect. Decline initially took the form of the disappearance of what we might call, after Frederick Engels, the 'reserve army' of Christianity: the least attached disappeared first. In 1900 most Methodist chapels, for example, had twice as many people attending every week as they had core members. The Church of England had an even larger penumbra. Interpreting the data is a little complex, because the significance of different measures of affiliation changed: for example, over the twentieth century communion became more frequent and communicating at Christmas became more popular, while communicating at Easter declined. Nonetheless the basic pattern of change is clear. In 1870 the vicar of Easington, County Durham, reported that over the year 1,050 people attended, that 210 took communion, and that the average attendance at communion was 71. In 1886 his successor reported average attendances of 120 in the morning and 360 in the evening. There were

Table 7.1. Christian adherence, Active and Nominal, Great Britain, 1914–2000 (as percentage of population aged 15 and over)

Type of adherence	1914	1963	1980	2000
Active	52	28	21	11
Nominal	48	65	68	44
Active plus Nominal	100	93	89	55
Neither Active nor Nominal	0	7	11	45

Sources: 1914, 1963, and 1980 data derived from C. Field, *Secularization Enumerated: Revisiting Britain's 'Religious Crisis' of the Long 1960s* (Oxford: Oxford University Press), table 9.1. 2000 'Active' data estimated from church membership data in P. Brierley, *UK Church Statistics 2005–15* (Tonbridge, Kent: ABC Publishers, 2015), table 1.1. 2000 'Nominal' data are 'affiliation' figures from British Social Attitudes survey 2000 <http://www.bsa.natcen.ac.uk/media/38958/bsa28_12religion.pdf> (accessed May 2017).

ninety-four 'occasional communicants', and seventy-six people took communion at Easter; this figure is generally accurate, because Easter Day Communication was regarded as the minimum requirement for an Anglican, and it was recorded in the Register of Services at the time. However, the number claimed as 'regular communicants' was only thirty-five.[17]

Over the course of the twentieth century the penumbra declined, so that by the 1950s attendance had fallen below membership for Methodists, and that pattern continued into the 1970s. Blackhall, County Durham, in 1974 had 203 members but only 40 people attended the morning service and 76 the evening, and many of those would have been the same people. Peter Lee Memorial had 208 members on its books, but the combined attendance at its two services was 100.[18] The same for the Church of England. In 1921 vastly more people attended than were on the electoral roll. In 1982 normal Sunday attendance in a sample of rural parishes was less than their electoral rolls.[19]

One of the main ways in which the churches influenced the wider population was through their Sunday Schools. In 1900, 55 per cent of the population under 15 were enrolled in Sunday School.[20] In 1965, the figure was around 20 per cent.[21] By the end of the century, it is just 5 per cent: less than the proportion of the adult population that attends church.[22] This is not because church attenders do not take their children; it is because a large part of the churchgoing public is too old to have children to take to church.

That church membership declined more slowly than attendance is interesting for what it says about self-image. Clearly many people are reluctant to give up membership, despite never attending. The many extant chapel minute books proffer various frustrated explanations for this nominalism. Some people were reluctant to see the chapel that their grandparents built and that they attended as children close and so paid their subs despite knowing they would next attend in a wooden box. This is not facetious: the wish to be 'buried from' the family chapel was for a generation an important consideration. But another consideration was that people were reluctant to admit to themselves (as much as to any imagined audience) that they no longer believed.

This is important, because it suggests an entirely different explanation for the differences in decline in various indices of religious interest from that given by those such as Grace Davie who seek to soften the blow of secularization by showing that people are still in some sense religious. In comparing two indices, Davie takes the higher one (claimed belief in God, for example) as representing the 'real' attitude and explains the lower one (church attendance, for example) as being due to auxiliary changes such as a general decline in the willingness to join associations. My argument is almost precisely the opposite. If we take measures such as religious identification, church attendance, and religious beliefs, we find them all declining roughly in tandem but with the latter two declining more quickly than the first. This gives me confidence that the primary force is decline in belief and that what needs to be explained is why some people are slow to admit they are no longer really interested. That impression is reinforced by the remarkably thin excuses given by former churchgoers when pressed as to why they stopped attending. One said that the church he had tried had been too cold. He did not try any others. Another person said he had moved house and had not yet found a church. He not tried any.[23]

Why some people are reluctant to abandon a nominal religious attachment is complex and I will not try to explain it beyond noting that, as people became more remote from the generation for which the faith was vibrant, as the proportion of the population that was churchgoing declined, and as the expectation of a church attachment went the same way as the rolled umbrella, dog racing, and the bowler hat, so it became easier to own up to a lack of faith.

To return to the main thread of my argument, the decline of the Christian churches over the twentieth century has produced a gap of between 20 and 44 per cent of the adult population, depending on whether we take the strongest or the weakest measure of religious interest. That gives us a rough sense of the size of the secularization gap and, as will become obvious when we return to possible estimates for the popularity of new expressions of religious or spiritual sentiment, rough is fine for our present purposes.

By way of further preliminary deck-clearing, we can note that non-Christian religions have made little difference to overall levels of religiosity. In the 2001 censuses (the religion questions differed in the Scotland, England, and Wales, and Northern Ireland versions), 5.36 per cent of the British population identified with a non-Christian religion. There are no data for these faiths corresponding to the figures for Christian church attendance, but a number of surveys suggest that about 50 per cent of such religious minorities claimed to be 'religiously observant'.[24] That is almost certainly an exaggeration; the same surveys show an impossible third of nominal Christians making the same claim.[25] So let us add 2 per cent to the conventionally Christian religious to allow for the proportion of the non-Christian population that can reasonably be guessed to be religious observant. The new religious movements of the late 1960s are irrelevant to such calculations. We have no data from the England and Wales census, but the differently worded Scottish version tells us that in 2001 there were fifty-eight Scientologists, twenty-five Hare Krishnas, and no Moonies; they would all fit on one big bus.[26]

The above is a long way round the houses, but it is important to be clear about just how much new religion or spirituality would be required to sustain the claim that religion is not declining but simply changing its shape. If new religious or spiritual expressions are to fill the gap left by the decline of the Christian churches, they would need to have been taken up by something between 18 and 38 per cent of the population.

THE RISE OF THE NONES

A second possible yardstick for testing the 'not-decline-just-change' position is the number of people who disclaim, or who decline to claim, any sort of religious interest. Field summarizes a very wide range of statistical sources to conclude that declaring one had no religion was almost unknown at the start of the twentieth century.[27] In 1983—its first year of operation—the British Social Attitudes survey gave 'No Religion' as 33 per cent followed by a steady rise to 47 per cent in 2011–12. The longest running of the major British social science surveys—the British Election Studies—starts in 1974 with 34 per cent saying they have no religion. In 2010 the figure was 48 per cent.[28] One 2016 poll has the 'No Religion' figure for white British respondents at over 50 per cent.[29] So a conservative estimate would put the proportion of people willing to say they had no religion as having risen over the twentieth century from perhaps 5 to at least 40 per cent. In case it be thought that reporting such assertions of identity is cherry-picking the data, we can add that all the indices for the religious sanctification of rites of passage show a similar trajectory. In the 1960s about 70 per cent of weddings were religious; in 2003 fewer than a third were, and humanist weddings had gone from 0.3 per cent of all non-Registry Office weddings in 2000 to 11.4 per cent in 2009. The state does not collect data on funerals, but we know that humanist celebrations were only 0.6 per cent of all deaths in 2000 but 5.4 per cent in 2009, and even funerals conducted by clergy have changed from being reminders of key religious themes to being largely secular celebrations of the life of the deceased.[30]

The actual numbers are less important than the rough scale. For the case that religion in Britain is not declining but merely changing its form to be plausible, the proportion of the population interested in new forms of religious and spiritual interest would have to have kept pace with the rate of growth of the percentage declaring they had no religion. Anything less would guarantee that the total of the religious (that is, the conventionally religious plus the unconventionally religious and the spiritual) would be outstripped by the growth in the secular. That is, religion would not just be changing; it would also be declining.

It was clear from Chapter 2 that the number of people directly associated with specific religious innovations (such as the new religious movements of the late 1960s) was tiny: often fewer than 1,000. Grand claims that suppose otherwise, when examined closely, invariably prove to have little foundation. For example, the BBC in 2003 reported there were 'as many as' (a nicely slippery formulation) 10,000 Druids. In 2010 the Druid Network—one of the best organized and most popular groups—reported 350 members.[31] The 2011 census in England and Wales showed 4,189 Druids—still not halfway to the BBC's figure.[32]

THE ZOMBIE OF PREVIOUS IMPIETY

The idea that modernization weakens religion obviously rests on the claim that, at whatever point in the past we use for our comparison—and I would take any time from the tenth to the end of the nineteenth century as that point—people were more religious than they are now.[33] It is sometimes asserted that just how religious were the people of the Middle Ages or the nineteenth century is an open question—the implication being that the correct answer is 'not very'. This is a stance that could be struck only by someone who knows little of the work of British historians, because religious beliefs and behaviour are probably the best-documented aspects of social life. The Christian Church (and post-Reformation, Christian churches) were assiduous in collecting and keeping data. We know precisely how many of the people of the village of Goodnestone-next-Wingham in Kent attended Mass at Easter 1676, because the priest recorded it in a report to his bishop in which he also explained the absences.[34] Many wills, from different times and places, survive, and they give a good indication of what the testators thought was important. Before the Protestant Reformation ended the belief that the living could hasten the souls of the dead out of purgatory and into heaven, almost all wills left money to enlist the living in the service of the dead.

> If we take four wills of 1499 ... we discover John Breteyn of Stotfold leaving measures of barley for the provision of candles to burn before images and for the repair of bells; John Lord of Millbrook leaving barley and a cow for candles and 20s towards the price of a great bell... Richard Curteys of Hill in Warden leaving barley for candles and the bells; and William Gere of Sharnbrook leaving 1s for the maintenance of the bells and lesser sums for lights to burn before the images in the church. These men were small farmers or country craftsmen; they had wives, sons and daughters; they did not have much to spare for the church; they gave generously of what they did have.[35]

We also have the obvious architectural testimony to the power of faith. Until the Victorian era the largest man-made structures were religious. We have the evidence, not just of the great cathedrals but also of the thousands of parish churches and of nonconformist chapels. When travelling, people oriented themselves by the spires and towers of churches, and churches gave us many of our place names. In Cheshire one can find Church Shocklach, Church Minshull, Church Lawton, and Church Hulme. Scotland has a similar pattern with 'Kirk' as in Kirk Yetholm, Kirkliston, and Kirkton of Auchterless. When clocks were rare, church bells marked the hours. They also announced deaths, as in John Donne's famous quotation: 'Send not to ask for whom the bell tolls.'[36]

The interiors of those churches and chapels offer further eloquent testimony to the power of belief. The iconoclasts of the Reformation stripped many of their interior furnishings, but sufficient remains to show us how seriously people took their faith. Important for those who could not read well, walls were covered with paintings of Bible stories, but the most compelling illustration was the 'doom': a vivid depiction of the hell that awaited those who failed to live the Christian life. An even more arresting mark of an almost macabre interest in the life post-mortem was the cadaver tomb: a stone coffin awaiting the recipient that was decorated with a life-size model of his skeleton eaten by worms, snakes, and toads. A man who paid for such a reminder of his eventual fate, which he looked on every time he attended church, was a man who took his religion seriously.[37]

The sceptic may say that much religious observance was driven by social pressure to conform, but that simply takes the argument on a slight detour before bringing it back on track. Some people might have doubted the Church's teachings (or more likely doubted the need for them to attend Mass or to pay tithes), but most did attend and did pay their tithes, which tells us that religion, as a social institution, was extremely powerful. If some attendance was 'mere' conformity, there must have been strong pressure to conform and that pressure must have come from those who believed. Social institutions, especially ones that consume considerable time and capital, are not invented and sustained for centuries by people who do not believe in them. And, unless we suppose that the Christian Church was unusually inept, it is difficult to see how a social institution with so much ideological power could dominate a society but fail to indoctrinate successfully the people whom it dominated.

One version of scepticism about the strength of the religious culture in previous centuries concerns the supposed political effects of religion. It is argued that the upper classes indoctrinated the common people to become religious in order to defuse such revolutionary potential as may have existed.[38] But even this requires that people believe.

Claims that the people of pre-modern or early modern Britain were not really that religious usually rest on just one authority: Keith Thomas's magisterial *Religion and the Decline of Magic*.[39] Thomas offers many examples of church courts trying to discipline people for unacceptable behaviour. Sometimes that involved an impious attitude to religious offices or disrespect for the Church, but more often it involved supplementing the Church's teachings with magic and superstition. In another context the difference between magic, superstition, and religion might matter, but when we are trying to gauge the extent of change between the sixteenth century and the present day they can be taken together. That some people in the past were deviantly religious is not the same as them being secular.

To summarize thus far, the secularization thesis is sometimes criticized for presuming some golden age of faith as the front end of its comparison.[40] It need not. It requires only that the people of the past be markedly more religious than they are now, and, although the zombie of inappropriate scepticism will doubtless return, the above should be enough for most readers to settle the matter.

CYCLES AND TRAJECTORIES

As part of my argument that the secular trumps the spiritual, I have shown that many of our religious innovations have gradually become more secular. It is possible to accept that case and still reject the secularization thesis. One could argue that such a process of religious attenuation is common and cyclical: it is not the first time once-radical religious movements have gradually compromised with the prevailing culture and it will not be the last. In its first centuries, Christianity itself changed from marginal underground sect to wealthy religious orthodoxy compromised by its association with power. In Northern Europe Martin Luther's Reformation settled into a comfortable slipper-wearing old age as the national Lutheran churches. When the Free Church split from the Church of Scotland in 1843, it was overwhelmingly evangelical. By the time it returned to the national church a half-century later it was largely liberal. The Primitive Methodists who reunited with the Wesleyan Methodists in 1932 a century after they had left what they then denounced as spiritually compromised were able so to do only because they had lost the radical edge that had earned them the sobriquet 'Primitive'. Seen in the context of that familiar pattern, Findhorn's loss of radical purpose and the drift of various new religious expressions from world rejecting to world affirming could simply be instances of a universal phenomenon rather than evidence of the secularizing influence of modernization.

The elaboration of definitions is tedious but they are useful for describing certain patterns of change. Sociologists use the terms church, sect, denomination, and cult to describe four very different ways in which religions can be organized and can present themselves. Unfortunately, scholars differ in their use of these terms, and scholarly usage differs from common usage. Hence some conceptual clarification is necessary before we can proceed.

The church type is exemplified by Christianity in Britain in the Middle Ages. It claimed a monopoly of representing the people to God and vice versa. As it had to encompass the entire society, it had to accept considerable laxity in religious observance, though it did not tolerate rebellion. It had a professional clergy that placated God on behalf of the common people and it allowed the transfer of religious merit from the clergy to the laity and from the pious to those who fell short. Those who feared for their souls could pay others to pray for them. It also had to be politically and socially conservative and to be on good terms with the ruling classes: it could hardly be radical and hope to retain its position of social domination.

The sect is a very different creature. It interprets the teachings of Jesus in a literal and radical manner. It is a small, voluntary fellowship of converts who live the divine law in their own behaviour and who reject the notion of merit transfer. It espouses ideals of frugality and poverty, it stresses the religious equality of believers, and—if it permits religious professionals at all—it makes no sharp distinction between them and the laity.[41]

The third type—the denomination—is either the church displaced or the sect grown old.[42] It is liberal and tolerant in its teachings. It accepts the validity of alternatives. It lacks radical fervour and it makes few demands of society as a whole and barely more of its own members. Although most Christian organizations describe themselves as churches, in practice those in the West are now denominations, because their ability to impose on the society at large has been eroded by factionalism and by the growth of religious freedom.

This book has been largely concerned with the fourth type of religious organization. The cult embodies tendencies towards religion of a strictly private, personal character. Its structure is loose. Its goals are those of personal ecstatic experience, salvation, comfort, and mental and physical healing. One joins a sect—an activity that implies that others have the right to confer or refuse membership and to set standards of performance—but one does not really join a cult. One simply picks up certain beliefs or ritual practices. In fact, to talk of 'a' cult is often misleading. Given that most cult organizations are almost passive providers of resources to people who make of them what they will, it makes more sense to talk of a 'cultic milieu'.[43]

We should note that this usage differs importantly from that of tabloid newspapers, which treat the sect and the cult as pretty much the same thing, differing only in degree of unacceptability. A sect is bad; a cult is very bad. For an example, consider the following *Daily Mail* headline: 'Religious status for Druids. The police trained to respect witches. Pagans are on the march—but are they harmless eccentrics or a dangerous cult?'[44]

How the four types of religion fit together and fit their environments is neatly summarized in Figure 7.1. What distinguishes the two *rows* is the status the organization claims for its core teachings. The church and the sect share the common feature of believing that it and only it has the saving truth: they are, in Roy Wallis's terms, 'uniquely legitimate'. Thus, Roman Catholics until recently, and the Exclusive Brethren still, are similar in the view that only they are going to heaven and everyone else is in trouble. In some settings, the Catholic Church acts more like a denomination, but the core principle of the Vatican remains unchanged. What it has is the truth and what everyone else has is heresy.

What distinguishes the two *columns* is how the outside world sees the religious organization. What separate the Catholic Church from the Exclusive Brethren are size and success. In many Christian countries, the Catholic Church has a monopoly, and in most others, it is a powerful force. Hence it is respectable. The Exclusive Brethren is a very small sect that is widely regarded as deviant. Indeed, it is so unpopular that it is currently being investigated by the Charities Commission, which has the power to remove the official status as a charity, which almost all religious organizations enjoy in the UK.[45]

Let us consider the second row. What the denomination—the Methodists, the Church of Scotland, and the Church of England are examples—and the cult have in common is that they do not claim a

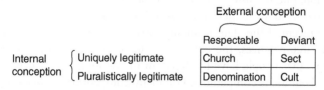

Figure 7.1. Four types of religious organization.

Source: R. Wallis, 'The Cult and its Transformation', in R. Wallis (ed.), *Sectarianism: Analyses of Religious and Non-Religious Sects* (London: Peter Owen, 1975), 35–49.

unique possession of the truth. They think they have something to offer, that you might be better off being a Methodist than a Baptist, but they recognize other organizations as being valid. Again, what separates them is the top line: the extent to which they have succeeded in establishing themselves. The Methodists are a respectable part of our social and cultural landscape; cults are not.

The above distinctions are based on clutches of characteristics that both are historical and logically cohere. However, while many organizations are very clearly of a certain type—Scientology is very obviously sectarian—others straddle the lines. The Baptist Church, for example, has denominational and sectarian elements. Some organizations vary with place. For example, the Catholic Church in Poland still tries to act as if it had the presence and powers of the medieval Church, while its American counterpart has largely and for a long time accepted its denominational status. Those qualifications do not prevent the four terms being useful, especially to describe change. Two patterns are common. It is the second one that is central to my thesis, but the first is an important part of the general background.

Church to Denomination

When all, or almost all, of the population belong to one religious organization, it is possible for it to see itself in the church form and to behave like a church. But, when a population becomes divided between a number of organizations, that fragmentation undermines the conditions for the church form in two ways.

If the state regards all citizens as being of roughly equal worth, it can no longer much privilege one religion over another. It has to become increasingly neutral. All but one of the colonies that originally formed the United States of America had an established church, funded out of taxation, but, because they were not the same church, the US Constitution offered the modern promise. It both guaranteed religious liberty and prevented the state from supporting any particular religion. In such circumstances, the church has to become a denomination. It accepts that people have the freedom to choose and that it is in the same boat as its competitors. Gradually competition between organizations reduced and inter-denominational cooperation increased.

Second, there is the social psychology of the pluralistic culture. It is easy to believe that your religion is absolutely right in every detail when there is no alternative. Every increase in competition makes that dogmatism more and more difficult to maintain. If the competing faith is carried by some subordinate minority, it can be dismissed as fitting only for 'people like that', but when small communities of socially similar people start to fragment so that, for example, some stay in the Church of Scotland and some go to the Free Church down the road and some attend a Baptist meeting around the corner and you live and work with these people, it becomes ever more difficult to insist that your own link with God is unique and the others are all wrong. Gradually the way in which people hold their beliefs changes, so that certainty and intolerance diminish, and we end up with the denominational position of supposing that most previously competing organizations are, in their different ways, doing God's work.

Sect to Denomination

It is common that once-radical sects, critical of the mundane world, lose their critical edge, drop stringent entry requirements, reduce the demands they make of members, and become generally become more liberal and tolerant.[46] There are a number of reasons for this.

The first generation of members sought out and voluntarily accepted the demands of the sect. They often made considerable sacrifices for their beliefs. The people who broke away from the state churches in England and Scotland in the eighteenth and early nineteenth centuries often suffered considerable political, social, and financial penalties. They had property confiscated, they were excluded from political office, and they were even threatened with the removal of their children. When one makes that kind of sacrifice, one has a lot invested and hence a great deal of commitment. But the children and grandchildren of the sect founders did not join voluntarily. They inherited their identity and, even when the greatest effort is put into socializing subsequent generations into the sect's ideology, it is almost inevitable that their commitment will be less than that of their parents.[47]

This is even more so the case if, as is common, the sect members enjoyed considerable upward social mobility. The case of the British Quakers is well known. Because their dissent from the state church precluded them from the professions and from public office, many Quakers were in manufacture and trade and they flourished, especially in the promotion of chocolate and tea as alternatives to alcohol: the Cadburys, Rowntrees, and Hornimans are examples. Their reputation for scrupulous honesty allowed the banks owned by the Barclays, Trittons, Backhouses, and Gurneys to prosper. As a result, every generation of Quakers was considerably better-off than its parents and hence had more to lose by remaining so much at odds with the world. Hence they faced greater temptation to compromise. Or, to put it another way, it is always easier to accept an ascetic lifestyle if you cannot afford anything else. And it is easy to be socially deviant when you have no social status or prestige to lose. The prosperous 'Gay Quakers', as they were known, became increasingly liberal Quakers, then moved into the evangelical wing of the Church of England, then the mainstream, and finally became secular like everyone else.[48]

But, even before the second generation matures, there may be strong pressures to moderate. Many sects are in some sense *millennial* or *millenarian*. Strictly speaking, the millennium is the Christian idea of the thousand years of paradise that will occur when Christ returns. Part of the spur for the initial enthusiasm of the sect is the idea that the end of the world is nigh and the saints have to prepare themselves for it. There is no expectation that the high levels of commitment displayed at the start will have to be maintained for long. Once a few decades have passed, and the world has not ended, the sect has to get used to a long future. Few of the new religious movements we have been considering were millennialist in the classic sense, but many shared the view that their task was in some sense final. In its early days, the founders of Findhorn thought they were about to be saved from the end of the world by Venusian spacemen. Later they saw themselves as the light that would transform the world.[49] The Moonies (aka the Unification Church) thought they were living in the times of the new messiah. When the first generation started to marry and raise families, the sect had to accept that commitment would be reduced and that the demands made of members had to be scaled down so as to fit into a conventional family life. The same happened with Hare Krishna and Rajneeshism.

So Where are the New Sects?

Although both patterns described above are commonplace, they differ in one important regard. The shift from church to denomination does not produce dissenting schism. Many conservatives will resent the church's loss of social domination, but such domination cannot be regained by schism. Indeed, schism is patently self-defeating, because it weakens the church and reduces further its claims to social power and prestige. And the dissidents lack the power to reverse the changes they dislike. They can fight for the restoration of a few peripheral elements. English conservatives have succeeded in restoring the Book of Common Prayer (BCP). Or to be more precise, they have had the BCP restored to the list of many permitted liturgical forms. But they do not even try to persuade parliament to restore the land tax funding of the Church of England or restore its powers to coerce conformity: non-Anglicans are not about to lost the right to vote, to hold public office, or to own property.

However, the sect to denomination pattern is to an extent cyclical. And this is what allows opponents of the secularization thesis to deny the significance of the changes documented in the previous chapters. As the Wesleyan Methodists lost their radical edge, some members broke away to form alternative Methodist movements that were, they believed, more faithful to the original intent. As the Brethren became more liberal and tolerant, the Excusive Brethren claimed to keep alight the original flame. When the once-evangelical Free Church of Scotland moderated enough to plan to merge with the Seceder Presbyterians, a group broke away to form the Free Presbyterian Church. When the combined Free Church/Seceder body returned to the national Church in 1929, another segment broke away and claimed to be the true Free Church. At the end of the twentieth century, both those already small bodies split along conservative and liberal lines.[50]

This is indeed a repeated pattern, and it may at first sight support the view that there is nothing terribly significant in the many cases of secular drift I have documented in the previous chapters. However, two things suggest otherwise. The first is that the cyclical pattern of sect-to-denomination drift involves decline. The numbers involved in each turn of the wheel are fewer and fewer. As a result of the Reformation, the entire national Church of Scotland (barring some very small dissident groups) became rigorously evangelical Protestant. When in 1843 evangelicals split off from the national church to form the Free Church, they took more than a third of the people. When conservatives dissented from the Free Church's increased liberalism, the two schismatic groups—the 1893 Free Presbyterians and the 1929 Free Church—together were only some 1 per cent of the size of the Church of Scotland.[51] The most recent schisms have been even smaller, involving only a few hundred people. The secular drift and conservative schism are not a cycle within an otherwise stable religious economy. It is the way that decline happens. The tide comes in and the tide goes out, but the high-water mark is lower each time.[52]

The other important observation is that the secular drift in the new religious movements of the late 1960s and in the cultic milieu of New Age spirituality has not produced significant new challengers. There is no new reformed ISKCON or TM or Divine Light Mission. The case for the cultic milieu is more difficult to establish because, by definition, it is already amorphous and fluid in organization. But the same rhetorical question can be posed. Where are the countercultural challenges to the Findhorn Foundation's abandonment of its original revolutionary purpose? Where are the British Buddhist organizations that reject the marketing of meditation as largely secular mindfulness? If I, and Jeremy Carrette, and Richard King and others, are correct in seeing contemporary holistic spirituality as a compromise with the secular, where are the more rigorous and countercultural alternatives?

INDIVIDUALISM AND RELATIVISM

Historians naturally dislike the details of their time and place being submerged in sweeping generalization, but it is reasonable to suggest that, since the initial victory of Christendom, attitudes to religious conformity have shifted through three distinct positions. In the Middle Ages it was taken for granted that we inhabited a unitary world and that there was one religious truth that, having been ascertained, should be imposed on everyone. Religion was not separated from such other forms of knowledge as what we would now call geography or metallurgy or astronomy: religion, like science, was either right or wrong. The post-Reformation fragmentation of the religious culture caused first an increase in violence and coercion and then the gradual growth of toleration. Dating this shift is difficult, because it occurs at different times in different societies, but the 1648 Peace of Westphalia is an important early marker. A series of treaties brought to an end long-running wars that had been at least in part informed by religion, and it established the principle that each state should follow the religion of its ruler and that each state should recognize the right of others to disagree. The toleration of disagreement within states took longer, in part because eighteenth- and nineteenth-century notions of nationalism supposed that a state's citizens or monarchic subjects should share a common culture.[53] But, especially in states with a high degree of religious diversity, two things allowed the growth of toleration: the spread of the proto-democratic idea that all people were in some sense much-of-a-muchness and the discovery that religious conformity was not essential for stability. In the UK, all the various Acts designed to impose uniformity were gradually repealed or ignored. The Roman Catholic Relief Act of 1829 can stand as a convenient marker of the final acceptance of religious freedom in the UK. Its primary driver was agitation in Ireland, but it also removed such disabilities as a ban from voting or holding public office from English and Scots Catholics. Reasons for supporting Catholic emancipation were many and varied. When the Duke of Wellington (then Prime Minister) threatened George IV that he would resign unless the Act was passed, he may have been swayed by his experience of commanding Catholic troops; he was certainly concerned with placating the Irish. Many Scottish evangelical Protestants supported emancipation for the less-than-generous reason that they thought it would make easier the conversion of Scots Catholics. Thomas Chalmers believed that his missionary work among the Catholics of Glasgow was hampered by their resentment at the lack of equality: deliver a level playing field and the true faith would conquer all!

It is important to note that toleration in this context concerned only social rights and social interaction and not truth. Like the Peace of Westphalia, it was an agreement to disagree in a manner that recognized the right of others to be wrong. Many minority religions supported the shift because it protected them from an oppressive majority: the logic that Thomas Jefferson used in 1802 to justify the separation of church and state to the Baptists of Danbury.[54] Although some Protestants were moving to the modern ecumenical position of supposing that a variety of apparently competing Christian views could all in some sense be equally valid, outright relativism was rare until the 1970s. The overall consequences of toleration were confined by religion being regarded as a unique form of knowledge. There were many religions; there was only one physics and one chemistry. Parents could withdraw their children from such collective acts of worship as schools retained because religion was a preference; they could not withdraw them from maths or chemistry.[55]

As explained in Chapter 2, the position of many New Agers is importantly different. It is not toleration in just the behavioural sense but epistemological relativism. It denies the possibility of one truth (except at the highest level of abstraction) and instead supposes that each of us has his or her own truth. This can come in degrees. At its most extreme, it denies the unity of knowledge in any field. Geography, metallurgy, biology, religion: every sphere of knowledge is relativized. A good marker for this attitude is the denial of the value or importance of professional training and formal qualifications. Does it matter if your healer has any formal training in anatomy? No; what matters is your experience. If it works for you, then it is correct. Intuition replaces knowledge.[56]

Such relativism is often justified by an appeal to egalitarianism. To insist on credentials is elitist. No one has the right to tell anyone else what he or she should believe. As the eloquent American quoted in Chapter 5 put it: 'Don't fuck with anyone else's business, you know.'[57] Why does this matter? It matters because it removes a necessary condition for the creation and maintenance of any shared religion. The mechanism may be conversion rather than coercion, but the growth of any form of religion or spirituality that has more than a handful of adherents who have coincidentally come to the same conclusions requires one person telling another what he or she should believe. David Martin, the most thoughtful critic of the conventional secularization thesis, nonetheless recognized the corrosive impact of relativism when he recounted the attitude of one of his grandchildren, who had expressed, without the expletives, precisely the same view as our American spiritual seeker: no one had a right to argue with someone else's beliefs. Martin added ruefully that such a position, if widespread, was the end of western religion.[58] And he is right.

SUMMARY

The major part of the evidence for secularization is not in doubt. Christianity has declined drastically, and various innovations in the Christian realm (such as the charismatic movement), interesting as they are, have not stemmed that overall decline.[59] The import of major world religions through immigration has made little impact on the religious composition of the UK—less than 6 per cent of the 2011 population were Muslim, Hindu, or Buddhist—and very little of that was the result of the conversion of the indigenous population. Furthermore, a good case can be made for arguing that those imported religions have made it less, not more, likely that the indigenous population will become more religious, because it has created the very strong impression that religion is alien. It is something that foreigners do.[60]

This book has addressed the rest of the UK's religious culture: the new religious movements of the late 1960s and the cultic milieu known variously as New Age, alternative, contemporary, or holistic spirituality. In statistical terms this realm is trivial, but that fact seems to have eluded those who wish to use either new religious movements or the New Age cultic milieu as proof that the British are as religious as ever they were. Such secularization deniers have also failed to appreciate the significance of the way those religious and spiritual innovations have changed. In defence of the case that the secular beats the spiritual, I have argued that:

a. the new religious movements of the late 1960s never recruited anything like the number of people needed to sustain the 'just-change' view;

b. the movements that did best were the least religious or the most secular;

c. world-affirming movements (which are, by and large, the most secular) did better than world-rejecting ones;

d. most of those that survived more than a decade did so by becoming more, not less, secular;

e. attempts to measure serious interest in spirituality have failed to find any evidence that it is in any conventional sense of the word 'popular'; and

f. while it is the case that eastern religious themes have proved attractive to some in the West, they have often been changed in ways that looks like capitulation to the West's secular culture.

The above may seem a long way to get to this point, but it is important that what may otherwise seem like a casual insult be well founded: the secular has indeed beaten the spiritual.

There is one final observation that has largely been overlooked by those who argue that new expressions of religious and spiritual interest are filling the gap left by the decline of conventional religion: the proportion of the population that rejects, or declines to claim, any description as religious or spiritual is growing at a rate that far outstrips any possible growth of interest in the religious and spiritual. If the less than 2 per cent of the population of Kendal that engaged in some putatively spiritual activity (which was actually not seen as spiritual by half of them) counts as the 'Spiritual Revolution', then the fact that, since the start of the twentieth century, the proportion of us who say we have no religion has gone from almost zero to almost half surely deserves to be called the 'secular revolution'.

This is for the reader to judge, but I believe the previous chapters have done enough to demonstrate three senses in which contemporary, alternative, or New Age spirituality has failed.

First, while it is the case that spirituality has increased in popularity as conventional religion has declined, that growth has not been anywhere like sufficient to support the idea that people have an essential need (probably rooted in biology) for something like religion. The decline of the Christian churches, by removing their power to stigmatize competing ideas as dangerously deviant, has created social space for alternatives. And such alternatives have proliferated. But the numbers of people seriously interested in them are very small.

Second, the general tenor of the alternatives that have proliferated has been 'eastern'. We see this both in the origins of many of the products popular in the cultic milieu (India for yoga, meditation and Ayurvedic medicine, Japan for Reiki, China for acupuncture, and so on) and in the underlying principles (reincarnation in place of the Christian heaven, for example, or karma in place of divine judgement). However, what prevents Colin Campbell's description of the 'easternization of the West' being entirely accurate is the fact that the western appropriation of eastern religious themes has been accompanied by a considerable reshaping of those themes. What we have actually seen is the westernization of the easternization of the West.

Third, the move from religion to spirituality has not had any great direct impact on public life. The reasons are simple. The individualistic epistemology of New Age spirituality prevents the sort of concerted social action that allowed William Wilberforce's eighteenth-century evangelicals to have influence well in excess of their numbers.[61] For all that New Agers talk about community, they have actually created very few enduring social institutions (such as schools, colleges, hospices, drug-treatment programmes, and charitable works).[62]

Even without social institutions, there could still have been a considerable social effect through changes to the lives of large numbers of individuals, taken severely rather than jointly. There has not been. Much spiritual transformation is in attitudes to circumstances rather than to circumstances themselves. The banker who learns to control his anxiety by practising TM's meditation for fifteen minutes each day does not cease to be a banker. His internal apprehension, but not his external reality, changes. Insight or est seminar training similarly does far more to reconcile people to their circumstances than to change them. True, a few bankers have chucked it in (after making enough to buy that smallholding in Wales) but much involvement in contemporary spirituality is sufficiently directed to states of mind that its effects are literally negligible, in the sense that everyone except those very close to the convert can neglect them.

A related reason why spirituality has little social impact is that such effects on behaviour as it does have are lost to sight when the changes that spiritual adepts make in their lives coincide with changes that other people make for entirely secular reasons. When the early English Quakers decided to demonstrate the equality of all believers in the eyes of God by refusing to defer to their social superiors, they made sure that their protest was noticed by adopting as the headwear they would not remove in the presence of their masters, hats with very wide brims. The changes that the seriously spiritual now might make to their behaviour—giving up stimulants, becoming vegetarian or vegan, displaying Tibetan prayer flags or Buddha statues, campaigning for animal rights, voting Green, reducing their energy consumption—are barely noticeable, because they coincide with what many others do for secular reasons.

All of this leads me to conclude that, as a supposed rebuttal of secularization, contemporary spirituality is a damp squib.

SOCIO-MORAL EVALUATION

Although sociology is mainly concerned with description and explanation rather than moral judgement, where claims to morality rest on sociological principles, some sort of evaluation is reasonable.

Many criticisms of the subjective turn in religion boil down to religious rivalry. The New Age is bad because it worships the wrong Gods or it worships the right Gods in the wrong way. As the existence or nature of God is beyond the competence of the social sciences, we can leave that aside.

Four putative faults are more properly our concern: the inappropriate personalizing of failure, the critique of expertise, an inappropriate denigration of social roles, and the inadvertent encouragement of sexual exploitation.

Although it often presents itself as countercultural, New Age thinking shares with the political right an unfortunate tendency to overlook social-structural obstacles to material prosperity. The claim that we create our own reality or that we can have or can be anything we want or that 'visualizing' some goal will deliver it ignores the blunt fact that there are social forces beyond the control of most of us. That African-Americans in the USA are vastly more likely than their white contemporaries to be charged with serious offences, convicted, and incarcerated is not a consequence of their lack of spiritual awareness or their failure to 'visualize'. It is a consequence of racism. That the contemporary working class in the UK has very little chance of upward social mobility is not a personal failing to be cured with Mindfulness Meditation or yoga. It is a consequence of the class structure created by capitalism and the ability of those at the top to pass their advantages to their children. The Findhorn Foundation may have prospered by 'divine manifestation', but the poverty of the UK's chronically ill is not explained by their failure divinely to manifest their needs. It is a consequence of the austerity policies followed by post-2010 governments. The attitudes of individuals may explain why one particular working-class child escapes the constraints of his or her upbringing, and social structures do change, but in any particular time and place there are structures that confine and limit. To assert that embracing some new expression of religious or spiritual sentiment will allow all or most adherents to defy social structures is not just bad social science; it is adding insult to injury.

A second reasonable criticism is that contemporary spirituality's insistence on the right of every individual to determine the truth, which is often operationalized as a reliance on personal intuition, undermines the principles that have driven the development of science, technology, and medicine. We can build bridges, tunnels, and tall buildings. We can create medicines that cure once-fatal ailments and replace defective body parts. We can steadily improve our understanding of the material world. All because we have developed attitudes, procedures, and systems that allow us gradually to replace error with truth. Philosophers of science still argue about what precisely distinguishes science from pseudo-science, but there is widespread agreement that systematic experimentation, comparison of large-scale datasets, training in, and building on, agreed principles, and testing of levels of competence are all significant. For the sake of brevity, let us call this 'expertise'. Quite rightly, none of my colleagues in the Molecular Chemistry department would pay any attention to my views on the structure of molecules (were I to have any), because I have no training or credentials in molecular chemistry. More concretely, no civil engineer will pay any attention to my views on the best ways to reinforce concrete, because this is a field of knowledge that I have yet to enter, let alone traverse. When contemporary spirituality, with its insistence that no one has any right to tell anyone else what to believe, strays into the material world—as it does when it shades into 'alternative' medicine or when it makes implausible claims for the power of the 'heart' (often presented as a superior source of judgement to the mind)—it not only makes dangerously mistaken specific claims but it also muddies the waters in a way that weakens our ability to continue our recent great advances in scientific knowledge. When incautious practitioners of the Bowen method of minimal massage claim that they can cure multiple sclerosis, they are endangering any MS sufferers who take those claims seriously enough to neglect the conventional treatments that are vastly better supported by the evidence. But there is a further danger: to the extent that approaches to knowledge that value intuition above expertise, the heart above the head, are promoted, understanding of, and commitment to, the rational pursuit of knowledge is weakened. Snake-oil cures threaten those taken in by them; snake-oil thinking threatens the science base of modern civilization. Some New Agers will respond that modern science and technology are destroying the world and making people ill. It is true that the rapid growth both of population and of our ability to exploit the planet's resources creates enormous challenges, but it is also true that only science offers ways of measuring precisely the deleterious effects of modernity and only science offers any hope of solutions. There are not enough smallholdings in rural Scotland and Wales to accommodate—at any standard of living—the population of British cities. And the spells of Kevin the White Witch might protect the Loch Ness Monster from prying eyes, but they will not protect the world's reefs from deathly bleaching or the oceans from pollution by plastics.

Thirdly, there are good sociological reasons to be critical of the New Age stress on authenticity. Authenticity is often presented as the superior alternative to relationships based on patterns of inter-locking social roles: master and servant, worker and boss, parent and child, doctor and patient, teacher and pupil. People who act as they do because they have been socialized into a particular role are not properly human; true humanity resides in the pre-social. Actually, such systems of interlocking roles are essential both for social order and for stable personalities. Any group larger than can regularly meet face-to-face requires that its members be coordinated by roles that direct their occupants and that shape the expectations of those who interact with them. For schools to function effectively, it must be clear to teachers and to pupils how they are supposed to behave and what they can expect from each other. Such regularity cannot be achieved by every teacher and every pupil working out, for themselves, how they are supposed to relate. Patients learn expect-ations of doctors and correspondingly doctors have expectations of patients. Social roles can be more or less confining, but they cannot be dismissed as 'inauthentic' without the very possibility of conjoint action being undermined. The Findhorn Foundation and the Samye Ling monastery were nearly destroyed at birth by their failure to impose limits on the freedom of those who wished to join them. They stabilized only when they imposed role expectations and coerced those who were reluctant to accept authority. This is not a defence of any particular kind of organization but it is a defence of *some kind* of organization, and organizations are simply systems of interlocking roles, differing only from those of, say, parent and child in having narrow goals.

A related justification for the efficacy of social roles is that they stabilize the personality and protect the individual. As social scientists as varied as Emile Durkheim, Arnold Gehlen, and Peter Berger have argued, the relative freedom from instincts that explains the enor-mous human capacity to innovate potentially creates serious prob-lems for the human.[63] Unlike other animals whose desires and actions are largely fixed by their instinctual apparatus, humans poten-tially inhabit a condition of 'world-openness'. Imagine away our childhood socialization, and we could wish for anything. Worse, it seems that the satisfaction of desires merely encourages the expansion and diversification of those desires. When I was a pedestrian, I wanted a car. When I got a Citroen 2CV, I wanted a car with four cylinders. When I got a small Vauxhall, I wanted a big Vauxhall. Now that I have a big car, I wonder if I might not be better off with three cars: one for the commute to the city, one for driving on the winter's snow and ice, and one for cruising down the motorways. The solution we have evolved is to institutionalize certain expectations. In the place of the internal skeleton of instincts, we stabilize the personality with the external skeleton of institutionalized norms and values. Modern societies are far more fluid than pre-modern ones; they are 'characterized by constant innovation, rationality and reflectivity, and by a corresponding sense of the unreliability and changeability of all social order'.[64] But the psychological problems such openness creates are not solved by claiming the problems are virtues that need extending rather than curtailing.

The protection of the individual is a less obvious function of social roles. What is clear from a detailed acquaintance with New Agers is that strivers after authenticity often seem to be extremely sensitive and vulnerable.[65] Given that many proponents of New Age philosophies assert the primacy of the unsocialized child over the role-constrained and repressed adult, it does not seem too critical to describe much New Age interaction as 'childish'. It might be that this tells us more about the personalities of those attracted to the New Age than about the principles of the New Age itself, but the sheer frequency of such references suggests otherwise, and a sociological understanding of the nature of roles offers a plausible explanation of the problem. The division of society into a variety of spheres, and the consequent fragmentation of roles, allows any individual a degree of freedom. Roles can be played 'tongue-in-cheek', with what symbolic interactionists call 'role distance'. We can sometimes limit our investment in any particular role. Clearly roles differ in the extent to which we permit or expect role distance. We would frown on a hospital chaplain counselling a dying patient or a father caring for a terminally ill child who too readily displayed that he was not thoroughly involved in his performance, but even for such roles we can see the virtue in allowing a degree of separation of self and performance. Indeed, for some such roles, it is common for us to teach the future occupants that they must not become 'too involved'. Role performance also allows us to use success in one role to offset failure in another. The middle-aged professor deserted by his wife can compensate for his failure as a husband by reminding himself how good he is at his job. The middle-aged academic who sees himself overtaken by his younger colleagues can console himself by remembering how good a father he is.

What is at stake in any particular interaction can be limited by two lines of defence. First, we can blame the role. I can deflect criticism of me as an academic manager by pointing to the constraints imposed on my actions by my university. Second, we can accept the criticism that we have failed to perform the role adequately. Though this comes close to threatening our selves, it is preferable to be a bad actor than to be a bad person. In any case, people whose actions are shaped by interlocking roles are simply not putting as much of 'themselves' out there as those who insist on self-disclosure and intimacy. To be constantly authentic is to be constantly exposed, and that is not good for individuals.

Fourth, the world of New Age spirituality can reasonably be criticized for its failure to live up to its advertised authentic moral superiority in the realm of sexuality. Paul Heelas, one of the pioneers of anthropological studies of what he called 'holistic milieu spirituality', said in support of it:

> First it can make a positive difference to everyday life, this in the sense of improving the quality of personal life ... And, second, the New Age can be highly effective in communicating and fuelling commitment to values. I personally think that many of these are good, indeed excellent values: to do with nature, humankind's (there are no 'strangers' in the New Age), equality (egalitarianism being an aspect of New Age perennialism), authenticity, love and so on ... values , if put into practice— can make a difference to the world. Serving as 'institutions', values have very considerable functional capacities. Whether acquired by way of Self-spirituality or by way of socialization, the fact remains that those New Agers whose own lives are *informed* by the values under consideration are in a good position to work to change what they take to be the failures of conventional morality.[66]

If it is indeed the case that New Agers are in a good position to change the failures of conventional morality, the sexually exploitative behaviour of Bhagwan Shree Rajneesh or Dennis Lingwood or Chogyam Trungpa or Peter Caddy would be a rarity. Instead, it seems commonplace. So how do we explain this abject failure?

One element is common to secular exploitation: the appeal of celebrity. Many want to be close to the spiritual leader (and that can be the world-famous guru or the Findhorn group focalizer) because he the leader. But in addition to what it shares with the secular world, the religious and spiritual world seems to offer four advantages (or temptations) to the exploiter additional to those that pertain in secular settings: the emotional state of clients, the logic of detachment, the logic of spiritual growth, and the unusually charged atmosphere of pious groups.

Many attenders at New Age group activities (such as the Findhorn Foundation's Experience Week) and clients of one-to-one practitioners engage because they have suffered a recent breakdown in a long-term relationship or because they have become aware of a general problem in their personal and sexual relationships, which they hope to solve by spiritual growth or healing. Hence, like the Christian clergy, New Age providers often interact closely with people who are abnormally emotionally fragile. Furthermore, close interaction is what the milieu mandates. To be emotionally continent and socially distant is to be repressed.

Second, a great deal of religious and spiritual teaching focuses on the need for liberation and detachment. It may be material possessions, long-term personal relationships, or adherence to social norms that one is supposed to give up. In many cases of abuse, the guru persuades credulous young men and women that their spiritual development is being hindered by their attachment to a spouse and the guru is doing them a favour by helping them to prove they can betray a loved one.

Third, religious and spiritual rhetoric provides a unique justification for seduction. Much mundane sexual activity is justified by a combination of insight and desire. People seduce reluctant others by persuading them that, despite what they think now, they will find the experience fulfilling or pleasurable or some such. You may think you should be faithful to your wife, or husband, or partner, but I can tell you *really* want to do this. More abstract or exalted justifications are rare, but they are not unknown. There was a spike in sexual activity during both world wars because people feared that they might not survive and so had better take the opportunity for sexual pleasure while it was still possible. Certainly, servicemen tried to seduce reluctant women with the appeal (quite realistic in the case of aircrew) that they might soon be dead and that women should sacrifice their virtue for men who were about to sacrifice their lives. Radical political activists have sometimes used the same logic of matching sacrifice to argue that women had an obligation to reward those who were giving their all for the cause. Conquering armies have sometimes used a similar justification for raping the conquered. In the Second World War, the Japanese used the euphemism that translates as 'comfort women' for the Chinese and Korean women who were forced to service their soldiers. Retribution has been used as a justification for sexual exploitation: in the closing stages of the Second World War, Russian soldiers justified their rape of German women as retribution for the suffering inflicted on Russia by German armies. In brief, there are a variety of rhetorics other than the pleasure to be experienced by breaking social conventions that can be used to justify persuading or coercing the reluctant into sexual activity. But, for those who entertain religious beliefs, religious language is far more effective than any secular alternative because it mobilizes forces far more powerful and offers rewards far more attractive than anything the secular world can provide: the guru can invoke the authority of the divine (you should have sex with him because God or the spirit of the Cosmos decrees it) and promise rewards in the next life.

Fourth, while to outsiders such claims seem too preposterous and self-serving to be plausible, their frequency suggests that there is something about the environment in which they are made that causes people to suspend their scepticism and thus allow the rhetoric to be persuasive. This generalization elides a lot of interestingly different variations on the theme, but we can recall the observations about the Findhorn Foundation's Experience Week. A group of people intent on, or hopeful of, finding either God or their true self can create an emotionally charged atmosphere. In the right conditions, for the inexperienced, trusting, or credulous, sexual and spiritual arousal can seem rather similar, and the unscrupulous can try to parley the latter into the former. There is nothing new about this observation. In their time, religious movements as diverse as the early Methodists, Moral Re-Armament (MRA), the early twentieth-century Holiness movement, and the Moonies have been accused of encouraging vice. The hearers of Wesley's hell-fire preaching screamed, cried, swooned, and fainted and hence showed a lack of control. MRA encouraged adherents to discuss intimate, often sexual, problems in small groups and thus encouraged a prurient interest in what should remain private. The Holiness movement, because it claimed that the 'second blessing' it offered meant adherents could not sin, encouraged more sin. And who knows what the young people in Moonie communes got up to! There is actually no good evidence that, for the bulk of those involved, breaking some social norms led to wholesale vice: the early Methodists, members of MRA, those who attended the Holiness conventions, and the Moonies were puritans. However, the case does seem plausible if we shift it from being a claim about the impact of spiritually charged atmospheres on typical participants to the much narrower assertion that such environments facilitated manipulative leaders in taking advantage of those of their followers who were particularly affected.

But Heelas is right that there is a credit side to the world of contemporary spirituality. In the magnificent complexity of the real world, it is always difficult to separate cause of change and symptom of change. A good case can be made for the following all being consequences of broader sociocultural changes of which our new expressions of religious interest are beneficiaries rather than stimulators. Nonetheless, contemporary spirituality could claim, by embodying the following principles, to have amplified their effect. One could argue that the spiritual form of environmentalism encourages its more popular secular partner. As a counter to the above charge of presenting the fate of the poor, ill, and dispossessed as a matter of personal failings, one may argue that the shift from the Christian notion of original sin to the New Age notion of original virtue promotes a more caring attitude, especially towards children and those adults whose disabilities render them somewhat childlike. It is no accident that those seriously interested in holistic spirituality are disproportionately found in such caring professions as primary school teacher, social worker, care worker, occupational, speech and physiotherapist, and nurse. As noted above, the ideological relativism of New Age spirituality poses some threat to the knowledge base and expertise that have given us science and technology, but, provided one keeps the dividing line between objectivity and personal preference in the right place, the insistence that no one has any right to tell others what to believe is liberating. Notions of sexual liberation may have been used as levers of sexual exploitation, but Wicca and other female-led elements of the New Age have made the holistic spirituality milieu less sexist than the society at large. For all that the New Age is wrong about a great deal, it is part of a movement towards a kinder and gentler society.

NOTES

1. J. Rutter, 'Save the carol', *Spectator*, 13–27 December 2014.
2. The case that the secularization of Britain is a sociological myth is actually made by Rodney Stark and two of his close associates; see the exchanges in S. Bruce, 'The Truth about Religion in Britain', *Journal for the Scientific Study of Religion*, 34 (1995), 417–30; R. Stark, R. Finke, and L. R. Iannaccone, 'Pluralism and Piety: England and Wales 1851', *Journal for the Scientific Study of Religion*, 34 (1995), 431–44; and S. Bruce, 'A Novel Reading of Nineteenth-Century Wales: A Reply to Stark, Finke, and Iannaccone', *Journal for the Scientific Study of Religion*, 34 (1995), 520–2. Stark believes that the demand for religion is basically stable, not because of biology, but because humankind is insatiable. Even if we gain all we wish, we wish for more. As rewards are scarce, we are always in the market for 'compensators' (which are both explanations of why the rewards have not materialized and promises that we will receive them in the future), and, because it can invoke the supernatural, religion will always be a more popular source of compensators than any secular philosophy.
3. I make this case at more length and Paul Heelas responds to it in *Hedgehog Review* (Spring and Summer 2006), 35–45, repr. in B. S. Turner (ed.), *Secularization* (London: Sage, 2011).
4. This is the theme of J. Carrette and R. King, *Selling Spirituality: The Silent Takeover of Religion* (London: Routledge, 2005).
5. J. Hall, 'No Place like OMM', *Scotland on Sunday*, 11 August 1997.
6. Carrette and King, *Selling Spirituality*, inside cover recto.
7. It is worth noting that the capitalism-corrupts-religion argument is almost the opposite of the explanation for differences in the extent of secularization in Europe and the USA that was advanced in the 1960s. Then senior social scientists such as Seymour Martin Lipset argued that social democracy (and in particular the existence of an effective welfare state) was the functional equivalent of religion and explained why the British and the Canadians were less religious than the Americans. See S. M. Lipset, *American Exceptionalism* (New York: W. W. Norton and Co., 1997).
8. Elmer Schwieder and Dorothy Schwieder, *A Peculiar People: Iowa's Old Order Amish* (Iowa City: Bur Oak, 2009).
9. In case this be seen as an argument with Colin Campbell, I should stress that he frequently makes the same point.
10. A. R. Jain, *Selling Yoga: From Counter Culture to Pop Culture* (Oxford: Oxford University Press, 2015).
11. Jain, *Selling Yoga*, 46–7.
12. Anon, 'Millions Stretch and Twist for Yoga Day', *Press and Journal*, 22 June 2015, p. 24.

13. A good case can be made for saying that the Hindu nationalist project involves considerable borrowing from the West. The Bhagavad-Gita has been elevated to a primary text status comparable to the Bible. The faith has been simplified. And it has become more monotheistic. All of which makes easier the political claim that there is a single 'Hindu' people that deserves to rule its homeland with little or no regard for the presence of other faith populations. See A. Rajagopal, *Politics after Television: Religious Nationalism and the Reshaping of the Indian Public* (Cambridge: Cambridge University Press, 2001).

14. C. Field, '"The Faith Society"? Quantifying Religious Belonging in Edwardian Britain, 1901–1914', *Journal of Religious History*, 37 (2013), 61.

15. P. Brierley, *UK Church Statistics 2005-15* (Tonbridge, Kent: ABCD Publishers, 2011).

16. S. Bruce, 'Appendix Two', in B. R. Wilson, *Religion in Secular Society* (Oxford: Oxford University Press, 2016).

17. All of these data are from my original research. I am grateful to the staff of the University Library, University of Durham, for providing access to the Diocese of Durham Visitation Returns from which the data are taken.

18. These data are taken from Methodist circuit records in the County Durham Records Office. I am grateful to the staff for their considerable assistance in accessing this material.

19. L. J. Francis and J. Martineau, *Rural Mission* (Stoneleigh Park: Acora Publishing, 2002), 55, and L. J. Francis, *Rural Anglicanism* (London: Collins, 1985), 172–3.

20. P. Brierley, *A Century of British Christianity: Historical Statistics 1900–1985* (London: MARC Europe, 1985), 41–8.

21. Wilson, *Religion in Secular Society*, 19–21.

22. Brierley, *UK Church Statistics*, table 14.4.2. See also C. Brown, *The Death of Christian Britain* (London: Routledge, 2001), 188.

23. P. Richter and L. J. Francis, *Gone but not Forgotten: Church Leaving and Returning* (London: Darton, Longman and Todd, 1998).

24. R. Gale and P. Hopkins, 'Introduction', in P. Hopkins and R. Gale (eds), *Muslims in Britain: Race, Place and Identities* (Edinburgh: Edinburgh University Press, 2009), 10.

25. To be clear, this figure cannot be correct, because it would produce a figure for church attendance (one of the main requirements for Christian observance) greater than that produced by claims made in surveys and vastly greater than anything the churches themselves suspect on the basis of their own data.

26. Pagan Federation, 'Pagans and the Scottish Census of 2001' <http://www.scottishpf.org/resources.html> (accessed May 2017).

27. Field, 'The Faith Society?', 60.

28. C. Field, 'Measuring Religious Affiliation in Great Britain: The 2011 Census in Historical and Methodological Context', *Religion*, 44 (2014), 373–6.

29. N. Hellen, 'Post-Christian Britain Arrives as Majority Say they have no Religion', *Sunday Times*, 12 January 2016.

30. C. G. Brown 'The People of "No Religion"', *Archiv für Sozialgeschichte*, 51 (2011), 44.

31. M. Beckford, 'After Thousands of Years, Druids are Recognised as Religious Group', *Daily Telegraph*, 2 October 2010. To clarify, the British state does not decide what is a proper religion. The report concerned the decisions of the Charity Commissioners for England and Wales to accept the Druid Network as a charity (which has important tax benefits). In the case of groups claiming to be religious, the Commissioners apply a substantive definition of religion, but the crux for charitable status is not whether a group is a religion but whether it demonstrably does good for some population beyond its own membership. In 2014 they considered withdrawing charitable status from the Exclusive Brethren, not because their status as religious was in doubt but because their introversion called into question their claims to benefit anyone other than themselves.

32. <visual.ons.gov.uk/2011-census-religion> (accessed August 2016).

33. It has not been dealt with in the text because it is not crucial to my argument, but some historians, notably Callum Brown but also to a lesser extent Hugh Mcleod, take the view that secularization is recent and is largely a result of social changes associated with the 1960s. See C. Brown, *The Death of Christian Britain* (London: Routledge, 2001), and H. McLeod, *The Religious Crises of the 1960s* (Oxford: Oxford University Press, 2007. While I accept that the rate of decline accelerated from the 1960s, I would argue that such acceleration was made possible by loosening allegiances over the previous two generations and that much of what we see in the last quarter of the twentieth century is the abandonment of what was by then a largely nominal commitment. See S. Bruce and T. Glendinning, 'When was Secularization? Dating the Decline of the British Churches and Locating its Cause', *British Journal of Sociology*, 61 (2010), 107–26.

34. P. Laslett, *The World We Have Lost* (London: Methuen, 1983), 66–77.

35. C. Richmond, 'Religion', in R. Horrox (ed.), *Fifteenth Century Attitudes: Perceptions of Society in Late Medieval England* (Cambridge: Cambridge University Press, 1994), 184.

36. Although best known as part of the poem 'No Man is an Island', Donne originally wrote this as prose in his 1624 Meditation 17, from *Devotions upon Emergent Occasions*.

37. There is a particularly detailed and moving description of the cadaver tomb of John Baret of Bury in C. Watkin, *The Undiscovered Country* (New York: Vintage, 2013), 1–13.

38. This story is told particularly about the supposedly pacifying effects of Methodism and other Protestant sects in the period when the British supposedly should have been emulating the French and the Americans in being revolutionary. See E. Halevy, *A History of the English People in 1815* (London: Penguin, 1937).

39. K. Thomas, *Religion and the Decline of Magic* (London: Weidenfeld and Nicolson, 1971). For example, Thomas is the only historian cited in Stark et al., 'Pluralism and Piety'.

40. P. E. Glassner, *The Sociology of Secularization: A Critique of a Concept* (London: Routledge and Kegan Paul, 1977).

41. The church/sect distinction was elaborated by Ernest Troelstch, a student of Max Weber. See E. Troelstch, *The Social Teaching of the Christian Church* (Chicago: University of Chicago Press, 1976).

42. H. Becker, *Systematic Sociology* (New York: John Wiley and Sons, 1932). This is not the more famous sociology of deviance Howard Becker.

43. C. Campbell, 'The Cult, the Cultic Milieu and Secularization', *A Sociological Yearbook of Religion in Britain 5* (London: SCM Press, 1972), 119–36.

44. X. Brennan, 'Religious Status for Druids. The Police Trained to Respect Witches. Pagans Are on the March.—But are they Harmless Eccentrics or a Dangerous Cult?', *Daily Mail*, 12 November 2010, pp. 47–6.

45. Elsewhere I have argued that, as our culture has become increasingly secular, the distinction between respectable and deviant religion has lost salience. The non-religious majority of the population now tends to see all religion taken too seriously as deviant. However, as this does not affect anything being said here, I will persist with the classic usage. See S. Bruce and D. Voas, 'Secularization and Typologies of Religious Organizations', *Journal of Contemporary Religion*, 22 (2004), 1–17.

46. Although his interests are judgemental as well as explanatory, the issue is ably discussed in H. R. Niebuhr, *The Social Sources of Denominationalism* (New York: Meridian, 1962). There are additional reasons, derived from Robert Michels's discussion of oligarchy, that are relevant to the evolution of long-lived Protestant sects but that are not germane here. See S. Bruce, *Religion in the Modern World: From Cathedrals to Cults* (Oxford: Oxford University 1996), 79–80.

47. Bryan Wilson correctly challenges the inevitability of compromise at the heart of Niebuhr's analysis. Not all sects lose their founding fervour, though typically their target changes from the failures of competing religious organizations to the dangers of secularity. See Wilson, *Religion in Secular Society*, ch. 12.

48. T. A. B. Corley, 'Changing Quaker Attitudes to Wealth 1690–1950', in D. Jeremy (ed.), *Religion, Business and Wealth in Modern Britain* (London: Routledge, 2006), 137–51.

49. In the late 1970s, the transforming light metaphor was common among Findhorn associates. See the articles in *One Earth* 5 (Spring 1978).

50. The splits also had specific triggers. For details, see S. Bruce, *Scottish Gods: Religion in Scotland 1900 to 2012* (Edinburgh: Edinburgh University Press, 2014), 119–24.

51. Precise calculation is difficult because, although membership figures for the Church of Scotland probably give a good indicator of its reach, the two Free Churches have traditionally had a large number of lifelong regular attenders who are not members. But the difference in size of the various schismatic groups is so great that we can be confident of the general point. See R. Currie, A. Gilbert, and L. Horsley, *Churches and Churchgoers: Patterns of Church Growth in the British Isles since 1700* (Oxford: Clarendon Press, 1977), table A.2.

52. I believe that I owe this observation (as much else) to David Martin.

53. This case is argued in E. Gellner, *Nations and Nationalism* (Oxford: Basil Blackwell, 1983). An interesting variant is the French Code Napoleon, which aimed to create a culturally uniform but *secular* citizenry and which is the basis for the current French objection to signs of religious identity.

54. E. S. Gaustad, *Proclaim Liberty throughout All the Land: A History of Church and State in America* (New York: Oxford University Press, 2003).

55. One way of describing what American sociologists sometimes call the 'culture wars' in the USA is to say that to varying extents US fundamentalists reject the separation of religion from other forms of knowledge.

56. It is often said that conspiracy theories allow ignorant people to feel clever. In a less critical voice, it is worth suggesting that various forms of modern quackery appeal to well-meaning people who would like to help others but who, for a variety of reasons, lacked the opportunity to train in real medicine. It is certainly the case that many New Age therapists, like Chapter 2's Dorothy Lewis, are people who worked in caring professions at the lower levels, retired early in frustration at the bureaucratic constraints of the job or their relatively limited autonomy, and then took a short or part-time course in some alternative therapy.

57. J. P. Bloch, 'Individualism and Community in Alternative Spiritual "Magic"', *Journal for the Scientific Study of Religion*, 37 (1988), 295.

58. Martin mentioned this at a 2000 seminar at Lancaster University where the Kendal study and the Scottish Social Attitudes survey were being planned.

59. It is a curious and unfortunate consequence of fashions in academic life that the popularity of the secularization thesis is inversely correlated with the popularity of religion. It was taken for granted in the 1960s but is now regarded as passé, despite religion now being considerably less popular than it was then.

60. This case is argued in S. Bruce, 'The Sociology of Late Secularization', *British Journal of Sociology*, 67 (2016), 613–31.

61. E. Howse, *Saints in Politics: The Clapham Sect and the Growth of Freedom* (London: Allen and Unwin, 1971).

62. Arguably the great exception are the Rudolf Steiner schools and the associated residential communities for adults with learning difficulties. However, those have grown and survived, not because the founder's spiritual ideas are popular, but because the schools and communities clearly serve a practical purpose. The spiritual background can readily be ignored by those idealistic young people who work in them, by the governments who subsidize them, and by the individuals who make generous donations.

63. For Berger, see P. L. Berger, *Invitation to Sociology* (Harmondsworth: Penguin, 1975); for Durkheim, see E. Durkheim, *Suicide* (London: Routledge and Kegan Paul, 1976); for Gehlen, see A. Gehlen, *Man in the Age of Technology* (New York: Columbia University Press, 1980).

64. P. L. Berger, 'Introduction', in Gehlen, *Man in the Age of Technology*, p. xi.

65. For a good example of the sexual and emotional vulnerability of a New Ager, see J. Boice, *At One with All Life: A Personal Journey in Gaian Communities* (Findhorn: Findhorn Press, 1989).

66. P. Heelas, *The New Age Movement* (Oxford: Blackwell. 1996), 207.

Index